LGHT
ON
RELATIONSHIPS

LIGHT
ON
RELATIONSHIPS

The Synastry of Indian Astrology

HART DE FOUW & ROBERT E. SVOBODA

MOTILAL BANARSIDASS PUBLISHERS
PRIVATE LIMITED • DELHI

First Indian Edition: Delhi, 2002
First Published by Samuel Weiser, USA, 2000

ISBN: 81-208-1834-2

Also available at:

MOTILAL BANARSIDASS

8 Mahalaxmi Chamber, 22 Bhulabhai Desai Road, Mumbai 400 026
41 U.A. Bungalow Road, Jawahar Nagar, Delhi 110 007
120 Royapettah High Road, Mylapore, Chennai 600 004
236, 9th Main III Block, Jayanagar, Bangalore 560 011
Sanas Plaza, 1302 Baji Rao Road, Pune 411 002
8 Camac Street, Kolkata 700 017
Ashok Rajpath, Patna 800 004
Chowk, Varanasi 221 001

Printed in India
BY JAINENDRA PRAKASH JAIN AT SHRI JAINENDRA PRESS,
A-45 NARAINA, PHASE-I, NEW DELHI 110 028
AND PUBLISHED BY NARENDRA PRAKASH JAIN FOR
MOTILAL BANARSIDASS PUBLISHERS PRIVATE LIMITED,
BUNGALOW ROAD, DELHI 110 007

CONTENTS

PREFACE

We offer this book to the public with some trepidation, knowing that it may fall into the chasm that separates astrology's two worlds. Many of our Western readers may hear in the tunes of our opus an echo of their own methods—tunes that fail, however, to speak truly to them of the Western style of horoscope compatibility analysis. Some of our Eastern readers, particularly those devoted traditionalists who believe the extant classical body of Jyotisha to be divinely inspired and hence perfect, may, in turn, find elements of our approach too innovative to suit their tastes. Too often the proponents of these two astrological paradigms approach each other with a wariness that more befits a sibling rivalry than an honest attempt to work together for the greater good of the whole family.

This volume presents a synthesized approach to horoscope compatibility analysis, developed over some years of experimentation. This approach blends the principles of compatibility analysis familiar to most practicing jyotishis with other, lesser-known techniques culled from Jyotisha's classical canon. Certain of these techniques are based on oral traditions that somehow were never incorporated into the classical works of antiquity. Others come from our direct lineage mentors of Jyotisha. Yet others have been nurtured from both Western and Eastern inspirational seeds into processes that have been validated over many years of experience. Our attempts to synthesize notwithstanding, we believe the foundations of the methods that we introduce here are firmly anchored in Jyotisha.

Many readers will find that the principles we advocate cohere in practice rather more readily than they may seem to in print. To minimize the risk of selecting illustrative horoscopes that merely selectively support our theses, we have purposely chosen a limited set of examples, testing each of our varied techniques on the same subjects to provide a fairer picture of how an actual relationship analysis might proceed.

We believe that we build on some of the best principles that the astrological traditions of both West and East have to offer. We pray that our readers will treat kindly our efforts to bring the two camps closer together.

ACKNOWLEDGMENTS

First and foremost, we, the authors, would like to thank the Jyotir Vidya, and its exceptional son Mantriji, our primary Jyotisha mentor. We thank Aletha de Fouw for the diagrams and charts, and acknowledge the following readers who examined and commented on the manuscript at different stages in its development: Aletha de Fouw, H. Friedman, Margaret Mahan, Brian Montague, Dr. Shankardev Saraswati, Bette Timm, and Dr. Claudia Welch.

BIRTH DATA SOURCES

All birth data for the charts used in this book originates from the birth records of the individuals or from birth charts used and verified by numerous prominent jyotishis.

INTRODUCTION

*Unos nacen con estrella y
otros nacen de estrelladas.*

*Some are born under a star, and
some are born seeing stars.*[1]

Life demands that we relate perpetually to our world. Our very existence depends on the regular intake of food, water, light, sound, love, and other "nutrients" that flow into us from sources outside ourselves. Each of us, in turn, influences our environment as we communicate, fabricate, move, excrete, create, and perform all the other activities that constitute our lives. When we disturb the balance of these exchanges, we disturb the foundations of our being.

Each of us also interacts continually with our social environment. We so crave to relate that we begin to encumber a child with relationship classifiers (sister, son, niece) from the moment it is born. New descriptors (friend, mother, employee, manager, grandma) continue to pile on as the child ages. Even renunciates define themselves in terms of the society they renounce. Indeed, spiritual development itself involves establishing a healthy relationship between the individual and a divine reality. None of us ever completely escapes becoming enmeshed in the web of human relationships.

Few of us marry with the intention of eventually divorcing, but today's high rate of divorce suggests that many of us marry without accurately appraising a proposed relationship's potential. Many are the vantages from which we may examine our relating selves, but few are as clear-sighted as the Indian system of divination called Jyotisha. Jyotisha ("the study of light"), often referred to in English as "Indian" or "Vedic" astrology, has condensed the best of classical Indian philosophy and culture into clues for understanding the process of how we relate. By re-

---

[1] Traditional saying in New Mexico.

flecting back to us insightful images of our manifold and convoluted relationships, astrology assists us in getting our bearings as we explore this difficult-to-chart territory.

Life is relationship, and how well or poorly we relate to our environment and to the people we encounter determines how happy or unhappy our lives become. The wise among us become mindful of how they relate, for every encounter with the "other" influences our pursuit of health and happiness according to its degree of success. Some people enjoy extremely strong attachments to their mothers, while others never even discover who bore them. Some individuals battle their bosses daily; others become the teacher's pet. To review dispassionately our interactions with the others in our world is to gain perspective that may illuminate our steps as we move forward in relating. Act before pondering and we are likely to find ourselves repeating and reinforcing unproductive patterns of relationship behavior.

The horoscope often provides indications of which relationships, whether those of business partners or romantic associates, will prove easy or difficult for an individual. Sometimes—even without the help of a horoscope—it is obvious to us as soon as we meet someone new how well we will get along. At other times, first impressions prove less reliable. Some combinations that seem hell-bound at first mature into enjoyable, supportive, long-term alliances. Others that start with great expectations under ideal circumstances end, finally, in disarray, disappointment or tragedy. Jyotisha is an excellent barometer for measuring relationship climate. It can often foresee which associations will generally enjoy clear skies and calm seas, and which are likely to be in for rough weather. Jyotisha also forecasts changes in the atmosphere of existing relationships, and can suggest whether these shifts are likely to be for the better or the worse.

While horoscopes reflect the full gamut of human experience, relationship questions are among the most frequent that astrologers hear from a client. A good astrologer can generally provide percipient answers to a wide range of relating queries, including: "Will I marry? Will I divorce? Will my secret affair be discovered? How will I get along with my children, my business partner, my new neighbor?" Jyotisha is still frequently employed in modern India to evaluate the likely success of all manner of business, marriage, progeny, and friendship relationships, including such exceptional liaisons as the question of which surgeon to select for an operation. In the following pages, we will touch upon several of these sorts of interactions. Most frequently, however, classical Jyotisha applies relationship analysis to a potential couple's marriage prospects. This, therefore, will be the main focus of this book.

As natural and necessary as it may be for humans to relate, few of the fundamental social rules of relating seem to be inborn. Most must be learned, a fact that has had our species agonizing since the dawn of human socializing. Rules that permit certain interpersonal relationships and prohibit others help societies preserve, protect, and defend their integrity. A society that loses the ability or the will to enforce its rules usually unravels quickly as a result. We have seen this frequently, both in traditional cultures traumatized by invasion or colonization, and in dominant cultures that descend into decadence. We see this very scenario acting itself out today in our own postindustrial, virtual-reality society.

As a society's rules of relating deteriorate, those members who seek relationship guidance are thrown back to their own inner resources. Today, most Westerners choose with whom and how to relate on the distressing basis of fleeting attraction or repulsion. "Follow your heart" and "trust your intuition" may be sage advice for the seasoned heart and the skilled intuition. If you try to choose a life partner in haste, however, on the basis of idiosyncratic desire, you may live to repent, for stable, lasting family ties cannot be built on fascination alone. Fortunately, mature astrological assessment of relationship potentials and pitfalls, using the time-tested techniques of Jyotisha, can often enlighten blind emotions and enliven feeble perceptions. Astrology appeared among humans while civilization still lay in its cradle, and has endured the growth and decline of all manner of human organization. The observations of many generations of astrologers have accumulated a rich mass of implications for every sort of affinity permutation.

Jyotisha emanated from one of the world's oldest known societies, and its practitioners have had ample opportunity to refine both the techniques and the spirit of their relationship analysis. A good *jyotishi* (practitioner of Jyotisha) respects the sanctity of both the human spirit and the traditions of Jyotisha, and aims to provide even-handed, humanistic assessments of relationship possibilities rather than to exploit tradition to fetter individuals, or to justify self-indulgent behavior with pop psychology. Because good relationships cannot be legislated by substituting one set of false ideals for another, there is little value in attempting to make our relationships work by returning to modes of organizing society that existed when our ancient religions and astrology arose. It is equally unwise to conform to modern mores that are cobbled together by committee into "politically correct" norms.

What astrology can do, when properly practiced and used, is to break down false ideals about relationships, thereby establishing a fuller context within which our relationships can spread their wings. When we act after carefully observing a relationship's unique dynamic, we facilitate that relationship's development in the direction it most wishes to develop. We do well to work to permit change, not to manufacture it, and to act always with discerning commitment in our relationships. Everyone urges commitment nowadays, and there is little doubt that irresponsibility is now a national pastime. Foolish commitment to a destructive relationship that can ruin us, however, is mere excess in the opposite direction. We don't regard commitment to alcohol or drugs as noble or praiseworthy, so why should we see commitment to a relationship situation that is bitter as somehow better? Responsible divorce should continue to find a place in a compassionate society, and awareness of why such divorce became necessary should be encouraged in the detaching partners. Intelligent astrological assessment of relationship can often help to clarify the difference between a relationship that is compulsive, but negative, and another that, with effort, can become positively rewarding over a reasonable period of time.

Commitment becomes essential once we find a fertile relationship situation in which we know we can grow, for patience is as necessary for a relationship as it is for an oak tree. Driven by two mutually exclusive drives—for union and for freedom—each human must find that space where this paradox eases into equipoise. Superb flavors arise when richly textured opposites juxtapose. Transmutation, whether of personal chemistry into relationship alchemy or grapes into wine, requires the passage of time. A matured mellow wine refreshes the palate as surely as an immature or chemically "aged" wine leaves an acrid aftertaste. Today's "experts" may emphasize how pain-free and trouble-free the "optimum relationship" must be, but relationships often grow best in soil that has been enriched with the manure of healthy tribulation, for the sweetness of the lilac is born from the rankness of the compost. To expect perfection in any human relationship is as futile as to expect perfection from human life. All of us are imperfect, and we all create imperfect relationships. We are best advised to erase from our minds any idea of "perfect balance," and dedicate ourselves instead to discovering how to usher a dynamic, working, living balance into our interactions.

One of the most massive of the many illusions that the New Age has foisted upon us is the illusion that we are all perfect. Like most delusions, this one is founded in the distortion of a fundamental truth, that of the perfection of the Absolute. Our animating principle is perhaps flawless, but the instruments that it animates and through which it acts are not. They are in fact quite flawed: senses that can perceive only a limited range of perceptions and minds that selectively distort or delete parcels of the data thus received, all within a body whose functions progressively diminish and ultimately collapse within less than a century. These instruments may, at best, achieve a relative perfection discernible through comparison: my body is stronger than yours, this relationship is better than the last, and so on. Undue comparison, however, is as sure a path to dissatisfaction as a reasonable acceptance of circumstances (including relationships) is the royal road to contentment.

Fate and Free Will

In the philosophical matrix from which this book draws its insights, every living being displays both fate and free will to an extent that is determined by its degree of self-awareness. Traits that seem almost engrained in our personalities often seem, in fact, to possess a life of their own; they appear to be "fated" to occur. Willpower alone can suffice to dispel weakly held misconceptions, but strongly held ideals, false or true, may resist all our efforts to alter them, especially if they operate on the blurred periphery of our conscious ambit. While our fate represents the sum of the impending effects of our past actions, our free will equals our potential to make and execute plans to improve our personal situation by performing present and future actions. The sum of all our actions is our *karma*. Here, we strip all the glib modern connotations from the word *karma*, and use it in its traditional Indian sense of action and, by extension, the effect of that action. The individual karmas that two partners bring to the dance floor work with the shared karmas that the couple generates by working together through the relationship's dance steps. A "good" partnership is one in which the two (or more) people involved act predominantly to facilitate each other's positive, beneficial karmas. In a "poor" relationship, the partners tend, instead, to activate one another's unhealthy, destructive karmas.

The sages of ancient India developed Jyotisha as a karma-measuring apparatus, a "karmascope" that can inform us where and when our karmas will permit ideals to be shared (and so things to be smooth) between us and those with whom we relate. Jyotisha can also disclose where these ideals will be at odds, in what areas substantial work will need to even out the bumps, and when a relationship may be in danger of breaking up. A relationship's depth is often a function of its length and its nature, and Jyotisha can help us structure our relationship dynamics by providing us with perspectives on when and in what way our relationships and their difficulties are likely to arise and dissipate.

If Jyotisha's general objective truths could somehow be made infallible, they would become the magic bullet that would lay low all possible relationship difficulties. This, sadly, is impossible, for true knowledge never appears to us imperfect humans in a wholly objective form, precisely cut and dried. Relational knowledge, in particular, is almost impossible to abstract into some unvarying rational form. Jyotisha's efficacy thus depends, in good measure, on the subjective skills—the knowledge, experience, and intuition—of the individual jyotishi. Jyotishical reasoning arranges and rearranges many different astrological factors, highlighting and juxtaposing them until a faithful image of reality coalesces within the jyotishi's consciousness. Good jyotishi's perform a strong act of personal power to animate a horoscope's realities and help dissolve any of the client's long-held unrealistic fantasies. In the pointed words of our Jyotisha guru, "To try to create the four-dimensional reality of a person's life from the two-dimensional symbols on a piece of paper is no joke."[2]

Relationship Analysis

In the context of relationship analysis, *janma* (natal astrology) examines the karmas that a couple bring forward into this lifetime, and *prashna* (horary astrology; literally, "question") evaluates the present karmic prospects of their relationship dance. Janma assesses the ways in which a couple will relate, and prashna evaluates whether or not the couple will actually pursue a relationship. Good jyotishis use janma to evaluate how well the habitual relationship propensities of two people may intermesh to support or undermine a relationship. They use prashna to inquire into the actual viability of a couple's current relationship prospects, as of the moment they appear for a compatibility assessment.

The distinction between janma and prashna comes into sharp focus when we consider how frequently we contemplate our potential compatibility with people who are never likely to enter into relationship with us. Just because your birth chart perfectly matches that of a famous and desirable person does not mean that you will end up in a relationship with them!

---

[2] Personal communication.

Those who approach Jyotisha for an assessment of relationship compatibility will ideally locate a competent jyotishi, one who will help them create accurate visions of relationship reality that embrace both the fundamental nature and the actual viability of compatibility. Client and jyotishi must feel a deep and genuine reciprocal rapport for this goal to be achieved, for the successful practice of Jyotisha involves the creation of a healthy relationship between the reader and the subject. A good client actively participates in the process of assessment, creating, via interaction with the jyotishi, a relatively positive or negative relationship karma. The satisfaction that you may obtain from a Jyotishical analysis of one of your associations will thus depend both on the jyotishi's skill and on how you and your partner's karmas affect that skill. The more you know about Jyotisha and its techniques, the better your "fit" with your jyotishi will be.

The guidance you gain from the techniques in this book will be generally reliable, and may occasionally be exceptionally precise, provided that you apply these tools according to their rules. The first of these rules is to accept Jyotisha for what it is, and not what you wish it to be. The vocabulary and style of expression of Jyotisha's knowledge rarely corresponds precisely with the modern expressions used to translate them from the Sanskrit. If you let your mind interpret Jyotisha's pronouncements through its preexisting reality filters, you will likely lose much of the very perspective that you have approached Jyotisha to gain.

As an example, take Jyotisha's preference for speaking in generalities. "Happiness" is one such generality that abounds in classical Jyotisha. If, when you hear the Sanskrit word *sukha* (happiness) in your Jyotisha reading, you think of every possible context in which happiness can occur, you can be sure that you are coming close to sukha's actual meaning.

The modern preference for specialization, however, tends to inhibit "progressive" people from comprehending a generalization like sukha. When a jyotishi says to a Westerner (or Westernized Indian), "You are unhappy about your mother; your fourth house is afflicted," the response frequently is, "Wrong! I love my mother and she loves me." If the jyotishi patiently explores the mother's condition instead of the quality of the emotional relationship of child with mother, however, a different picture often emerges. Even if child and mother share love for one another, the mother may still have been sufficiently emotionally distraught, neurotic or psychotic, chronically ill, exceedingly poor, or otherwise personally dysfunctional to have had a rough time in the world, and to have unconsciously impaired the child through her circumstances.

Conversely, even when a client has had an unhappy relationship with his or her mother, both parties may have been materially comfortable, and the mother may have led a thoroughly happy and satisfying life from her own point of view. Any of these, or the many other, permutations of your mother's life experience, as well as your experience of your mother and her life circumstances, may enhance or diminish your state of "mother-sukha."

Clients who are educated and astute enough to appreciate what a jyotishi means when speaking of something like "mother-sukha" facilitate the jyotishi's ability to dig deeper into the matter at hand. Make Jyotisha into a commodity to be supplied on demand, however, and you will get astrological advice of the same quality as the personal care you might get from an overworked modern physician. The same tendencies that have conditioned the modern general public to consult general practitioners chiefly to get referrals from them to medical specialists are now also beginning to influence Jyotisha. The yen for specificity is forcing jyotishis to reach for that level of astonishing divine inspiration that makes the difference between a "you will travel during this period" prediction and a "you will go to New Jersey from Vancouver for the marriage of your third-older sister" pronouncement. While such proclamations may astonish, they can also uproot the budding relationship between jyotishi and client, a relationship that must develop if the client ever hopes to gain from the jyotishi a "big picture" overview of the direction and momentum of his or her life.

Another rule of relationship analysis—perhaps the most important of all—is never to use Jyotisha as a careless excuse to break a relationship. Jyotisha was designed to enhance your sense of responsibility, not to promote the kind of irresponsibility that a certain man—let us call him Jack—displayed with a certain woman, whom we can call Jill. Jack and Jill had enjoyed themselves on their first date together. On parting for the evening, they were mutually interested in enjoying another rendezvous, until the day they met by chance in a supermarket. Jack happened, on that day, to have in his pocket a mass-produced copy of one of Jyotisha's compatibility tables. When he used this table on the spot to gauge their mutual compatibility, he found that their stars did not properly align. He promptly announced to his astounded companion that their date was off, for Jyotisha clearly foretold that they must be incompatible. Jill told us later that she had never felt so insulted in her life.

By bringing their karmic interaction to an ungraceful close, Jack created new karma for himself, whose painful results he will eventually experience. If Jack continues to misuse Jyotisha in this shallow way, he will dig
himself into an ever deeper relationship hole, creating future misery without
realizing why or how. If, like the arrogantly cavalier Jack, you extract one
thread from an item of attire and proclaim it to be the whole garment, you
can expect that thread to be woven into the shroud of your relationship life.

Some Closing Thoughts

A few works on the subject of Jyotishical compatibility analysis already exist in English. None that we have seen thus far, however, are really acces-
sible to the modern Western student of Jyotisha. Hence this book, parts
of which present selected astrological methods that have been used successfully for centuries by Indian jyotishis. We have also developed and included other methods of interpretation that have not been mentioned
explicitly in Jyotisha's traditional texts. Our main inspiration for leaving
Jyotisha's conventional path was its traditional point system for cross-
comparisons of horoscopes. This system, though widely used (especially
in southern India) for comparing horoscopes of prospective marriage partners, is so complex and ethnocentric that it is not very user-friendly to the
average Western-trained mind. We do present this traditional point system, for highly motivated readers will find much to feast upon therein, but
we go beyond it for those who want a simpler, yet no less reliable, means
of interpretation.

We have also deliberately limited the extent to which we discuss examination of the seventh house of the natal horoscope of two individuals
who seek to become involved with each other. We have included only that
natal chart material that we believe is essential to meaningful compatibility
analysis, for our purpose here is to focus on relationship skill. Our readers
can pursue methods for determining the outcomes of those relationships
(via analysis of the seventh house, the lord of that house, and its
significator) by way of Jyotisha's standard methods, which are outlined in
several texts (including our *Light on Life*).[3]

A nodding acquaintance with the principles presented in *Light on Relationships* will make it easier for you to understand the Indian relationship

---

[3] Hart deFouw and Robert Svoboda, *Light on Life: An Introduction to Indian Astrology*
(London: Penguin, 1996).

paradigm and to scrutinize the skills of the jyotishis that you may consult for relationship advice. If you are astrologically inclined, a thorough study of this book's techniques and examples can provide you with valuable tools for evaluating all types of human relationships. We do focus, however, on "marital" prospects in this book, expanding "marriage" from the customary legally binding contract to include such modern marriage-like dynamics as "live-in" and "common law" arrangements. While we generally limit our comments on marriage to "standard" one male—one female arrangements, our techniques should also be applicable to less typical, but equally responsible and committed, relationships.

Our conscious intent in this book has been to help our readers better understand how they relate to the many notable "others" in their lives, that enhanced comprehension may sweeten their lives. We do not try to provide either one-size-fits-all explanations for why some people fail to relate well, or instant solutions for relationship makeovers. Too many people seek truth only until they locate a convenient theory that seems to explain everything about everything. Astrology often seems to serve this purpose—"If I am a Scorpio and my chosen mate is a Gemini, it is no wonder that we don't get along." This sort of "astrology" lets us use prefabricated horoscope interpretation to save us from having to make meaningful changes in our lives. We recommend that you resist this temptation, just as, in this work, we have resisted the temptation to try to create one grand "unified affinity theory."

In the ancient parable of the blind men and the elephant, each man drew a mistaken conclusion about the elephant's totality after perceiving a different part of the pachyderm. The elephant of Jyotisha is so wonder-filled that only blind men could expect its reality to yield to a single point of view. This volume is a book of essays, each presenting one perception of that pachyderm. Hopefully, they will unite within you into a handsome tusker. Enjoy employing each viewpoint in the context of the elephant from which it has been drawn, without seeking a foolish consistency that may drive you to twist these views into some uncomfortable "symmetry." Jyotisha, a faithful celestial mirror of life, is no more symmetrical than the life it mirrors. Take pleasure in each vista, and let your soul supply the inspiration that will revive that elephant. Atop it, you may then tour your relationships enjoyably and effectively, probing for the happiness that lies within them.

BHAVA AND RASA

$$The$$ first stop on our tour of Jyotisha's techniques for evaluating relationships is at the conceptual border that separates skillful divination from educated guessing. Several new and beautiful Sanskrit words will board our vehicle at this stop. Even if you have no facility for languages, your appreciation for and enjoyment of Jyotisha will greatly benefit if you will take the time to make the acquaintance of a few of these words.

SUKHA

Sukha, which most translators render as "happiness," literally means "good space." More than the exclusively emotional state that many of us think of when we think of "happiness," sukha is a state in which all the many "spaces" of a life are "good." These include (but are not limited to) the physical space of the body, the fiscal space of the bank account, the psychological space of the mind, the living spaces in one's home and community, the communal spaces that compose a society, and the moral space of the soul. A couple in relationship shares many spaces, each of which contributes to the overall condition of their mutual sukha.

Sukha appears in a life only when internal satisfaction blends with external plenty. A person who is emotionally optimistic, but living the life of a beggar without suitable amenities, may be "happy," but possesses no more sukha than the rich man whose heart has shriveled. Sukha is a relationship that develops when you are able to convert the circumstances in which you find yourself into satisfying experiences. Sukha may be associated with and may promote *shanti* (peace), but it does not, in and of itself, guarantee peace, for sukha may require quite an effort to establish and maintain. A person may spend so much time and effort juggling the realities of life that there is no time to be peaceful, despite the satisfaction that sukha may provide.

Sukha is one of those useful generalizations that support classical India's multivalent mode of thinking. A jyotishi who says, "Your fourth house being afflicted, you have had no sukha of mother," utters a general statement whose potential specific interpretations are many. The facts of the parent and child's life together may have been at fault (perhaps the mother died early, or gave the child up for adoption, or had a truly wretched life), or the shortcomings may have derived from their personal acts (the child may have abused his mother, or been beaten by her). While both may have been generally healthy, peaceable, and well adjusted, they may simply have been a poor match for one another. The child may have been unhappy with the mother, or vice versa, or their relations, though cordial, may have been dry and unsatisfying. Astute clients will intuit that their personal situation is likely to reflect any of these scenarios, to different degrees. Because this perception of sukha is complex and textured, you may obtain a tolerably accurate representation of your relationship with your mother. Understanding some of the complexity of the underlying flavor of this relationship, however, will provide you with a background against which you can interpret the specific incidents that have made up your lifelong interaction.

A good jyotishi will know in which areas of life sukha is likely, and in which of our relationships sukha may tend to elude us. Many of us spend our lives searching blindly for sukha, when just a small investment of time and energy studying Jyotisha's maps can show us reliable paths that can lead us thence. When we unroll them, we find these maps to sukha are written in the language of *bhava* and *rasa*.

BHAVA AND RASA

A *bhava* is a state or condition. Depending on context, a bhava may be a state of existence, a state of mind, or a state of karma. Your natal horoscope is a snapshot of your bhava, the overall state of your karma, at the moment of your birth. An horary chart is an outline of your karmic state at the moment you query a jyotishi about some aspect of your life. Jyotisha distinguishes three degrees of intensity for "fated" karmas, intensities that may apply to one, many, or all areas of a person's life. *Dridha* (fixed) karmas give fixed pleasurable or painful results, because they are so difficult to change that they are practically immutable. *Dridha-adridha* (fixed/unfixed) karmas, good or bad, can be changed with considerable effort through the concentrated application of creative will. They give fixed or unfixed results, according to the amount of effort employed toward the goal of change. Bhavas that display *adridha* (unfixed) karmas produce results that can easily be altered by the concentrated application of creative will.

Karma is such a complex business that astrologers divide horoscopes into twelve smaller *bhavas* (astrological houses, in this context), each of which defines the state of karma of one portion of your life: children, career, home, education, relationship, and so on. Taken together, these twelve horoscope bhavas house the totality of your external existence—your objective experiences, the things that "actually happen to you" in the world—as they are experienced by the internal states of your being, your subjective perceptions of those events. When a skillful jyotishi reads your horoscope, he or she first teases the bhavas apart, to analyze them, then carefully recombines them into a narrative that describes for you both the skills that you bring to certain areas of your life and the outcomes you can expect through the operation of those skills.

Frequently, we find that careful application of good skills will produce good results. We also all know of cases, however, where consistent hard work produces little or no practical result during a lifetime. And we have all heard of those who found the heavens showering blessings on them simply because they happened to be in the right place at the right time. Vincent van Gogh provides us a good example of how dramatically skills and outcomes can be mismatched in one life. Recognized now as one of the fathers of Modern Art (a testimony to his skills), he was an abject professional failure during his lifetime (the outcome that he personally experienced when he used those skills). He focused on his art to the exclusion of all the other bhavas of his existence, so much so that, when the weight of his internal experience of his external rejection became unbearable, he took his own life. Someone else in a similar situation, someone better able to withstand external rejection, might have taken a more philosophical view of his plight and settled down resignedly to a quiet life of composing canvases in Arles.

The difference between van Gogh's subjective perceptions of the events of his life and the subjective perceptions of this hypothetical other represents differences in their *rasas*. Our rasas (juices, essence) are what we experience as a result of our bhavas. Individual bhavas produce individual rasas, and the overall bhava of life produces an overall rasa that is the "expression in juice" of that life's unique flavor. *Rasa*, in Sanskrit, means "juice," in all senses of that word. Water, lymph, blood plasma, semen, other tissue juices, fruit and vegetable juices, meat soup, metals in general and the metal mercury in particular, and taste (both in the mouth and in the mind) are all rasas, all "fluid realities." The flavors of the juices that make up our bodies and minds combine to create our personal emotional rasas, the subjective perceptions that are the juices that water our souls.

While an existence bereft of emotions is dry and tasteless (in Sanskrit, *rasahina*), bitter emotions (like those of profound grief, extreme fear, and intense possessive jealousy) make for a bitter, mislived life. Unpalatable rasas can kill, as they killed van Gogh. Even romantic love, the ideal to which so many of us aspire, can, when unbalanced or misguided, destroy all hope of the happiness it promises. Love is wonderful, but merely being in love may not inspire a couple to develop a consensus over mundane issues, like who will pay the rent and who will wash the windows. Many people today are so afraid of the potential peril of their emotions that they label emotion "unnatural, untruthful," and try hard to eliminate it from their lives. Emotion is, in fact, so natural and so expressive of the truth of what lies within us, however, that very few people ever completely escape its coils. Why should we seek emotional emptiness when, with a little emotional intelligence, we can discover healthy ways to know and manage our emotions? Our relationships with others can improve dramatically when we learn to think as much of their rasas as of our own. Emotionally intelligent individuals know that their own lives become richly satisfying when the lives of those with whom they interact are richly satisfying as well.

Although bhava and rasa are causally related, they are not identical, just as the tree differs from the seed that gives it birth. Differing bhavas can sometimes produce very similar rasas, as was the case during the Impressionist period of painting, when men and women with vastly different life milieus (suggesting widely varied horoscopic patterns) succeeded in creating a body of work that is substantially uniform in rasa. On the other hand, similar bhavas can sometimes produce very different rasas. An Indian and an American with the same horoscopes will, for example, respond to their *grahas* (the "planets" of Jyotish) in different ways, due to differences in their upbringings and social environments. Moreover, their genetics will differ, as will the palms of their hands. Two people with identical bhavas are still two different people, who will probably respond differently, even to life events that are comparable.

The rasas you create from your bhavas is often determined by the choices that your current and evolving internal physical, mental, and emotional grooves encourage you to select. These grooves, which in turn, generally—but not exclusively—are determined by your pre-existing karmas, which can be read from the twelve bhavas of your horoscope. The more you escape from these pre-existing grooves, using your will or initiative karma to actively transform your bhava raw material into enjoyable rasas, the less these grooves will be readable in your natal horoscope. Delicious rasas make for a delectable life, a life of sukha. Rasas arise from a dynamic interaction between fate and free will, between the karmas we have brought with us into this life and the ones we are performing now. Jyotishis attempt, in their analyses, to evaluate how easily toothsome rasas can develop in your existence, how "fated" they will seem to be. Jyotisha also estimates how easy it will be for you to use your initiative karma, your "free will," to transform potentially disruptive situations into satisfying experiences.

A truly satisfying life is *rasatmaka*, filled to the brim with pure, refreshing emotions that permeate the very core of your being. The richest lives, those filled with greatest sukha, are those lived by the handful of spiritual giants among us. These emotional geniuses learn to reunite the fragmented bhavas of their lives into one coherent, focused bhava they "cook" into one singular, sublimely tasty, spiritual rasa. One such man of God, Sri Ramakrishna Paramahamsa, made his life rasatmaka by coddling all his bhava-moods into one *maha bhava* ("super bhava"), a *samadhi* (spiritual trance) in which he went mad with uncontrollable love and joy. From his *maha bhava samadhi*, Ramakrishna distilled *parama rasa* ("supreme rasa"), the transcendental flavor of God-consciousness that became, for him, a daily diet. In this, he followed his namesake, India's divine cowherd, Krishna, that paragon of rasatmaka-ness who is chock-full of blissful emotion.

As with ordinary people, so with saints: comparable rasa-states can arise from disparate circumstances. Sri Ramakrishna and St. Francis of Assisi lived in distinct times and countries and followed dissimilar paths. Because they dedicated themselves to unifying their very different bhavas, however, they were each able to distill from their experiences similar states of parama rasa. Any sort of spiritual bhava can produce results when followed sincerely, though only those unified bhavas that can be guaranteed to create unselfish states will ultimately relate to divinity. Adolf Hitler's unified, but egotistic monomaniacal, bhava unification, for example, does not qualify. Some of the bhavas that India's saints and sages have perfected over the millennia in their quest for relationship with God include:

- *Shanta*, the serene affection of a loving wife for her husband;
- *Dasya*, the humble devotedness of an obedient servant for his master;
- *Sakhya*, the friendly camaraderie of two near-equals;
- *Vatsalya*, the maternal ardor of a mother for her child;
- *Madhurya*, the intensely fervent craving that a passionate woman feels for her lover;
- *Virodha*, the intense hatred of God and everything for which God stands.

Every couple reflects, at any particular moment of its relationship life, some bhava. If they preferentially indulge in one bhava to the exclusion of others, it will eventually become a habit. Healthy bhavas create grooves that facilitate the production of ever healthier rasa, and ever deeper sukha; unhealthy bhavas do the opposite. Healthy or not, two people who form a relationship habit tend to return to it, for it comes to form the chief source of that relationship's rasa. Even a couple whose relationship seems essentially "dysfunctional" to observers may be experiencing substantial subjective enjoyment through their interaction. They may, in fact, so condition themselves to bickering that they refuse to consider new ways of relating, for fear of sacrificing what juice they have learned to suck from the situation.

Some years ago, one of us went on a joint vacation with a married couple who squabbled incessantly from sunrise to sunset about what seemed like trifles. They debated what to have for breakfast and where to have it, which way to face the chairs on the beach, the cost of the vacation versus the value received, the age and condition of his bathing suit, what she said to a waiter, on and on, ad nauseam. Some of these tempestuous arguments displayed an intensity that made their companions so distinctly uncomfortable that they resolved never to commit casually to a future vacation with any other couple. Astonishingly, however, on the way home, the couple turned to their fellow travelers and said enthusiastically "That was fun! Let's do it again soon!" Twenty years later this couple still seems inseparable; quite naturally so, for who else would so enthusiastically accept such a quarrelsome sentence for life?

Despite such examples of couples who find ways to extract a workable outcome from poor relating skills, belligerence is rarely an effective relationship bhava. Rasa gets poisoned by the venom of selfishness, and purified by the nectar of benevolence. Each of our thoughts and actions transmutes bhava into rasa within us, the rasa becoming sweeter as the motives become purer. Healthy rasa begins to ooze into our lives when our bhavas, our normal states of being, get "well cooked."

Ramakrishna found ecstasy in his relationship with his goddess. Any of us can taste the flavor of that ecstasy, even if on a smaller scale, in our own relationships, if we are willing to refine our one-pointedness. Life is like a lasagna: raw materials that may be only modestly savory on their own can develop a superb flavor when they are combined in the right order and baked in an appropriate vessel at a reasonable temperature for a judicious length of time. Most of us require rasa-cookery classes to optimize our rasa-experiences, however, for uneven bhavas produce lumpy rasas. Only good luck (previous good karma) can guarantee that a pleasingly sweet rasa will arise between two people who have not consciously learned how to generate healthy rasa within themselves.

The many arts and sciences handed down from ancient India seek, through their varied disciplines, to generate this sort of ecstasy-flecked rasa, the sort of healthy rasa without which no life is well lived, alone or in relationship. The *Dasharupa*, a classical work on dramaturgy written by Dhananjaya, avers that "there is no subject that cannot succeed in conveying Sentiment *(rasa)* among mankind."[1] The *Dasharupa* describes five types of *svada* (enjoyment) that arise from nine rasas, the last of which is the "peaceable rasa." Dhananjaya maintains that the peaceable rasa is the ground on which all the other rasas play. Peace of mind is, to him, an experience of the "permanent *state*" *(sthayin bhava)* that produces tranquillity, eliminates cravings for the pleasures of the senses, and promotes repose in the knowledge of the absolute reality.

One prerequisite for peace of mind is usually (but not always) peace of body, for, of all our sense impressions, the tastes in our food influence our physiology most. All our sensory inputs are food for us, no doubt, and all contribute to our rasas. Physical food is fundamental, however, for it creates our physical bodies. Food is just one more inanimate object to us until it enters our internal environment, at which point its flavors and other qualities

[1] Joseph Campbell, *The Inner Reaches of Outer Space* (New York: HarperCollins, 1986), p. 138.

begin to interact with our pre-existing rasas. Chilies and lemons look wholly innocuous while they sit on the plate. They are neutral to us until we taste them, at which point, they communicate their realities to us. The Sufis say that those who taste, know, and one can know quite a lot about most people by learning which food tastes they prefer. One branch of Ayurveda, India's classical healing art, details the effects on body and mind of the six tastes that form the most important source of rasas. A couple who eats together is more likely to stay together than one whose dietary habits are mutually disagreeable, for their dietary rasas influence the very rasa they are trying to produce together.

We all tend to seek in our environments (and thus, often, from our partners) the rasas that we cannot produce within ourselves. Our genes and chromosomes determine those rasas we can manufacture internally and that we have to extract somehow from the world without. While mystics like Ramakrishna learn to obtain within themselves every rasa that they require, the rest of us look mainly outward for the rasas we feel we lack. We search for rasa in each substance and action that we encounter, and each encounter offers its rasa to our main rasa. All these rasas, whether derived internally or externally, combine to form the overarching rasa of the moment. Rasa (subjective experience) and bhava (objective condition) interact continually, reinforcing or counteracting one another in a perpetual dance of potential and attainment.

Those who surrender to the indiscriminate dictates of their desires put themselves at the mercy of their rasas, sinking eventually beneath the waves of that ocean of emotion. Those who choose instead to maneuver through their rasas find themselves creating their own "fluid realities." The word *rasa* indicates both the flavor of one's life juice and the juice itself, and a well-lived life usually produces rasas that are healthy both in quality and quantity. A life of bitterness desiccates the overall level of rasa in the organism (making that being *rasabina*) and pollutes whatever juice is created with misery-filled, ego-centered emotions.

Ayurveda seeks to achieve healthy sentiments and enjoyments by purifying, strengthening, and refining the body's physical rasas through application of *rasayana* (rejuvenation; literally, "the path of rasa"). Practitioners of Tantra like Ramakrishna turn rasayana into the *sadhana* (spiritual discipline) of *rasa vidya* (alchemy). Rasa vidya teases and manipulates substances into elixirs that, when consumed, judiciously transmute fragmented, limited personal rasas into a personal *parama rasa*.

India's other aesthetic pursuits, including music, dance, and architecture, focus on the rasas of the mind. The many *ragas* of Indian music, for example, are bhava-refining fires (the word *raga* also means "rage," "passion,"
"redness," and "inflammation"). When talented Indian musicians play
ragas, they so construct the rhythms and harmonies that, by the end of the
performance, the crude bhavas of their listeners have brewed within them
into graceful, elegant, satisfying rasas. Some dedicated musicians turn their
craft into a sadhana; a select few ride their music all the way to the state of
maha bhava.

Two people who have been educated in how to tread the path of rasa
together can work to transmute their personal rasas into a mutual,
transpersonal parama rasa. Any sincere couple can pilot music, art, poetry,
or some other shared pursuit into a sublime shared bhava whose rasa can
provide them lifelong satisfaction, provided that they are willing to invest the
time and energy necessary to achieve that transformation.

For you as an individual to extract successfully the rasa of your potential from the dross of your false ideals, idiosyncrasies, and ignorant habits is,
in itself, the achievement of a lifetime. For you to succeed at creating a mutual rewarding rasa with another being—a savor that you both share, but
that is simultaneously distinct from you both—is something so truly wonderful that it occurs only rarely without the expenditure of sustained effort.
That effort is truly worth while, however, if the couple is truly compatible,
for the two can find in one another keys to unifying their bhavas that they
might never have found otherwise on their own.

The word *couple* may be a singular noun both in English and in Sanskrit, but very few couples ever reach the stage where they become a true
"singularity." How often it is that one person finds delight and the other dis-
may in the selfsame situation! Rasa flows better when those who try to create it are aware of their own bhava preferences and understand how their
own internal mental grooves may incline them to make certain choices and
avoid others. Understanding personal preferences enhances a couple's
awareness of their mutual bhava-rasa alignment options. Jyotisha can help a
couple achieve this.

Unlike humans, animals are driven wholly by their inner grooves, their
instincts. These grooves make them predictable. Humans have free will, the
choice to hop out of their grooves. That choice, however, is activated only
when one becomes aware of one's grooves. As long as you ignore your
grooves, you will conform to them, so your experiences of your existence will

seem "fated." If you permit your natural proclivities to distort your relationship bhava because you are unwilling to examine your ruts soberly and act on
what you find, do not be surprised if your relationship rasas lose their savor.

AURAS

How relationships develop for you will depend on how well your mutual
rasa flows. Mutual compatibility is one key to how much time and energy
will be required to achieve the desired rasa. When two people share "chemistry," their every interaction tends to promote intensifying passion (raga),
which will quickly concoct their bhavas into an intoxicating, captivating
rasa. Two people whose "chemistry" is completely off often, with their every
interaction, develop an ever-deepening mutual revulsion *(dvesha)* that can
drive them apart, reducing daily their potential for shared success at "relationship alchemy." Relationship chemistry is just that: a function of rasa
permutation, of the chemistry of our "fluid realities." The raga and dvesha
that we experience today conditions our potential responses tomorrow. As
one of these two motivators gains momentum in a relationship, it guides our
experience of that relationship ever more firmly into the one or the other
groove: passion or revulsion.

As you better understand the intensity (fixed, fixed/unfixed, unfixed)
of the pre-existing karmic grooves that encourage you to conform to your innate tendencies (the parts of your behavior that are "instinctual" to you),
you will better understand how to maneuver your way across your personal
relationship landscape. Unfixed relationships are blank tablets on which you
may write any story you please. Fixed relationships are those in which no
amount of personal effort on your part is likely to produce much of a change.
How your fixed/unfixed relationships play out depends on how seriously
you exercise your free will to plan and execute an *upaya* (astrological remedy), of which many appear within Jyotisha's traditional corpus.

Your karmic ruts influence every aspect of your existence. The condi-
tioning they produce often determines how your organism interacts with its
environment and how it perceives those interactions. We can view and
interact with these encounters in any number of ways, each of which may
express some relative truth, including examination of electrochemically determined behaviors or psychological propensities. Here we emphasize the classical perspectives on human demeanor that ancient India developed. Moreover,
when we do discuss psychology, we will be less interested in what things may
"mean" to you than in whether or not they work for you. Obsessive searches

for "meaning" all too frequently do little more than make it more difficult to relate personally to the relationship. Healthy relationships are living beings, and no living being responds well to being poked, prodded, or vivisected. End-less analysis can, in Thomas Moore's words, "dry out a relationship with the drive toward understanding."[2] No rasa? No relationship!

We prefer to evaluate human interchanges in terms of the attraction or repulsion of *auras*, the fields of energy that surround living organisms. Auras are more subtle structures than body tissues. They are, therefore, more pervasive and, hence, truer representatives of reality than most physi-cal representations. Jungian psychological and physiological types, though better approximations of the classical Indian paradigm, still only approxi-mate aura reality. We use "aura" as a translation for the Sanskrit term *chaya*, which can mean "shadow," "reflection," and "luster." The human aura is fun-damentally all these things; it is the shadow that matter creates when illu-mined by consciousness, and the luster that radiates when consciousness reflects itself in the mirror of matter. Aura is the difference between the lus-ter of the living and the pallor of the dead.

Auras arise wherever consciousness makes itself apparent. Each of us actually has several different auras, one for each of many "bodies," or sheaths *(koshas)*, that nature fabricates as consciousness penetrates and per-meates increasingly denser matter. The passage of awareness through the space that surrounds a sheath creates an aura in that neighborhood, in the same way that the passage of electricity through the wire filament of a light-bulb produces light. Each sheath develops its own luminous aura. Ulti-mately, all these radiances intermingle to form the aura of an organism. Organisms project their auras with the help of *ojas*, an exceptionally subtle form of rasa. This makes an individual's aura an exceptionally subtle expres-sion of his or her personal rasa.

Each sheath represents consciousness expressing itself at a different level of matter. Five sheaths are commonly described in classical Indian traditions:

- Sheath of food *(annamayakosha,* the physical body);
- Sheath of prana *(pranamayakosha,* the body in whose channels prana, the life-force, moves);
- Sheath of manas *(manomayakosha,* the astral or subtle body; loosely, the mind);

---

[2] Thomas Moore, *Soul Mates* (New York: HarperCollins, 1994), p. 25.

- Sheath of wisdom (*vijnanamayakosha*, the causal body, where karmas are stored);
- Sheath of bliss (*anandamayakosha*, the greater causal body).

These five sheaths, each with its own awareness, embrace one another more tightly than the petals of a rosebud. *Prana* is the power that strings body, mind, and spirit together like beads on a strand of breath (the Chinese call it *chi*). *Manas* is the perceiving and thinking mind, the controller and director of the senses. The sheath of prana (some call it the etheric body) connects the sheaths of food and manas and permits them to operate together. The sheath of wisdom is your personal karmic depository. It determines how your body and mind develop, subject to the influences of the sheath of bliss, which holds the karmas you share with your family, neighbors, and fellow citizens. "Self- awareness" in most everyone is a conglomeration of the awareness of the five subtle bodies into one overall personal awareness. This occurs via the action of the "integrating awareness" (*ahamkara*, the I-forming power of con-sciousness), the power that makes you *you* by identifying with all the self-images that these awarenesses create.

The subtler a sheath, the more influential it will be to your overall awareness. The condition of your physical body is, thus, sure to influence your mental state, but your body generally influences your mind less than your mind affects your body. Your mind, in turn, is strongly swayed by the condition of your causal body. As your karmas ripen, they project into your astral body, where they induce you to achieve or avoid certain ends. Your mind then directs your etheric body to coordinate and energize your physi-cal body to carry out certain schemes and evade others. This system permits your stored karmas to be worked out without your conscious mind ever needing to be aware of the process. We thus have an ancient Indian forerun-ner of the modern, often blurry, notion of the mechanism of action of the human unconscious. This sophisticated Indian notion is as crucial to Jyotisha as modern psychology has become to Western astrology.

AURAS AND RELATIONSHIP

Most everything we have said for bhava and rasa holds true for the aura as well. Each of us is born with certain instinctual "grooves" that contain and mold our auras. Some of these grooves are amenable to change when suffi-cient willpower is applied to them in a diligent and directed way. Others, and the rasas they produce, change with the greatest of difficulty. The union of the physical, pranic, mental/emotional, causal, and greater causal rasas that our physical, pranic, mental/emotional, causal, and greater causal bhavas produce creates the one rasa that generates the one aura that we bare to the world. For centuries, Ayurveda and Tantra have understood how important it is to begin life on the right foot, with healthy bhavas and rasas and healthy grooves into which to pour them. Your overall aura becomes pure and coherent only when the bhavas and rasas on all levels of your being develop a coherent, harmonious, fully interpenetrated relationship.

Ancient techniques teach couples how to align themselves, that their offspring may be properly aligned with them and with the world into which they are born. When two people coordinate their breathing, they coordinate their prana. This can then be used to influence a child's sex, and to direct the development of its personal physical and mental constitution that it may enjoy a fundamentally healthful foundation for its life. Creatures like hummingbirds, who breathe hastily, live fleetingly; slow-breathing creatures, like the elephant and the tortoise, endure. Haste makes waste, in all life's venues. Healthful sexual adjustment is less a matter of orgasmic apportionment and more an affair of how a couple learns to share and exchange prana, thoughts, and food. In short, their sheaths must harmonize.

Alignment and rhythm are as essential for the creation of a healthy relationship as they are for the creation of a child. Any two individuals are bound to align well in certain walks of life and misalign in others. Each misalignment translates into a potential conflict. When a couple's sheaths of food are seriously misaligned, one will feel a physical revulsion for the body, or perhaps the diet, of the other, a situation that is highly unlikely to promote marital harmony without compromise on both parts. One of our clients reports that his Korean mother had to keep her kimchi (the delicious Korean relish of cabbage, chilies, and garlic) in a refrigerator in the garage, out of the range of her redneck American husband's nose. A crude solution, perhaps, but one that worked.

If the sheath of prana of one partner fails to align with the sheath of manas in the other, disturbances of prana and mind become likely in both, for what disturbs prana disturbs mind, and vice versa. Once prana and mind are disturbed, the physical body finds it difficult to remain balanced, and this imbalance will soon spread to the remaining sheaths as well. Whether these confrontations become relationship breakers, or merely force the members of the partnership to review their ideals that they may "straighten up and fly right," depends greatly on the degree of aura misalignment. This, in turn, is a matter that can often be judged with the help of an Indian horoscope, as we will see in detail below.

THE GRAHAS AS AURA MANIPULATORS

The nine *grahas*, the "planets" of Jyotisha, produce within you aura vectors that speed you in particular directions. Your horoscope is a map of your overall aura, for you can only be born at the moment when the aura created by your causal body resonates strongly with the auras created by the position of the nine grahas in the sky. The nine grahas are much stronger than you, thus your personal aura usually strongly reflects the grahas that molded you at birth. One person may have a Saturnine look, another may project a lunar "something." These looks can frequently be verified from the horoscope, which often accordingly displays a strong and prominent Saturn or Moon.

Satisfying predictions can be made of how well the auras of the owners of two birth charts will mesh by comparing the positions of the grahas in their horoscopes. Where these graha forces are powerful and negative, they will shape you at their will if you do nothing to try to modify them, for they are likely to overrun even your sincerest efforts to intercept them, unless your personal energy is very strong. In such cases, only judicious application of skillful occult and spiritual means (upayas) can thwart the worst of these graha influences (though they are still likely to affect you to some extent). By improving the conditions that the grahas create within you, upayas can sometimes improve your relationship.

Indians have, for centuries, consulted astrologers when their children reach marriageable age, that they may find a well-meshed match for each child. Most Westerners do not yet have access to such advice. If, on astrological evaluation, you find that you have wed someone whose aura fails to parallel yours properly, do not, for heaven's sake, rush out and get a divorce! Nor should you seek to divorce your parents or your children or your other family members solely on the basis of astrological misalignment. Seek first to discover how you can remedy the situation, to create alignment where little exists, before you abandon the situation. Learn how you react, how your partner reacts, and how your reactions blend.

Any two people who interact affect each other's auras. Even sleeping next to or breakfasting with someone allows that someone's aura to influ-

ence yours. The longer and stronger the influence, the more you will be affected. That is why we commonly see that couples who spend lots of time
together start to look like each other, particularly if their time together is
harmonious in the main. In healthy relationships, the auras of the two partners begin to blend. On the other hand, spending long periods with someone with whom you do not relate well can often cause your auras to learn to
chronically repel one another. Poor aura integration is one explanation for
the observed fact that a sports team that lacks cohesion, even if its players
are supreme talents, can often be beaten by another more cohesive team of
lesser lights.

Since everything has an energy field, any two related things (animate
or inanimate) influence each other. How well the auras of two things interact (which can often be determined through Jyotisha) determines whether
this influence acts on you for better or for worse. Jyotishical theory has it
that the nine grahas pervade every aspect of our environment, surfacing in
the nine numbers of our base ten numbering system (from which issues a
digital world's reality) and in the many qualities that gratify or disgust our
senses (which are very sensitive to auras).

Take, as an example, the sense of sight, which sees auras as colors.
The nine grahas of Jyotisha appear visually in our world as the seven colors of the visible spectrum, plus the two invisible, but cognizable,
"hues"—infrared and ultraviolet—that appear at either end of the spectrum. Most people remain unaware of how influences like the dark (Saturnian) decor of a room can enter them like a noxious fume and create
depression, for such linkages are rarely obvious to the casual observer.
The task of Jyotisha is to make these influences more evident, that they
may be remedied.

Suppose that a jyotishi informs you that the position of the grahas in
your horoscope suggests that a red car will lead you into trouble. What he
means is that, when you spend time in a red car, its aura enters you. It,
when added to your aura, creates a strong field of "redness." If that field becomes strong enough to overwhelm the equilibrium of your awareness, it
may then attract you into a potentially detrimental "red" situation.

Red vehicles are not inherently bad, of course. Not all people are "al-
lergic" to red cars, and driving autos of a scarlet hue may even benefit some
people. Even if red cars are potentially detrimental to you, you probably
don't need to decline every offer of a lift in a car that happens to be red. If
you cannot afford any other conveyance, you may well be better off cau-
tiously driving your antiquated red clunker around town, instead of doing

without transportation altogether. But your horoscope suggests that, since red is a color that you digest with difficulty, the likelihood of untoward events occurring in your life increases the longer you interact with your crimson car.

Every substance and action in your environment reflects some quality or other of one or more of the nine grahas. The more you associate yourself discerningly with places and things whose qualities agree with your aura, the more harmony will accrue to you and your aura. Associate instead with places and things that are less agreeable to your aura, and the likelihood of problems will multiply.

SATSANGA AND KUSANGA

The principles of *satsanga* and *kusanga* link harmony with aura agreement, particularly in the context of interactions with other people. Complexities multiply when two living beings mingle auras, for their powers of volition and choice introduce more variables into the encounter than inanimate objects can muster. Surrounding yourself with people whose auras agree with yours is an essential, but not a sufficient, condition for a happy and healthy life. You must also ensure that you interact primarily with people who are "true"—who, by and large, unselfishly pursue altruistic goals in their lives. When you overexpose yourself to "bad" people—those whose juices are one-pointedly selfish—some of their selfishness may rub off on you. This is the basis for the Sanskritic distinction between satsanga ("true blending") and kusanga ("bad blending").

Trouble may, of course, arise even when two fundamentally "good" people interact, if their auras fail to mesh. What is satsanga for one person may well be kusanga for another, if the rasas don't agree. We have all experienced situations in which we simply find ourselves disliking someone in a strongly "intuitive" way. Such repulsion may merely represent your reflexive response to sensory cues in the other that somehow displease you. How can such a behaviorist explanation, however, account for those sudden bedeviling sensations of malevolence that force you to turn around to confront a seemingly innocuous, nonthreatening person. Were you "seeing" that person through the back of your head? Did you overreact to some unconscious auditory or pheromonal signal of theirs? We suggest, instead, that it was your auras that clashed.

As a general rule, auras that mesh well promote in us a sense of raga, of excited enthusiasm, while auras that clash augment the experience of dvesha, repugnance. Raga "drags" you into involvement with those whose auras are agreeabls to your own. Dvesha spurs you to flee in disgust from those whose aura is incompatible with yours. When we find positive alignments between the grahas in two horoscopes, we confidently expect raga to bring the couple closer in this context. When, instead, we discover grahas that are negatively disposed to one another, we expect that, in those arenas of life, the couple will be prone to dvesha.

While intuitive likes and dislikes occur in any sort of coupling—parent and child, business partners, good friends—they are perhaps most pronounced in romantic pairings, for sex profoundly enhances aura intermingling. Sexual caresses can whisk auras into a state of exceptional openness. Those who seek to unite their physical bodies alone, no matter how pleasing that union may be, will find their relationships determined for them almost unconsciously by the very aura interactions that they try to ignore. Those who are able to achieve some greater level of sexual exchange, by accident or design, do so only because they also somehow succeed at intertwining their deeper sheaths as well.

Sometimes, a couple whose "aura chemistry" is off will feel an unaccountable revulsion for one another when they are sexually intimate, even though they desire each other and cooperate reasonably well. All the congruence of manners and actions in the world can still leave two people feeling sexually disappointed, devitalized, cheated, or disturbed if their auras disagree. Sometimes, people go so far as to blame their partners for negligent behavior when they have done no more than to unknowingly precipitate experiences of disharmony via their sexual auras.

Similarly, aura misalignment is a better explanation for some cases of total misalignment of parents with children than is an assumption of poor parenting skills or psychological pathologies. Occasional misunderstandings are inevitable in any relationship, of course, at astrological moments when graha forces encourage auras to grow apart. Some parent-child misunderstandings, however, seem to begin at birth and carry on to the end of life. We suggest that you can hardly expect to enjoy a healthy "feel" for your children if your auras fail to align properly. Jyotisha can usually determine which parents and children may have immense difficulty getting along. Jyotisha's analysis then permits the parent to begin to ask, "What can I do to make some sort of harmony grow here?" instead of, "What's wrong with me?" or "What's wrong with this kid?" Though the situation may prove very hard to alter, realizing its nature can help to create a useful framework for the relationship.

Indian metaphysics suggests that, in certain cases, such misalignments occur at the moment of the child's conception. For example, if either member of a couple whose copulation results in pregnancy ardently visualizes someone other than his or her mate at the moment of climax, the intense aura activation thus caused will likely attract a soul aligned with the energies of that "other." The resulting child may then go on to have such different features and characteristics from its parents that it and they will have little common ground between them—which is a reliable recipe for misunderstanding. Such major misalignments can often be partially realigned through the eating of or abstinence from certain foods, the wearing of gemstones, the recitation of mantras, or other techniques of upaya.

Good relationships are generally more effortless when the two relaters have similar "feels" for the world, similar ways of seeing and relating to their environments. You should, therefore, ideally connect yourself with those people whose auras complement and thus benefit your own, people with whom your raga impels you to interact. You gain little and stand to lose much, however, when fear of failure leads you to refuse all meaningful interaction with people whose horoscopes suggest a relationship of less-than-effortless enjoyment with you. While this is particularly true of those with whom you are more or less obligated to interact (like blood relatives), it applies to everyone in your life, including a spouse you may have married before you were introduced to Jyotisha. After all, shotgun weddings sometimes endure long after love-marriages have become bitter memories.

It may also be true that you are unable to will yourself into a perfect relationship with anyone or anything just because you want to. Sometimes, it is simply not productive for two people to interact when they do not get along, despite pop psychology's assurances that someone who "gets under your skin" is showing you something in yourself. When two auras are so incongruous that the very textures of their perceptions differ, what will their possessors find to share? Even if two such people do somehow succeed at relating despite their dvesha, will that relationship be the best use of their energy and talents?

ASCENDANTS, MOONS, SUNS, VENUSES

Jyotisha provides a way to answer such queries, by determining the salient qualities of a person's various auras, and then comparing and contrasting these qualities with those produced by the sheaths of another. It does this by reading the physical body from the Ascendant, the astral or subtle body from the Moon, and the causal body from the Sun. Each of these factors rules different aspects of life, and a positive alignment between a pair of factors in two horoscopes suggests that those subjects will enjoy good potential to align those life aspects when they relate together.

Of the four varieties of functional alignment (described in detail later), the strongest attraction is that of "opposites." From magnetism to sexuality, we find nature teaching us by example that opposite polarities attract. In humans, this attraction often flows from a fascination (raga) with how our significant others differ from us. When, for example, the Ascendants of two horoscopes are in opposite constellations, the two people involved are generally most attracted by their "mutually opposite but complementary" circumstances in life, their external projections into the world, one of the things ruled by the Ascendant. This often takes the form of a natural and powerful appreciation for each other's physical body and/or habits. This is a generality, of course, for two people whose Ascendants oppose may allure one another in many different and not-always-predictable ways. We have found it to be generally (and often specifically) true, however, that attractions between two people with opposite Ascendants are based in physicality of one sort or another.

Similarly, when the Suns of two horoscopes occupy this alignment, they suggest (in general, and sometimes with great specificity) a natural complementarity of the couple's causal bodies, or souls. Two Suns that relate thus indicate that, at the foundations of their beings, the two people involved often hold different, but fundamentally complementary, things dear. In our culture, these "things" may be their "essential values"; in other places it may be their "true philosophy"; yet elsewhere, it may be their religion. For all, however, the Sun is the factor that motivates from the level of "soul."

When the Moons in two horoscopes sit opposite, there is likely to be a meeting of the emotional minds. When Venus, the marriage significator, is situated opposite in two charts, the two will be drawn to each other by mutual desire. Healthy people crave the rasas they lack. Moons that are opposites indicate an instinctual mutual emotional craving, a raga, for each other. Despite their differences (or even because of them), the two will show an innate "taste" for one another's rasas, in the same way that one person may have an inborn "taste" for sweets (despite being diabetic) and another may have a "taste" for spectator sports (while being a couch potato).

When two Venuses interact positively, each will see the other as an appropriate vehicle for enjoyment *(bhoga)*, in whatever fashion. The Moon represents instinctive tastes, and Venus represents the desire for some specific pleasure that is "enjoyable"—that is, both able to and fit to be enjoyed. While Venus may attract you to a certain play, movie, or restaurant, the Moon will help determine whether or not you get from that experience the taste that you crave. In this context, Moon represents bhava, the raw material from which a rasa may be created, and Venus, the graha that always seeks to balance and harmonize, represents the means through which you seek to create that rasa. As with the Ascendants and Suns, these general statements are often, but not always, specifically true.

Other possible combinations frequently occur, both between people and inside an individual, for Jyotisha is a complex study. Suppose Mr. X has such an instinctual craving (Moon) for ice cream that his body (Ascendant) becomes addicted to it, so addicted that he salivates each time he thinks of it (Venus saying, "Ice cream is a good way to obtain enjoyment in life!"). Here, Moon is the bhava, the spontaneous pleasure X derives from his ice cream. Venus extends this bhava into rasahood, extracting from a crude bhava a rasa that may, depending on the individual, be coarse or refined. At this point, the philosophical Sun sees no reason to demur.

All goes well until Mr. X visits his family physician and learns that he has diabetes. From now on the grahas, though they will continue to perform their assigned roles, will deliver messages with new implications for Mr. X's awareness. On the Moon level, his previous raga for ice cream has mutated into a continued passion for it, which alternates with a spontaneous but conditioned dvesha, a revulsion to it. Meanwhile, Mr. X's Ascendant/body probably still craves the sweets, there may be a desire on the Sun level to be a good boy and obey the doctor's advice, and Venus may be telling him that ice cream consumption is still the right way to enjoy life. Replace "ice cream" with "Ms. Y" in the above equations, and you quickly realize that there is no end to the possible ramifications of the interactions of these four important factors.

We can, of course, extend this principle of graha alignment to the other grahas. Two Mercuries who are opposites will often indicate complementarity of intellect, and two Jupiters as opposites point to complementarity of knowledge and wisdom (which may manifest in spiritual practices, or in approaches to providing wise counsel to one another). Complementarity does not necessarily mean similarity; it can also mean that the two complement each other in the functions that the graha indicates. One member of a couple with complementary Jupiters may, for example, be strongly attracted to the regular practice of religious ritual, while the other member, though uninterested in personal ritual performance, may obtain spiritual satisfaction by providing aid and comfort to the performance-oriented spouse.

Two Marses who are opposites suggest that the two people involved will find a mutual meshing of their preferences for types and intensities of activity. Mars represents challenges, and a couple for whom Mars is complementary may find that their tastes for demanding leisure-time physical activities agree (even if one is a professional parasailer and the other simply enjoys packing the parachutes). Such a couple is also likely to deal cooperatively in confrontations, for example, he will not cringe when she is dressing down the inept waiter. Two Saturns as opposites will promote mutual understanding of the diverse things that create feelings of responsibility, particularly around issues of human suffering and the tragedies of life. The one may, for example, be able to provide effective, structured support to a strategy that the other develops to handle the fallout from a death in the family. Opposite Saturns will also promote cooperation around the mundane affairs and details of the couple's life (such as, who keeps the accounts, how the household chores are allocated, and how extended family or career burdens are managed).

If, however, we focus mainly on how interpersonal relationships are born and develop, we must look principally to the Ascendant, Sun, Moon, and Venus. The general circumstances, souls, minds, and desires of two individuals must somehow meet if their liaison is to proceed from simple intersection to true connection.

CULTIVATING THE RASA

Life is relationship, and a successful life requires a successful rasa. How much satisfaction you extract from life depends on the aplomb with which you relate and the wisdom you use in establishing relationships. Tweaking your natural bhavas into submission (by repainting your car, say) can only form part of the process. Changing your physical circumstances will likely change your physical aura to some degree, but it is not likely to affect your astral aura greatly, and it will have, at best, a minor effect on your "causal aura," the beliefs that are created by your karmas. The (usually unconscious) beliefs that "trickle down" from the causal level are the ones you most need to change if you want to transmute your crude bhavas into tasty rasas. A musician may play all the right notes with the proper phrasing and emphasis. If those notes lack the right emotion, the audience will remain unmoved. To focus on technique alone is to ignore the energetic intermingling that actually creates the rasa. This is why most self-help books, tapes, and seminars fail to help their audience. When they do succeed, they succeed because the auras of the instructor and the student somehow mesh to generate some raga.

Jyotisha strives to prepare an admirable astrological rasa by working, not from the general ("Taurus people are tight with their money") to the specific ("Oh, you are a Taurus, are you? Let's go Dutch!"), but from the specific to the general. Jyotisha first discerns the pattern that lurks within a long list of seemingly disconnected factors, then seeks to make that pattern cohere in an accurate image of an individual's reality. Like those computer-generated 3-D images that suddenly become apparent to you when you look through them in a particular way, a Jyotishical image springs into being when you look "through" the raw data to the karmic mechanisms behind their curtain.

Once an image has formed, many seemingly irrelevant pieces will constellate around it, engendering a narrative of the horoscope's owner origins, present reality, and fortune. The astrological image is the chairman of the board whose directors are Jyotisha's principles. It is the focus around which information orders itself, like the seed around which an oyster forms a pearl or the sky a snowflake. Remember this as your conscious mind reads the subsequent chapters of this book, and allow your subconscious and unconscious minds to focus on the image around which those principles will coalesce. Use what you read to examine your own relationships, and allow the aura of the words to penetrate your own, that it may aid your relationship rasa to flower and flow.

2

RELATIONSHIP SKILLS

S*ynastry* is the art of comparing the horoscopes of the participants in a relationship, assessing aura interaction with an eye to promoting a smooth, durable relationship dynamic. Whether a proposed relationship is appraised in foresight, or an existing union in hindsight, synastry's consistent goal is to promote mindfulness among the relaters of the inherent strengths and weaknesses of their relationship pattern. Conscious awareness of relationship habits encourages useful inclinations to be more selective and productive, and undermining tendencies to be modified or terminated. The insights of synastry contribute, thereby, to enhanced sukha, encouraging the spaces of a relationship to become more rasatmaka, more filled with the nectar of understanding.

SYNASTRY AND NATAL ASTROLOGY

Effective though it may be, synastry is a secondary method, a derivative of the primary natal, or birth-chart astrology. Synastry, which is usually used in astrology when two horoscopes are brought together for a specific proposed relation, does not address the crucial question of how well or poorly each of two individuals are likely to relate independently with the world as a whole. That question falls within the purview of natal astrology. Natal astrology provides insight about an individual's ultimate patterns in the marital sphere, and synastry comments on how that person will interact with the particular partner that he or she does marry. Natal astrology can describe, in a general sense, an individual's overall experience in the many categories of relationship, including liaisons with siblings, children, and

business partners, while synastry offers detailed evaluation of these relationship categories. Synastry describes how a person interacts with a particular brother or sister, as opposed to how that person experiences his or
her siblings collectively.

The several techniques used to pursue synastry's aims require us to
assess horoscopes interactively, by transferring the grahas of one chart into
the chart of another. These methods effectively "add" two independent
charts together to measure what the two produce as an aggregate. Astrologers East and West have used this hypothetical transferring of grahas from
one horoscope to another over many centuries to assess the degree of harmony that two people create when they interact. We introduced this concept of synastry at the end of the previous chapter, when we briefly
described what can happen when one person's Sun, Moon, or other graha
occupies the *rashi* (any of the 12 astrological constellations) opposite to that
of another person's Sun, Moon, or other graha.

Synastry is, thus, based more in symbolism than in astronomical fact,
given that none of the grahas can be in more than one position in the sky at
a time. Being distinctly symbolic, synastry is rather more theoretical than
natal astrology. Synastry says to two people whose horoscopes mesh mag-
nificently according to its rules, "You two are likely to have a blissful life together, provided that you actually get involved and that your individual natal
horoscopes each promise satisfaction in relationship." Other methods,
prashna in particular, are employed to answer the vital question of whether
those people can or will get involved. Many people whose birth charts intertwine perfectly are people who will never meet, or who, if they do meet, may
not enter into relationship for one reason or another.

Even those couples who do actually get involved and whose horoscopes intertwine uncommonly well through synastry may experience serious friction when they interact, if their individual birth charts display
difficult relationship patterns. Because every couple is formed of two individuals, each member of the union contributes his or her own individual
karmic relationship baggage from the past. Synastry can provide flavor—it
can show how a specific match can improve, or disturb the situation that the
seventh (marriage) bhava of a horoscope promises—but it is unlikely to independently transcend the overall karmic conditions described by the individuals' natal charts. Experience suggests, moreover, that a person whose
individual horoscope indicates poor possibilities for happy relationships will
typically attract someone with similar prospects. In such situations, the
partners often find themselves spurring one another along the path of mutu-

ally unpleasant relationship adventure—their karma—through which opportunities will arise to learn beneficial lessons.

This tendency for "birds of a karmic feather to flock together" does
not mean that all difficult relationships are doomed. We also know from experience that some difficult relationships do endure and do become mutually
satisfying. In certain instances, horoscopes that are well suited to each other
can actually mitigate some of the personal tendencies to relationship disrup-
tion that may afflict the individual partners. The key that unlocks the shack-
les of relationship misery appears when one or both partners commit to
cultivating a cooperative state that is appropriate for the relationship, be it
dasya (humble devotion), sakhya (friendly camaraderie), or some other. A
cooperative bhava can promote the development of a rasa that is suitable for
that pairing, a rasa that will both assure for the couple the best they can
achieve in that relationship and pave the way for future relationship sukha.

People with mediocre or neutral patterns in their individual birth
charts usually attract partners with similar tendencies. Those with brilliant
birth-chart indications customarily encounter companions who catalyze
their successful relationship karma. Try though they may to remain together, two people whose individual natal horoscope's success potentials do
not agree will usually find themselves drifting apart, whatever the implications of their synastry may be. Natal-chart analysis thus usually supersedes
synastry, especially if the natal chart displays fixed relationship karma. One
of us once predicted the impending divorce of a young and poor woman on
the basis of the single fact that, while she had brilliant *yogas* (astrological
combinations) for money and eminence in her horoscope, her husband had
a less than mediocre birth chart. How could these two people possibly share
a destiny? Indeed, within a year of this prediction, a paramour who was
more socially prominent and moneyed than the husband impregnated the
woman. She got a divorce, married the paramour, had the child, and now
lives an elegant existence that is aligned with the promise of her horoscope.

We do not detail here the results that are likely for any particular
natal horoscope. We focus, instead, on the proficiency an individual may
display in pursuit of a relationship's eventualities. A couple's relationship
success is one thing, and the innate ability to relate that the two people
bring into their relationship is something else. Sometimes two people who
love one another enough to marry find, soon after the wedding, that the
marriage just isn't working out. If they part, but remain good friends, we
may conclude that the relationship outcome achieved through that matri-
monial karma was far less favorable than were the relationship skills they

brought to the relationship. Another couple that marries and stays married, while fighting continually, provides an example of a different scenario: poor skills overlaying an enduring result.

Skill contributes to result in any arena of endeavor, but (as van Gogh discovered) superlative skill is no guarantor of success. Both union and management, when they sit down to negotiate, are likely to bring their best negotiators to the table. This may promote, but cannot, in and of itself, secure, negotiation success, for inexplicable impasses sometimes occur. At other times, two people can sit down in a restaurant and sketch out on the back of an envelope the outline for a partnership that goes on to develop into a multinational business that grinds to a halt only when one partner dies. Our good intentions and our ability to act skillfully notwithstanding, life remains a gamble, for the clouds of the unforeseen always loom on the horizon of our conscious ambit.

Synastry aims to make that gamble a reasoned wager, rather than a blind throw of the dice. An "aggregate horoscope" can show us which couples are likely to discover a shared bhava from which they can milk a contentment-yielding rasa. Mutual compatibility facilitates the development of the ardor (raga) that engenders ambrosial rasa while minimizing the potential for the emergence of the repugnance (dvesha) that can defile and poison their "fluid reality." Poorly matched charts can, by intensifying disruptive relationship tendencies, diminish the relationship success that is promised in the individual horoscopes. Exceptional insight may sometimes be required to balance the contradictions that can arise between analysis of two natal charts independently and an analysis of the synastry of the two.

Sometimes, people who generally do not interact with others at all well find themselves in good and lasting relationships. Some skillful relaters, on the other hand, always seem to find their relationships coming to a close. Pop psychology admonishes us that, since skillful work always brings results, if you have not yet achieved your desired goal, you must not be working skillfully enough. Jyotisha teaches us otherwise: at times, success can be wholly effortless; at other times, no amount of work can salvage a situation, at least in this lifetime. Jyotishical analysis plots a "skill-outcome" graph whose greatest attainments appear in the "excellent outcome + exceptional skill" quadrant, and, whose most notable failures litter the "inferior outcome + limited skill" enclosure. Mixed results occur in the mixed sectors: propitious outcomes with poor skills, and unfavorable outcomes with superior skills. Natal astrology plots the outcome axis of this graph; synastry generates the skills axis.

For our purposes, we define relationship skills as the manner in which people habitually relate to significant others in their lives, and relationship outcomes as the final result of such important relationships. While astrological analysis of relationship skills often indicates what a person is likely to do when confronted by a relationship crisis, relationship-outcomes analysis indicates whether or not a person is actually likely to be involved in ongoing, satisfying interpersonal relations. Skills determine the habitual way of dealing with the challenges of life; outcomes depict the results of those challenges. Though the world's two best chess players may have comparable skills, only one will win the world championship. Both are skillful, yet they experience divergent outcomes.

Among the bevy of astrological details that Jyotisha uses to evaluate the outcome of a marital relationship, three factors are primary: the seventh bhava, the lord of the seventh bhava, and the *significator* of the seventh bhava. The *significator* of a bhava is that graha which has the greatest natural affinity with that bhava's life themes. Later in this chapter, we will provide an overview of the method of outcome analysis. Here, we will focus on skills analysis.

Relationship-skills analysis is achievable through the methods of synastry and through those of natal astrology. Ideally it combines the two. This chapter outlines skills analysis within a single natal chart. The next two chapters will supply tools for constructing an insightful analysis of the level of interactive skill among the owners of two natal charts.

Examining relationship skills from an individual horoscope by the method about to be described requires the use of several of Jyotisha's core concepts: relative graha placement, the nature and strength of the grahas, friendship and enmity between grahas, bhava rulership, and other affiliations of the grahas.

RELATIVE GRAHA PLACEMENT

Grahas in a horoscope can be placed relative to one another in any of seven possible ways (see figure 1, page 38):

One-One	Four-Ten
Seven-Seven	Five-Nine
Two-Twelve	Six-Eight
Three-Eleven	

A One-One relationship is present when two grahas tenant the same rashi. Seven-Seven means that the two grahas sit in rashis that are opposite one another in the zodiac by constellation. A Five-Nine relationship is a situation in which the grahas are five rashis and nine rashis away from each other. For a Three-Eleven placement, we count, depending on where we begin, either three or eleven rashis between the two grahas. In a Four-Ten placement the two grahas are four and ten rashis apart. In a Six-Eight configuration, they are six and eight rashis apart. A Two-Twelve placement exists when the grahas occupy neighboring rashis. All counting is inclusive. Note that we use the Sanskrit term *rashi* here to indicate one of the twelve constellations of Jyotisha. These begin with Aries and end with Pisces. Though Jyotisha's twelve rashis have the same names, in English, as the twelve signs of Western astrology, they do not represent the same astronomical reality. The signs of Western astrology are tropical; the constellations of Jyotisha are sidereal. When we wish to indicate one or more of

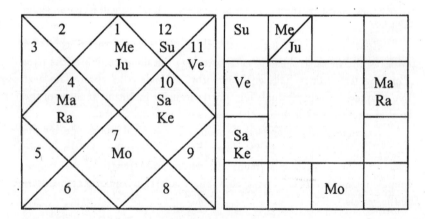

One-One Me-Ju, Ma-Ra, Sa-Ke
One-Seven Me-Mo, Ju-Mo, Ma-Sa, Ma-Ke, Ra-Sa, Ra-Ke
Two-Twelve Ke-Ve, Sa-Ve, Ve-Su, Su-Me, Su-Ju
Three-Eleven Sa-Su, Ke-Su, Ve-Me, Ve-Ju
Four-Ten Me-Ma, Me-Ra, Ju-Ma, Ju-Ra, Ma-Mo, Ra-Mo, Mo-Sa, Mo-Ke, Sa-Me, Sa-Ju, Ke-Me, Ke-Ju
Five-Nine Mo-Ve, Su-Ma, Su-Ra
Six-Eight Mo-Su,

Figure 1. Relative planetary placements.

Jyotisha's twenty-seven sidereal lunar asterisms, we will also call them by
their proper Sanskrit name: *nakshatra*.

The great astrological authority Maharishi Parashara, in his astrological magnum opus, *Brihat Parashara Hora Shastra*, offers some hints for inter-
preting graha placements. These comments, though made in the context of
astrological timing, can reasonably be extended to relationship analysis.
Maharshi Parashara states that:

- Grahas in Three-Eleven and Five-Nine relationships will cooperate with
  each other;
- Grahas in Two-Twelve and Six-Eight relationships will be disinclined to
  cooperate with each other;
- Grahas in One-One, Seven-Seven, and Four-Ten relationships will powerfully influence each other, in ways that will depend on the natures and
  the strength or weakness of those grahas.[1]

Parashara's hints have been expanded by jyotishis who followed in his
footsteps into a variety of specific principles. The renowned astrologer
Mantreshwara, who thrived some five centuries ago, offers this example in
his book, *Phaladipika*:

> If there should be enmity between the lord of a bhava and that of
> the Ascendant due to natural or temporal causes, or their being
> posited in the 6th or 8th places with respect to each other, envy,
> rivalry or jealousy will arise to the native with the person de-
> noted by that bhava during the transit of these grahas. But if
> there should be friendship, natural or temporary, between the
> aforesaid two grahas, one ought to predict new friendship being
> formed when those grahas conjoin in their transit.[2]

Although Mantreshwara speaks here in the context of astrological timing, we
can again reasonably extend his comments to a more static pattern of relationship analysis. Mantreshwara asks of Jyotisha how and when happy or unhappy
relations between two grahas will fructify; we inquire as to the conditions that
will create those relations. Mantreshwara's aphorism reinforces Parashara's
notion that, when two grahas are posited Six-Eight to one another, they will
give inimical results for the indicated relationships. Similar verses can be

---

[1] Maharishi Parashara, *Brihat Parashara Hora Shastra*, vol. II (Delhi: Ranjan, 1984), ch.
52–60.
[2] Mantreshwara, *Phaladipka* (Bangalore, India: Yugantara Press, 1961), 16:34.

found for several other relationships, but all conform to Maharshi Parashara's tenets of who will cooperate with whom.

Let us use Indira Gandhi's horoscope (see Chart 1, page 41) to illustrate these graha relationships in greater detail. Mercury and Sun occupy the same rashi (Scorpio) in Gandhi's chart, which puts them in a One-One relationship to each other. Moon-Saturn, Sun-Jupiter, and Mercury-Jupiter occupy opposite rashis. Their relationship is thus Seven-Seven. Four Two-Twelve relationships appear here: Mercury-Venus, Sun-Venus, Venus-Moon, and Saturn-Mars. These positions are Two-Twelve, because, when we count from either Sun or Mercury toward Venus, we count only two rashis (Scorpio, in which Mercury and Sun sit, and Sagittarius, in which Venus resides), while, if we count from Venus to Sun/Mercury, we count through all 12 of the rashis. A similar situation prevails for Saturn-Mars and for Venus-Moon.

Three Three-Eleven relationships also occur: Mercury-Moon, Sun-Moon, and Jupiter-Saturn. Sun-Mars, Mercury-Mars, and Jupiter-Mars are the three Four-Ten placements. Three Six-Eight configurations exist—Saturn-Venus, Venus-Jupiter, and Mars-Moon—as do four Five-Nine placements—Sun-Saturn, Mercury-Saturn, Moon-Jupiter, and Mars-Venus. Note that, by excluding Rahu and Ketu, the total of such relative placements among the remaining seven grahas will always be 21. Rahu and Ketu are usually excluded, because they do not own any bhavas. Thus, they can only indicate relations as natural significators and never as bhava lords, a fact whose explanation appears later in this chapter. The other seven grahas do, however, indicate specific relations, both as bhava lords and as natural significators.

NATURE AND STRENGTH OF THE GRAHAS

Having examined the relative placements of the grahas, we now consider their nature and absolute positions. No matter how effectively the partners in a relationship may interact, the magnitude of the results obtainable from their relationship depends on the intrinsic attitudes and the inborn strengths of those partners. The same thing can be said of the grahas: no matter how effectively their relative placements may enable them to interact, exceptionally malevolent or weak grahas are unlikely to bring much practical benefit to the interaction. There is, thus, no guarantee that a favorable relative placement between two grahas will be workable, unless both of those grahas are also innately strong and benign toward each other. Mantreshwara's dictum thus alludes to the enmity and the friendship of the grahas due to natural or temporal causes.

Rashi Chart

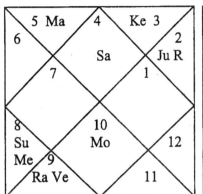

Navamsha Chart

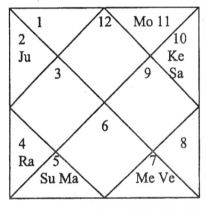

Planetary Positions		Vimshottari Dasha		
LG	29°CA47'	SU	28 Oct. 1913	Yogi Point SC 13-09'
SU	04°SC08'	MO	29 Oct. 1919	
MO	05°CP41'	MA	28 Oct. 1929	Yogi – SA
MA	16°LE22'	RA	28 Oct. 1936	
ME	13°SC15'	JU	29 Oct. 1954	Avayogi – MO
JU	14°TA59'R	SA	29 Oct. 1970	
VE	21°SA01'	ME	29 Oct. 1989	Duplicate Yogi–MA
SA	21°CA49'	KE	29 Oct. 2006	
RA	10°SA34'	VE	29 Oct. 2013	Daghda Rasis
KE	10°GE34'			AR & LE

Chart 1. Indira Gandhi.

For our purposes, there are two varieties of grahas: the benign and the malevolent. These two groups are the astrological incarnations of satsanga and kusanga (see page 26). The benign grahas are the natural benefics of traditional Jyotisha: Jupiter, Venus, a well-associated and well-aspected Mercury, and a Moon that is more than 72° distant from the Sun, particularly if it happens to be waxing. The malevolent grahas are the traditional natural malefics of Jyotisha: Saturn, Rahu, Ketu, Mars, Sun, a badly associated and badly aspected Mercury, and a Moon that is less than 72° from the Sun, especially if it is waning. With this preponderance of malefics, it is no wonder that relationships can be so demanding!

Assessing a graha's strength can involve a taxing array of technical factors. It can take a lifetime of ardent study and keen-minded practice to perfect the ability to make accurate snapshot assessments of graha strength. Our work is made somewhat easier in this respect by being able to rely on the 80/20 rule. It is well-known that, in most organizations, 80 percent of the work is done by 20 percent of the people, and the remaining 20 percent of the work is completed by the other 80 percent of the workforce. Likewise, a few serviceable precepts will instantly and accurately portray the strength of the grahas in 80 percent of all horoscopes. The other 80 percent of the rules exist to service the other 20 percent of horoscopes, the birth charts that give up their secrets with greater difficulty. Here is our hard-working group of precepts. Grahas are strong when they are:

• Exalted;
• In their own rashis;
• In a friend's rashi;
• Retrograde;
• In a good bhava ("good mood," as when tenanting the first, fifth, ninth, fourth, seventh, or tenth bhavas and, somewhat less so, the second and eleventh bhavas);
• Flanked by natural benefics alone in each of their adjacent rashis;
• Associated with and aspected by natural benefics alone.

Grahas are weak when they are:

• Debilitated or fallen;
• In an enemy's rashi;

- Combust (too near the Sun, in particular within 6°);
- In a bad bhava (in a bad mood, so to speak, as when they reside in the sixth, eighth or twelfth bhavas);
- Flanked by malefics alone in each of their adjacent rashis;
- Associated with and aspected by natural malefics alone;
- Defeated in a planetary war (Mars, Mercury, Jupiter, Venus, or Saturn within 1° of longitude of each other, the planet with the higher celestial latitude winning the war).

Although graha strength and weakness can usually be assessed easily and efficiently with these two short lists, a graha's influence for better or worse multiplies as indicators of its strength or weakness accumulate. A benign graha that occupies its own rashi in a good bhava aspected by only benefics will give far better results than one that possesses only one form of strength. Likewise, a compounding of undesirable results is to be expected when a malevolent graha is debilitated in a bad bhava aspected by malefics. A graha whose indicators are contradictory (for example, when it is exalted in a good bhava, but is also combust and aspected by both a benefics and malefics) will require very careful evaluation. Typical horoscopes, which are fortunately free of such complexities, readily lend themselves to direct planetary strength or weakness evaluation via the simple lists above.

FRIENDSHIP AND ENMITY BETWEEN GRAHAS

As with humans, two grahas are much more likely to cooperate with one another if they are friends, or at least neutrals to one another. Table 1 (page 44) displays the vital relationships of the grahas of Jyotisha in detail.

Every serious student of Jyotisha must memorize these relationships. To reduce memory work to a bare minimum, divide the grahas into two groups, the first composed of Sun, Moon, Mars, and Jupiter and the second of Mercury, Venus, and Saturn. Note that grahas in the same group are usually friends (or are at least neutral to one another), but they treat grahas of the other group as enemies, or neutrals at best. There are only three exceptions to this rule: the Moon has no enemies, and has Mercury for a friend; Mercury has the Sun for a friend; Jupiter is the enemy of no other graha.

Table 1. Graha Relationships.

GRAHA	FRIENDS	NEUTRALS	ENEMIES
Sun	Moon, Mars, Jupiter	Mercury	Venus, Saturn
Moon	Sun, Mercury	Venus, Mars, Jupiter, Saturn	None
Mars	Sun, Moon, Jupiter	Venus, Saturn	Mercury
Mercury	Sun, Venus	Mars, Jupiter, Saturn	Moon
Jupiter	Sun, Moon, Mars	Saturn	Mercury, Venus
Venus	Mercury, Saturn	Mars, Jupiter	Sun, Moon
Saturn	Mercury, Venus	Jupiter	Sun, Moon, Mars
Rahu Ketu	Not specified by tradition, although some jyotishis use the friends, neutrals, and enemies of Saturn for Rahu and those of Mars for Ketu.		

BHAVA RULERSHIPS AND OTHER AFFILIATIONS OF THE GRAHAS

While the first bhava of a horoscope always represents the subject's very own self, the various other bhavas signify specific significant others in life. Of these, the second bhava indicates the many members of the extended family unit. Here the word "family" is used in its most comprehensive sense to include parents, grandparents, uncles and aunts, brothers and sisters, children, cousins, and nieces and nephews, even though many of these familial others are ruled more specifically by the horoscope's other bhavas. Use the second bhava to assess the general conditions of this "family." For instance, a well-placed second bhava is likely to indicate that your overall relationship with your family is harmonious, despite your disgust for Uncle Harry and your frequent arguments with your elder sister.

The third bhava of a horoscope rules siblings, especially younger ones, as well as cousins and neighbors. The fourth bhava is the place of ancestors, particularly of the mother and the maternal lineage. The fifth bhava indicates the state of natural or adopted progeny and of students, if any. Open or known enemies, such as litigants and competitors, along with uncles and aunts, especially maternal ones, are sixth-bhava people. The sixth bhava also indicates valued pets, an arena of important relationship for many people. The seventh bhava of a horoscope indicates all important socially, and usually legally, contracted life partners, including particularly the spouse and important long-term business partners. Guides and mentors, the father, and foreigners are ninth-bhava types. The tenth bhava indicates authorities, like the government or one's boss, and, according to some authorities, it is the place of the father. The eleventh bhava indicates friends, associates, and according to many, elder siblings.

Though the eighth and twelfth bhavas are generally not used for the purpose of assessing specific relationships, they do represent potentially important others that bring implied problems, difficulties, and traumas into your life. The eighth bhava points to your surgeon, your tax collector, your bankruptcy trustee, your mortician, even your executioner, and a host of other potential tormentors. The twelfth bhava, which is most often used to indicate secret enemies, is also associated with reclusive religious aspirants, social workers, humanists, foreigners (though less markedly than the ninth bhava), and all those others that cause you major expenses and losses of time, energy, or money.

A graha that has a natural affiliation with a certain class of individuals becomes the natural significator for those individuals in a horoscope. In Jyotisha, the Sun represents the father and other authority figures, like employers. The Moon stands for the mother and other maternal figures. Mars denotes siblings, especially younger ones, and open enemies. Mercury betokens uncles and aunts, adopted relations, business partners, and friends. Jupiter signifies children, teachers or advisors, and older siblings. Venus indicates your spouse and lovers in general, as well as your friends. Saturn equals employees, secret enemies, and foreigners. Rahu points to both the maternal grandparents and foreigners; Ketu rules the paternal grandparents.

Maharshi Parashara teaches an alternate scheme of signification that rotates the signification of the parents among four grahas, based on the criterion of a day or night birth. In this little-used method, the Sun is the significator of the father for births that occur during the day; for night births, Saturn becomes the paternal significator. Venus is, likewise, the significator of the mother for day births, while the Moon signifies the mother for night births. This principle, though it is used infrequently in modern Jyotisha, is occasionally useful. Another tradition that is both useful and frequently employed, especially in northern India, emanates from the astrological text known as the *Bhrigu Nadi*, which makes Jupiter the significator of the spouse in female horoscopes, while reserving Venus as the spouse significator in the birth charts of males.[3]

---

[3] The *Bhrigu Nadi* is a manuscript in Hoshiarpur, Punjab, India, which to our knowledge has never been published.

RELATIONSHIP PATTERNS

Now that we have reviewed relative placements of the grahas, graha nature and strength, friendship and enmity among those grahas, and graha affiliation rulership, we are ready to trek further into the territory of relationship analysis. Our next step is to distinguish more clearly the difference between relationship skills (which determine how habitually well or poorly we relate to significant others in our lives) and relationship outcomes (which are the ultimate fruits of our significant relationships).

The skills that an individual brings to a relationship are examples of *vasanas.* A *vasana* is a psychic residue that lingers in the substance of the mind *(chitta)* as one result of the performance of a karma, which is (in this context) any action of body or mind and its concomitant effect or result. Every action we perform creates for us both an eventual appropriate reaction that we will experience as an effect of the action and a vasana that will facilitate that experience. As each karma ripens, its vasana serves as a ready-made entry path into the conscious mind for that action's effects. These paths, which appear in the form of desires and inclinations, act as the conduits along which the effects of our previous actions project themselves out in the theater of the world.

Vasanas develop from the portion of our past karmic inheritance that has caused us to take birth in this lifetime and from the karmas we performed during this incarnation. Like karmas, which, you will recall, may be fixed, fixed/unfixed, or unfixed, vasanas may be strong, middling, or weak. Repeating the same sorts of actions, good or bad, provides us with many copies of the same vasana. This encourages ruts to form in our mental, etheric, and physical landscapes. The deeper these ruts become, the more likely we are to fall into them and travel in their direction, swept along by an irresistible vasana momentum that speeds us in the direction of the karmic reactions those vasanas encourage us to experience. Deeply furrowed channels make for strong vasanas; lighter grooves represent vasanas from which we will have less difficulty emerging. Since, ordinarily, vasanas from the past strongly influence our ability to plan and execute actions in the present, past karmas and vasanas act as pointers toward future experiences.

A natal horoscope reflects both the vasanas that help to structure many experiences of life and the karmas from which those vasanas arise. While vasanas represent the way in which we approach our environment, karmas are the interactions that transpire between us and that environment. Those who are "loners" have vasanas for preferring seclusion to society.

When they act on them (a karma), they discover that their seclusion rein-forces their "predilection for aloneness" vasana. Similarly, a woman who finds herself getting involved with older men may be both experiencing the karmic results of a previous vasana and, through those experiences, reinforc-ing that vasana, thereby encouraging her to continue getting involved with older men in the future.

Generally speaking, the results that we experience in a relationship derive from the nature and intensity of our karmas, and our innate relating abilities and tendencies arise from our vasanas—a cycle reminiscent of the proverbial chicken and egg. Those components of sukha measured mostly by gross external circumstances—for example, physical attractiveness and socioeconomic status of the marital partner—are analyzed through horoscopic outcome analysis, for they depend on the examination of the nature of a person's karma. The portion of sukha that depends more di-rectly on subjective reality—on the attitudes that the one person trains on the other during the course of their interaction—are assessed through horoscopic skills analysis, for they depend mostly on the nature of the vasanas.

RELATIONSHIP-OUTCOME ANALYSIS

The karmas we perform determine the results we experience. Jyotisha makes available to us a formidable array of methods for estimating the na-ture and intensity of a person's karma from a horoscope. These include bhava analysis, examination of yogas (astrological combinations), *varga kundalis* (the horoscope's harmonic subcharts), *ashtaka varga* (the eightfold interrelationship of the grahas), *dashas* (timing segments and sequences), and *gocharas* (transits).

Fortunately, the 80/20 rule once again serves us well here. Roughly 80 percent of horoscopes provide insightful snapshots of the fixed, fixed/unfixed, and unfixed nature of their relationship karma via simple analysis of the strength or weakness of the three factors already mentioned earlier in this chapter: the bhava, the lord of the bhava, and the significator that rules the relationship in question. The full strength of these three factors implies desirable fixed karmas, and their complete weakness suggests undesirable fixed karmas. An ample mixture of strength and weakness among the three salient factors indicates fixed/unfixed karmas; nondescript placements sug-gest unfixed karmas.

Karma analysis applies equally well to any of the twelve bhavas of a horoscope. When, for instance, we assess a person's marital karma, we look to the conditions of the horoscope's seventh bhava, the lord of that seventh bhava, and that bhava's natural significator. If these three factors—the seventh bhava, the seventh lord, and Venus or Jupiter (the natural spouse significators for males and females, respectively)—are strong and unafflicted, desirable marital experiences become very likely indeed. Should all three factors be weak and distressed, marriages are unlikely to last, or are likely be filled with undue stress.

For a stark comparison of relationship outcomes, contrast the horoscopes shown in Chart 2 (page 49) and Chart 3 (page 51), those of writer Anais Nin and actor Paul Newman. These two cases belong to the 80 percent group of straightforward birth charts, and our selected 20 percent of rules work well here. In both charts, the conditions of the seventh bhava, the seventh lord, and the significator of marriage all point toward the eventual outcome—a difficult and stressful one for Nin, an enduring and happy one for Newman.

The seventh bhava of marriage in Nin's horoscope is influenced by the aspect and occupation of the natural malefics Mars, Saturn, and Rahu-Ketu, without being influenced by any natural benefic. Jupiter, the lord of the seventh bhava, occupies the sixth bhava direly combusted by the Sun, flanked by the malefic Saturn on one side and the malefic Ketu on the other. This being a woman's chart, these confluent weaknesses and afflictions are doubly meaningful, since Jupiter also becomes the significator of the seventh bhava. Moreover, Nin's seventh bhava has a *dushkriti yoga*, a "miscreant combination." Dushkriti yoga exists because:

- Her seventh bhava is both occupied and aspected by malefics;
- The lord of her seventh bhava occupies the sixth bhava and is combust;
- Her seventh bhava is not influenced by any benefics.

The famous text, *Phaladipika*, describes two of the effects of a dushkriti yoga as ". . . deprived of a spouse and will indulge in the spouses of others." Indeed, Nin's unusual married life and her numerous extramarital affairs are well documented. The bottom line: here is fixed karma for marital misery by conventional standards, karma that encourages Nin to be *sukhahina* ("lacking in good space") in her married life.

Rashi Chart

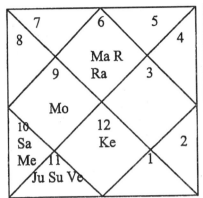

Navamsha Chart

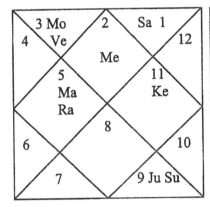

Planetary Positions		Vimshottari Dasha		
LG	14°VI 14'	KE	14 Jan. 1899	Yogi Point CP 20-42'
SU	09°AQ33'	VE	15 Jan. 1906	
MO	07°SA49'	SU	15 Jan. 1926	Yogi – MO
MA	23°VI 40'R	MO	15 Jan. 1932	
ME	13°CP32'	MA	15 Jan. 1942	Avayogi – ME
JU	07°AQ51'	RA	15 Jan. 1949	
VE	29°AQ43'	JU	15 Jan. 1967	Duplicate Yogi – SA
SA	11°CP19'	SA	15 Jan. 1983	
RA	25°VI 55'	ME	15 Jan. 2002	Daghda Rasis
KE	25°PI 55'			SC & LE

Chart 2. Anais Nin.

Newman's chart, on the other hand, has three natural benefics (Jupiter, Venus, and Mercury) aspecting the seventh bhava, on which no malefic influence falls. Mercury, the lord of his seventh bhava, aspects it, conjoined with two natural benefics (Jupiter and Venus) all of whom are in the excellent first bhava. Venus, the significator of marriage, occupies that praiseworthy Ascendant in the company of the two benefics, Jupiter and Mercury. Although the aspect of Saturn on both Mercury and Venus diminishes the brilliance of the other combinations, the preponderance of evidence is very favorable for happy, enduring marriage sukha over the course of most of his life.

In fact, Newman has the reverse of Nin's combination, a delightful astrological combination, which *Phaladipika* terms *kama yoga*, a "desire/passion combination." Kama yoga exists in Newman's horoscope because:

- The seventh bhava is aspected by benefics;
- The lord of the seventh bhava occupies a kendra while associated with benefics;
- The seventh bhava is not afflicted by malefics.

According to *Phaladipika*, kama yoga gives in part ". . . the desire to have nothing to do with the spouses of others," and indeed, Newman has a long-standing reputation for devotion to his wife. Here, the bottom line is a happier one: it is a rare instance of fixed karma for marital sukha. Rarely in our world, however, is sukha unalloyed by some quota of misery. In Paul Newman's case, Saturn's influence did put a pebble into his relationship shoe by ending his short first marriage. Perhaps it was the excellent graha vasana alignments (explained later) that Newman shares with Woodward that prevented this pebble from bruising the heels of that long-married couple.

The method described for Nin and Newman, which entails the evaluation of bhava, lord, and significator, is outcome analysis. While outcome analysis can often predict the outcome of an event—in this case, a relationship—it does not address the abilities, good or bad, brought to the execution of that event. Investigation of competence in action, which we call skills analysis, requires an evaluation of how well or poorly certain grahas are placed in relation to the lord of the Ascendant. It is to this topic that we turn next.

Rashi Chart

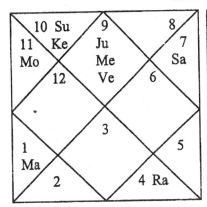

Navamsha Chart

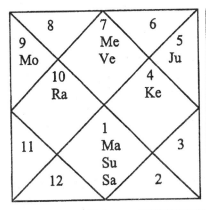

Planetary Positions		Vimshottari Dasha		
LG	20°SA23'	RA	16 Feb. 1922	Yogi Point AQ 25-24'
SU	13°CP13'	JU	17 Feb. 1940	
MO	08°AQ51'	SA	17 Feb. 1956	Yogi – JU
MA	00°SC50'	ME	17 Feb. 1975	
ME	20°SA30'	KE	17 Feb. 1992	Avayogi – SU
JU	16°SA04'	VE	17 Feb. 1999	
VE	21°SA36'	SU	17 Feb. 2019	Duplicate Yogi – SA
SA	20°LI 54'	MO	17 Feb. 2025	
RA	21°CA28'	MA	17 Feb. 2035	Daghda Rasis
KE	21°CP28'			CP & LE

Chart 3. Paul Newman.

RELATIONSHIP-SKILLS ANALYSIS

Though our emphasis on skills analysis alters somewhat the thrust of standard outcome-oriented Jyotisha, it is but a simple extrapolation of the principles from *Brihat Parashara Hora* and *Phaladipika*, mentioned earlier in this chapter. Here is the method in brief: To discern how well you will interact with the many "others" in you life, evaluate the positions relative to one another of the lord of the Ascendant and the lord of the bhavas that represent those others. For example, to discover how skillfully you relate to your children, analyze the relative placement of your horoscope's first and fifth lords, since the lord of Ascendant represents you and the lord of the fifth bhava represents your children. Similarly, view your skill with your friends from the relative positions of your first and eleventh lords, your relationship with your boss from that of your first and tenth lords, your skills with your enemies from the connection between your first and sixth lords, and so on. The seven relationship patterns described earlier suggest the lines along which specific relationships evolve.

We can simplify our discussion of skills analysis by introducing three very useful Sanskrit terms: *lagnesha* ("lord of the lagna," the *lagna* being the Ascendant), *karyesha* ("lord of the effect/purpose"), and *karaka* ("agent, doer"). The lagnesha is the lord of the Ascendant; the karyesha is the lord of the bhava whose effect you wish to analyze. For marriage, the karyesha is the lord of the seventh bhava, for brothers and sisters it is the lord of the third bhava, for the mother, it is the graha ruling the fourth bhava, and so forth. Since the karaka is whichever graha "acts for" or signifies the relation inquired about, karaka is frequently translated as "significator." The karaka for the father in any horoscope is the Sun, for the mother it is the Moon, for children, Jupiter, and so on.

Vasana analysis on the basis of a single horoscope follows three patterns: those based on lagnesha and karyesha (described in the first of the three sections that follow), those based on lagnesha and karaka (described in the second of those three sections), and those based on *sambandha* ("affiliation," described on page 61).

The Relative Placement of Lagnesha and a Karyesha

We have already noted that one insightful way to estimate the relationship vasanas in your horoscope is to compare the relative placements of the lagnesha with a karyesha. Lagnesha represents you, and karyesha represents the significant other in question. A bhava's lord is its prime indicator, its executor, which makes lagnesha the chief factor that determines how well or poorly you will relate to life in general. A strong, well-placed lagnesha that is influenced exclusively by benefics will, all other factors being equal, find it immensely easier to interact with others than will a weak, poorly-placed lagnesha. Evaluating the ways in which lagnesha and karyesha interact can indicate how the shared karmas of two individuals will be executed, regardless of the outcome.

The seven relative graha-placement patterns suggest that, when lagnesha and karyesha are Five-Nine or Three-Eleven to one another, you will want to cooperate in the relationship that karyesha rules, no matter what the outcome of that relationship may be. If, however, lagnesha and karyesha are Two-Twelve or Six-Eight to each other, you are more likely to bring (consciously or subconsciously) a "bad" attitude to that same relationship. Lagnesha and karyesha in mutual One-One, Seven-Seven, or Four-Ten placements exist in cases of dynamic interactions that require more analysis than do the other purely harmonious or inharmonious dispositions.

Even if two grahas relate well to one another through their relative placements, they should be both benign and relatively strong individually for them to freely collaborate. Under such conditions, they will still not necessarily cooperate completely unless they are friends, or at least neutrals, to one another. Take, for example, Venus and Sun, which are dire enemies. Since Venus is the enemy of the Sun and the Sun is Venus's enemy, their animosity is reciprocal. Venus always rules the first bhava in a Taurus Ascendant, and Sun rules the fourth bhava of mother. As a statement of general principle, the mutual enmity between Venus and Sun will always tend to foment disagreements between Taurus children and their mothers.

The particular stage to which these disagreements progress depends on the relative graha placement and on the strength or weakness of Venus and Sun in the horoscope of the concerned child. Suppose that Venus occupies Pisces, its exaltation rashi, in the eleventh bhava, and Sun occupies the rashi of Taurus in the first bhava, thereby creating a Three-Eleven pattern relative to one another (see figure 2, page 54). In such a case, the two grahas are strong by being in good bhavas from the Ascendant, while they concurrently are in good bhavas from each other. One drawback is that the Sun occupies the rashi of its enemy. The rashi placement of the Sun is counterbalanced, however, by the powerful rashi placement of Venus in its exaltation rashi. These predominantly positive indications are likely to reduce, or perhaps even prevent, the general discord that the reciprocal animosity of Venus and Sun promotes from becoming severe enough to destroy the mother-child bond.

If, however, Venus occupies Virgo and the Sun sits in Libra, Venus, though in a good bhava, is weak by virtue of being debilitated. The Sun is very weak, being debilitated and also in an obstructive bhava from the Ascendant (see figure 3, below). Moreover, the two grahas are now in a Two-Twelve placement to one another. This suggests that the mother and child would be likely to have such a poor relationship, such mutual dvesha, that they might even break off relations with one another. The strong Venus-Sun enmity will render this mother-child relationship exceptionally tempestuous, unless some mitigating factor, such as the aspect of a strong Jupiter on one of the grahas, comes into play.

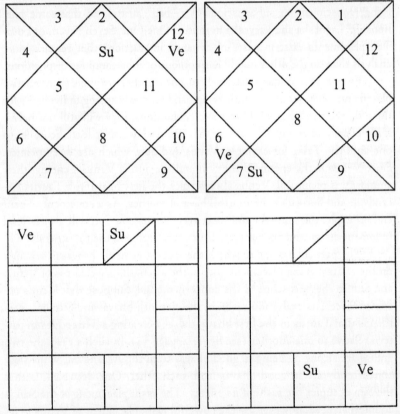

Figure 2. Three-Eleven
relative graha placement.

Figure 3. Venus in Virgo
with Sun in Libra.

By extension, two grahas like Jupiter and the Sun, who are reciprocally innately friendly, will, when participating in a Six-Eight or a Two-Twelve placement, be less obstructive to one another than will two enemies who share the same placement relative to each other. Though the relationship signified by such a Jupiter and Sun may still be turbulent, the subjects are likely to try to be mutually magnanimous, much like two friends trying to resolve their differences. Conversely, two friendly grahas in a harmonious relative placement are more likely to purr than are two enemies.

In a unilateral situation—when one graha is the enemy of the other, but the second graha is neutral to the first—the one who is the enemy may act inimically toward the neutral graha, while the neutral graha may tend not to reciprocate the enmity. For example, Table 1 (page 44) shows that Mercury is inimical to Mars, while Mars is neutral to Mercury. In a Virgo Ascendant, Mercury rules the first bhava and Mars rules the third bhava of siblings. No matter where these grahas sit relative to one another, the subject (represented by Mercury) will tend to have enmity for the siblings (represented by Mars), but the siblings will tend not to reciprocate this ill will. This archetypal pattern for a Virgo Ascendant will be exacerbated or ameliorated depending on the actual placements of the grahas relative to each other in a particular horoscope. Similarly, for a Cancer Ascendant, in which Moon rules the first bhava and Venus rules the eleventh bhava of elder siblings, the subject (Moon) will often bear animosity toward any elder siblings. These older brothers or sisters will not be likely to retaliate, however, because Table 1 (page 44) informs us that the Moon is inimical to Venus, but Venus is neutral toward the Moon.

The interaction of the grahas as rulers of the twelve bhavas for each of the Ascendants according to their relationships as friends, enemies, and neutrals seems to provide a worthy field of investigation into the archetypal nature of primary human relationships. For instance, a cursory examination of the friend-enemy relations between the first and third lords (third bhava = younger siblings) and the first and eleventh lords (eleventh bhava = older siblings) of the twelve possible Ascendants shows at least one-sided enmity in all but six cases of the total of twenty-four combinations. No lagnesha of any of the twelve Ascendants is reciprocally friendly with the lords of either the third or the eleventh bhavas. This situation seems to reflect the frequent rivalry that arises among siblings. The six exceptions to this minimum standard of one-sided hostility are:

- For a Gemini Ascendant, third lord Sun is Mercury's friend, and Mercury is neutral to Sun;
- For Sagittarius and Capricorn Ascendants, third lords Jupiter and Saturn are mutually neutral;
- For a Leo Ascendant, eleventh lord Mercury is neutral to Sun, and Sun is Mercury's friend;
- For Aquarius and Pisces Ascendants, eleventh lords Jupiter and Saturn are mutually neutral.

Proceeding with our musings on universal rather than specific relationship themes, we discover that the diametric opposite to the previous condition of animosity among siblings appears in the relations that exist among the grahas that rule an individual (lagnesha) and his or her children (fifth lord) or father (ninth lord). All such relationships are, at least, friendly from one side, and several are friendly from both. Why so? One potential explanation is that, unlike siblings, who usually have the protection of parents to "referee" their rivalries, the child/parent bond must involve amicability because of the child's vulnerability and dependency on the parent. Given the long, arduous commitment on the part of a parent to rearing a child, that parent must be friendly to the child, or the child to the parent, in order for the relationship to survive the demanding responsibilities inherent in the parent-child dynamic. The child must often exude a certain "entrancing" charisma if it is to keep the parent interested enough to remain engaged in parenting.

The most variegated interactions of all arise between the lagnesha and the mother (fourth lord). Relations between the first and fourth lords in the twelve Ascendants run the gamut of possibilities, from the mutual enmity of a Taurus Ascendant to the mutual friendship of the Leo, Libra, and Aquarius Ascendants. The Cancer Ascendant even provides us a condition of friendship from one side and enmity from the other. Perhaps the mother-child relationship is so diversified because of its prevalence in human upbringing, for babies who lack all semblance of a mother figure rarely survive. After all, if someone is the predominant presence in our lives, we will strive to establish a powerful relationship with that person. In India, the ubiquity of the mother principle has led her to be deified in many forms: as the benevolent Saraswati, the prosperity-granting Lakshmi, the ascetic Parvati, and the devouring Kali. Our relationships with our mothers, who are usually the parent with whom we are most involved biologically and sociologically in our formative years, can, and do, take any or all of these forms astrologically.

Moving from the consanguineous to the contractual, we uncover the fact that the lords of the first and seventh bhavas for every Ascendant can never be anything better than neutrals to each other. In several cases, they are open enemies. For the pair Aries-Libra, Mars, and Venus are neutrals, as also for Taurus-Scorpio. For Gemini-Sagittarius, Mercury is the enemy of Jupiter, but Jupiter is neutral to Mercury. For Cancer-Capricorn, Moon is the enemy of Saturn, but Saturn is neutral to the Moon. For Leo-Aquarius, the Sun and Saturn are mutual enemies. Finally, for Virgo-Pisces, Mercury is the enemy of Jupiter, but Jupiter is neutral to Mercury.

By refusing to allow the lords of the first and seventh bhavas ever to become friends, the formulators of Jyotisha perhaps wished to send us a message about how inherently arduous it is to develop a truly harmonious covenanted relationship. Making a marriage or a business partnership work is tough, they seem to be saying, particularly when we compare the relationship of the lagnesha with the marriage and business partnership karyesha, and with the grahas that indicate blood relations. Only in relationships with siblings do we approximate the degree of extremity that first-seventh connections display.

It is truly rare to get to know the "contracted other" as well as we get to know our blood relatives. Love them, hate them, or avoid them, we typically have a longer period of time in which to get to know our blood relatives. Moreover, we usually commence our relations with them when our minds are more pliable and less judgmental. Contracted relationships, like marriage or business partnerships, commonly begin only in adult life, when we are forced to learn how to blend our already developed (and often rigid) patterns of interaction with someone else's already evolved patterns. Children are a special case: their innocence and pliability tend to soften our own accumulated stiffness as we participate in their development.

Our methods of skills analysis become particularly important when it comes to cultivating greater awareness of how we habitually relate socially. The ambassadors of Israel and Syria may hold differing views of reality, both publicly and privately, but when negotiating, they will, if they aim to make their discussions productive, attempt to relate to one another in a courteous and businesslike manner. In this, they resemble two grahas that, though intrinsically enemies, enjoy a harmonious relative graha placement, like Five-Nine or Three-Eleven. Two grahas that are reciprocally inimical and occupy an inharmonious relative graha placement, such as Six-Eight or Two-Twelve, are more likely to remain openly hostile, like the ruthless terrorist and the officer of the law in pursuit.

Similarly, grahas that are friendly and occupy a harmonious relative graha placement are akin to two leaders who respect and admire one another, while sharing similar views. They will display their mutual affinity openly, and are likely to interact effortlessly. Two grahas that are friends, but whose relative graha placement is inharmonious, resemble two politicians whose values and views agree, but whose personal "chemistry" is off. Their mutual antipathy will often prevent them from cooperating, even when it would be to their mutual benefit to do so. We can, with a little imagination, characterize all our many social interactions along these lines—from our genuine, loyal friends to our casual acquaintances, from our open, sworn enemies to those people whom we detest but we choose to tolerate anyway. All our interpersonal contacts can be analyzed effectively by this means with the aid of a horoscope.

The Relative Placement of Lagnesha and a Karaka

The lagnesha and a karaka relative to one another in any one of the seven placements will imply results that are similar to those expected from the identical mutual placements of lagnesha and a karyesha. A person will thus be inclined to relate skillfully with the individual indicated by a karaka that occupies the third, fifth, ninth, or eleventh bhavas, as counted from the lagnesha. Similarly, the person will suffer diminished ability to relate constructively to the party signified by a karaka that occupies the sixth, eighth, or twelfth bhava from lagnesha. Thus, in Indira Gandhi's chart (see Chart 1, page 41), Jupiter, the children karaka, occupies the fifth bhava, as counted from first lord Moon, which suggests that she possessed good relationship skills with her children.

The lagnesha-karaka relationship, though consequential, is usually not as influential as is that between lagnesha and a karyesha. One situation in which a karaka does assume great importance, however, occurs when the lord of the Ascendant owns another bhava as well, which occurs whenever any of the five true planets rule the Ascendant. When Gemini, for example, becomes the Ascendant of a horoscope, Mercury rules both the Ascendant and the fourth bhava of the mother. For a Gemini Ascendant, the lagnesha and the karyesha are identical. Thus, one cannot be assessed in relation to the other. We can, in such and in similar cases, only evaluate the relationship that exists between lagnesha and the karaka.

These principles of lagnesha placement relative to a karyesha and/or a karaka encourage us to coin a name for two sorts of relationship yogas. We may call the situation that occurs when multiple grahas create harmonious "skill" placements with the Ascendant lord a *susambandha* ("good relationship") yoga. Such a yoga promises generally good relationship skills in life. Conversely, relationship difficulties are likely to abound in a life when a large number of inimical dispositions occur between the lord of the first bhava and other grahas in its horoscope. This we can call a *dussambandha* ("poor relationship") yoga. These combinations, in turn, suggest some general principles for the interpretation of relationships with significant others from a single horoscope:

- A person is likely to have an inborn ability to relate well with those people indicated by the bhava(s) that are ruled by any grahas that occupy the third, fifth, ninth, or eleventh bhavas, as counted from the lord of the Ascendant;
- The stronger these grahas are, the greater the rapport will be. If the grahas are friendly to the Ascendant lord, the rapport will be further magnified;
- The influence of natural benefics on the pertinent grahas will further enhance this rapport;
- The same series of principles applies (to a reduced extent) to the people indicated by a karaka placed as above.

And:

- A person is likely to have difficulties relating with those people indicated by the bhava(s) that are ruled by grahas that occupy the sixth, eighth, or twelfth bhavas, as counted from the lord of the Ascendant;
- The weaker these grahas are, the greater the difficulties will be;
- If the grahas are inimical to the Ascendant lord, the difficulties are magnified;
- The influence of natural malefics on the pertinent grahas will further enhance these difficulties;
- The same series of principles applies (to a reduced extent) to the people indicated by a karaka placed as above.

Figure 4 illustrates a susambandha yoga. It shows the birth chart of a man to whom relationships come easily. When we count from Ascendant lord Mercury, we note that Mars and Moon are in the desired Five-Nine relationship with Mercury, while Jupiter and Saturn are in the desirable Three-Eleven relationship. All these grahas are, moreover, well placed in the natal chart. This suggests that the third, fourth, fifth, sixth, seventh, eighth, and eleventh bhavas, and the people ruled by them, will all be predisposed to fall into an aligned relationship with the subject.

Note that the harmonious relative graha placement of the Moon, as karaka of the mother, and Mercury, the lagnesha, reinforces the harmony already evident from the excellent placement of the lagnesha and Jupiter, who is, here, the karyesha of the mother. Similarly, Jupiter's excellent placement in relation to lagnesha Mercury, as karaka for children, reinforces the already excellent relative graha placement of Saturn—the karyesha of children in this horoscope—with the lagnesha. A confluence of positive placements exists here (that is, both a karyesha and a karaka relate well to lagnesha), which reinforces our certainty that his skills in this arena are superlative. A confluence of negative placements would reinforce a verdict of scant skill at relating.

Furthermore, since Venus occupies the same rashi as Mercury (a One-One relationship), the two grahas modify each other—they are mutual friends, one sitting in the sign of a friend and the other occupying its own rashi, in a good bhava, unaspected by any malefic. Under these ideal circumstances, we can add Venus to the long list of grahas that create a desirable relationship with the lord of the Ascendant. We can thus add the

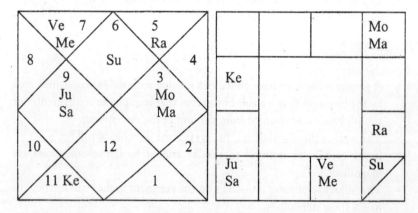

Figure 4. Susambandha Yoga

people indicated by the Venus-ruled second and ninth bhavas to the list of people with whom the subject will be inclined to have aligned relationships. In fact, Sun is the only graha that occupies the sixth, the eighth, or the twelfth bhava from lagnesha. We may, thus, conclude that the one class of people this man is *not* likely to align with easily is the twelfth-bhava group of secret enemies and those who cause him major expenses of time, energy, or money.

This type of analysis provides general indications of the tenor of the relationships that a person will have with significant others during his or her life. It does nothing however to preempt any conclusions that analysis of a particular bhava, its lord, and its significator may prompt us to draw. Even those with the best of relating skills sometimes stumble in their relationships due to their karma. In this case the individual has had serious disagreements with his elder brother, although his attitude toward this brother remains conciliatory.

Outcome analysis attributes the described results to the conditions of the eleventh bhava, its lord, and Jupiter, all of whom represent older siblings in this horoscope. The eleventh bhava is hemmed in between Rahu and Mars, and the natural malefics Mars and Saturn influence both the Moon (who is lord of the eleventh) and Jupiter, the significator of older siblings. Though these afflictions paint a clear portrait of the difficulties to be faced, the Five-Nine relationship that the Ascendant lord and the eleventh lord create nevertheless enables him to bring innately good relationship skills to bear on the situation. This permits us to conclude that he will continue to try to find some way to resolve his differences with his older brother, no matter what may transpire between them.

Sambandha

Sometimes, the two bhava lords under consideration enjoy a sambandha (special affiliation) in a horoscope. In the context of relationship-skills analysis, the individuals represented by the two grahas that participate in a special affiliation are compelled to relate to each. Their compulsion to relate may cover the spectrum of determined human relationship, everything from undying or unrequited love, to unremitting hatred, to obsession—depending on the condition of the grahas involved in the sambandha. Though the notion of sambandha is one that can, in Jyotisha, cover a broad spectrum of indications, we distinguish only three varieties of sambandha for our purposes here: mutual aspect, one-sided aspect, and exchange of bhavas.

Mutual aspects occur between any two grahas in a One-One or a Seven-Seven relationship, and in the single special case when Mars is ten rashis from Saturn and Saturn is four rashis from Mars. Mutual aspects cause the players represented by the grahas to be impelled to relate; the aspect incessantly stimulates them to become actively and reciprocally involved in relationship. The overall tenor of the relationship still depends, however, on the general strength or weakness of the two grahas involved, on their friendship, enmity, or neutrality to one another, and on the bhavas they rule.

In one-sided aspects, the aspector pursues the aspectee, who may resist if he or she is stronger than the aspector. Jupiter, Saturn, and Mars can all provide one-way aspects—their "special full aspects." These special aspects are five and nine rashis, counted from Jupiter's horoscopic position, four and eight rashis, counted from the position of Mars in any horoscope, and three and ten rashis, counted from Saturn's position in a chart. For example, when Jupiter occupies Taurus, Saturn occupies Virgo, and Venus occupies Capricorn, Jupiter exerts one-sided aspects on both Saturn and Venus by virtue of its special aspects to the fifth and ninth rashis from its own position. Similarly, when Saturn occupies Cancer and the Moon occupies Virgo, Saturn throws a one-sided aspect on the Moon. In this instance, the influence is not completely one-sided, however. It is balanced, to some extent, by virtue of the Moon dispositing Saturn (i.e., the Moon owns the bhava in which Saturn sits). This is also a type of sambandha, one that eludes our narrow definition of that term. When Mars aspects a graha in the eighth from his position, the person that Mars represents will pursue the other. Since the two grahas are Six-Eight, however, the other will tend to want to elude the pursuer. Tinges of masochism may appear if the pursuer's graha is poorly placed.

When two grahas exchange bhavas, the situation is enhanced if the grahas are in mutually good positions to begin with. If they are, instead, Six-Eight, the exchange will provide a tenuous means of resolution for the problem. Indira Gandhi's horoscope (see Chart 1, page 41) exemplifies this. The exchange of the lords of bhavas six and eleven made her friends tend to become enemies and her enemies, friends. Raga became dvesha, and dvesha raga, repeatedly in her life. Her enemies and friends frequently showed enmity toward one another, which tended to benefit her own political position. Though her skills at handling her friends and associates were often questionable, she usually found a way out of her predicaments, thanks to the exchange. Ultimately, however, the negative implications of the sixth bhava won out, and an enemy who appeared to her in the guise of a friend did her in.

RELATIONSHIP ALCHEMY: OUTCOMES AND SKILLS WORKING TOGETHER

When we merge these two factors—a relationship's potential outcome and the skills likely to be available to apply toward achieving that outcome—we can hope to obtain a useful image of that relationship's overall process. Take, as an example, the horoscope shown in figure 5, in which the lord of the third bhava occupies the ninth bhava from the Ascendant, from which it aspects the third bhava. In this situation, we expect generally good results for the third bhava of siblings based on the general precepts of Jyotisha, because the lord of the third aspects the third and occupies a most desirable bhava. Since the lord of the Ascendant occupies the tenth bhava in this chart, we also expect good results from the Ascendant, since the tenth bhava is fundamentally a good bhava and, once again, the lord of the first bhava aspects the first bhava.

Considering, however, that, in this position, the lord of the Ascendant creates a Two-Twelve relationship with the third lord, we must expect this person to display poor skills at relating with those siblings. "Good results" or a good outcome may mean that he or she and the siblings will interact

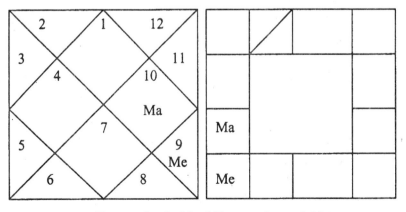

Figure 5. Lord of third bhava in the ninth bhava
from the Ascendant.

and maintain successful relations in spite of it all. "Poor skills" may mean that their interactions will often prove rancorous, frosty, or otherwise dysfunctional, irrespective of the outcomes. When indications of outcomes and skills fail to complement one another, a convoluted and complex relationship dynamic becomes likely. "Good results" here may also indicate that the siblings are healthy and successful in their own right. They may have sukha (that is, their "spaces" may be good). The subject may also be successful in his or her own life, but despite (or perhaps because of) this separate success, may still be unable to speak a civil word to the siblings in their ongoing relationship. A well-placed third bhava suggests siblings that are somehow well placed in life. It does not necessarily suggest that those siblings will align themselves seamlessly with the subject.

As a contrasting example take the horoscope in figure 6, in which the lord of the third bhava occupies the eighth bhava from the Ascendant, influenced by every natural malefic. This position promises a poor outcome in the matter of siblings. If there is a sibling (and there may not be), he or she is likely to have some intrinsic weaknesses, or may face a life filled with obstacles. Such obstacles to sibling sukha may occasionally fail to influence the subject directly (and if he or she is unmoved by them, is that relationship not poor?), but such troubles will more likely form an important part of why the relationship between the two is so troubled.

Note that, while the Ascendant lord here continues to occupy the tenth bhava, it now sits in a Three-Eleven relationship to that third lord,

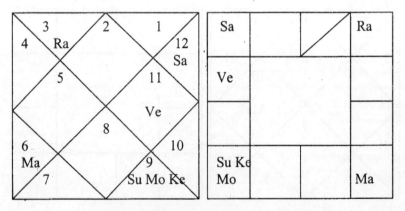

Figure 6. Lord of third bhava in the eighth bhava
from the Ascendant.

which promises that the individual's skills at relating to siblings will be generally good. One way in which such a situation may play out is when those concerned live geographically distant from one another, thereby promoting a sense of isolation. This may make regular interaction difficult (a poor relationship outcome), but may also make it likely that, whenever they did get the opportunity to be together, they would continue to attempt relating harmoniously, picking up where they had previously left off. Or perhaps a sibling's afflicted health may engender suffering that the individual tries to ameliorate, while trying to console the brother or sister about it. Both the obstructed outcome and the innately good relating skills are reflected in this reality of the relationship.

Karmas (outcomes) and vasanas (skills) are the twin polarities that interact to create our lives. "Woe is me!" mourns the lover who, after sacrificing everything for the loved one, is callously jilted in the end. "Love is blind!" proclaims the kindly, but jealous, businessman on hearing that his ex-wife has taken up with his pitiless rival. "Life is bliss!" coo the couple who have discovered in one another a mutual ambition to grow old growing berries in the wilderness. "I'll get you for this!" scream wealthy antagonists over the heads of their lawyers, their interaction in divorce becoming far more intense and meaningful than their marriage had ever been.

Astrological geometry plots these karmic dramas along life's x-axis and vasanas along its y-axis. Those who have the alchemical eyes to see find curves jumping out at them from these graphs of existence. Though it may be difficult, initially, to align the internal and external manifestations of a life with some accuracy, the beauty of well-practiced Jyotisha is that it refuses to retreat to the narrow safety of either psychological interpretations or mundane predictions. A skillful jyotishi takes up karma and vasana in both hands, as a weaver lifts up warp and weft, and weaves from those threads a life-pattern that the client can identify as his or her own. From this union of inner and outer, come images that can transform you, can spur you to invest the energy needed to climb out from the ruts of your karmas and vasanas and turn your feet in new and healthier directions. What is required is the courage to face reality, and the determination to engage that reality without trying to escape it, fight it, or ignore it.

Figure 7 illustrates how relationship alchemy can work (see page 66). It gives the fictional (and admittedly challenging) chart of several potential relationships between bhava lords and karakas. First, we will analyze the Ascendant lord, then we will examine that lord's placement relative to the various grahas that represent key significant others in their capacity as either karyesha or karaka. For this purpose, we will take the rulerships of the bhavas in their natural order.

In this horoscope, first lord Sun sits exalted in the ninth bhava, conjoined with Mercury, the lord of the second bhava of family. Most members of a family actively influence one another, but this One-One sambandha promises that this person and his or her family will influence each other to a substantially greater extent than most. Like two grahas who occupy the confines of the same rashi, they will be compelled somehow to interact, even if only through a calculated awareness of the other occupants, as are passengers thrown together in an elevator. As always in a One-One placement, we must ask whether this interaction will be to their mutual benefit or to their detriment.

One positive factor here is that the Sun is Mercury's friend and Mercury is neutral toward the Sun. However, even though these two grahas are benignly disposed toward one another and occupy a good bhava, they are associated with the psychic, but befuddling, nodal axis and are aspected by the natural malefic Saturn. Moreover, Mercury is combust within 6½°. Also, both Saturn and Mars aspect the second bhava. Add to these malefic influences on the second bhava and its lord the fact that the Sun-Mercury union occurs in the eighth bhava, as counted from the second bhava. These many destabilizing influences suggest that the outcome of family interactions in this case is likely to be rocky overall. The fact that the first and second lords sit together in a good bhava suggests, however, that the individual is likely to maintain these relations and perhaps even to

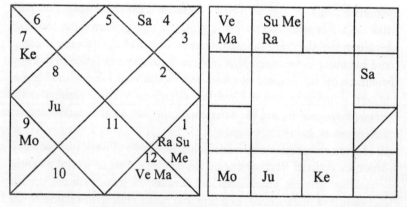

Figure 7. Relationship alchemy at work.

consistently attempt to improve them. Such relations will likely be imbued with a motivated and well-intentioned search for resolution, because the grahas have good relations with each other—friendly in the case of the subject (Sun) toward the family (Mercury), and neutral in the case of the family toward the subject. Like two people locked together in a room, the two grahas involved will eventually work out some way in which to relate, however convoluted the process may be.

Remember, the outcome of a relationship with any particular individual is determined by the condition of the bhava that represents that individual, its lord, and its significator. Your skills at relating are indicated by the relative pattern of placement that exists, between the two grahas that represent the interacting parties. Mars and Saturn aspecting the second bhava here imply that the outcome of the family relationship will be rocky. The fact that the lords of the first and second bhavas are associated implies ongoing active association. Something similar will happen with friends, for in this horoscope, the eleventh bhava of friends, which is also owned by Mercury, will tend in the same direction as the second bhava, particularly since that eleventh bhava is aspected by Mars. Though these relationships with friends will certainly be stormy, they are likely to continue, particularly since the union of lagnesha and karyesha occurs, in this case, in the neutral eleventh bhava, as counted from the eleventh bhava.

Venus, lord of the third bhava of siblings, occupies the eighth bhava in the company of the malefic Mars. Ketu occupies the third bhava. Because Venus occupies an undesirable bhava, as counted from the Ascendant (which predicts the outcome), and because the Sun and Venus exist in a Two-Twelve relationship (which predicts the skill), there are likely to be significant challenges in relationships with siblings. The shared antipathy that exists between the Sun and Venus (who are mutual enemies) evinces an antipathy that will be somewhat attenuated because Venus is exalted, and because the benefic Jupiter aspects Venus into his own rashi in the eighth bhava. This exaltation of the third lord suggests that the siblings will possess their own inherent dignity or status in life. The exaltation will not materially alter the outcome, however, since the Sun (which here signifies the native) is also exalted. That both significators are exalted promises that all concerned will be strong-willed, both in general and in their relationship with one another.

The fourth bhava indicates the mother, and the fact that the lord of the fourth, Mars, has gone to the obstructive eighth bhava suggests some difficulties in outcome with the mother. Like Venus, Mars is in the twelfth bhava from Ascendant lord Sun, which implies conflict in skill with the mother. Unlike Venus, however, Mars has a friend in the Sun, which may suggest a soft spot for the mother that is unlikely to be extended to the siblings. The mother may reciprocate the sentiment, because she is represented by Mars, who is friendly toward the Sun. A similar dynamic applies to the ninth bhava (which represents the father), which is also ruled by Mars.

The situation with the father is, however, more stressful than that with the mother. Mars occupies both the twelfth bhava from the ninth and the eighth bhava from the Ascendant, whereas, for the mother, though Mars tenants the eighth bhava from the Ascendant, it at least sits in the favorable fifth bhava away from the fourth bhava of mother. Also, the ninth bhava is aspected by Saturn and occupied by Rahu, whereas the fourth bhava contains the benefic Jupiter. Some sense of camaraderie and shared experience will exist with the father, because of the Mars-Sun friendship, but it will be less than will exist with the mother.

Jupiter rules the fifth bhava of children for Leo Ascendants. Jupiter is strong in this chart, because he occupies an angular bhava and a friend's rashi, though his position in the twelfth bhava from that fifth bhava does detriment his influence somewhat. The Six-Eight relationship that Jupiter and the Sun share puts poor ability to relate to offspring at the root of the tensions that may arise here between the subject and his or her children. At least the Sun and Jupiter are mutual friends, which will make for some good will amid the fundamental tension implied by poor relationship skills.

Saturn, the lord of the seventh bhava, occupies the twelfth bhava (as counted from the Ascendant). This placement disturbs Saturn doubly, as the twelfth bhava from the Ascendant is also the sixth bhava as counted from the seventh bhava. Moreover, Saturn and the Sun, who are mutual enemies, form a Four-Ten relationship, with Saturn additionally aspecting the Sun by its special tenth aspect. In the natural zodiac, the fourth and tenth bhavas represent private life and public life, respectively. A Four-Ten dynamic often brings private/public issues to the fore in the relationship. When, as here, it is stressful (because they are enemies, and because Sun is weakened by a malefic's aspect), it can indicate deep disagreements over how to apportion the couple's lives between the requirements of the home and the outer world. Here, the one-sided aspect of the astringent Saturn will tend to make one partner feel that the other somehow is restricting full personal expression and external environment. This one-sided sambandha also suggests that partners tend to pursue the subject in a one-sided manner, perhaps detrimentally (since Saturn is Sun's enemy). A thankfully beneficial influence is Jupiter's one-sided aspect on Saturn, which softens the latter and greatly diminishes the potential for active malevolence.

Our general analysis of this horoscope thus suggests that this person will have considerable difficulties in the arena of relations. These difficulties become particularly likely because the lords of the third, fourth, fifth, sixth, seventh, eighth, ninth, and tenth bhavas are all located in stressful positions, when counted from the lord of the Ascendant. Eight of a possible eleven bhavas are thus afflicted—we exclude here the Ascendant, which is our point of reference. When such a plurality of grahas exist in poor relations with the Ascendant, we can generally conclude that the person is unlikely to bring good relating skills to many types of relationships. This is, thus, an example of a dussambandha yoga. In fact, were it not for the benefic aspect of Jupiter on Mars, Venus, and Saturn, these relationships would likely be even more difficult.

Further Examples

In Richard Nixon's horoscope (see Chart 4, page 70), the Sun and Mars occupy the fifth bhava in a One-One relationship. Recall that grahas in a One-One relationship actively influence each other, in ways that depend on their natures and placements. Here, both grahas are strong: they occupy the fifth bhava, a good bhava from the Ascendant, in Sagittarius, which is ruled by Jupiter, a mutual friend of both. Sun and Mars are mutual friends, and Mars is not combust. Our conclusion: Nixon and his mother enjoyed an intense (intense because both Sun and Mars are fiery and in a fire rashi) but satisfying relationship. This seems to have been the case, since it has been reported that Nixon thought of his mother as a saint.

Another salient relationship feature of Nixon's horoscope is that only one graha occupies the sixth, eighth, or twelfth bhavas, as counted from lagnesha Sun. The almost complete susambandha yoga thus created was most useful for a politician. Unfortunately, the barrier to a complete susambandha yoga is the karaka of enemies, Saturn, who sits in the sixth bhava, as counted from Nixon's lagnesha. Saturn is also noteworthy here, as he happens to be the lord of the sixth bhava of enemies. Nixon's much-publicized crude diatribes and illegal maneuvers against his political enemies offer clear evidence of his poor relationship skills with adversaries. Despite his achievements, the questionable skills he brought to bear on his opponents led to his downfall, and earned him the pejorative nickname "Tricky Dick."

Rashi Chart

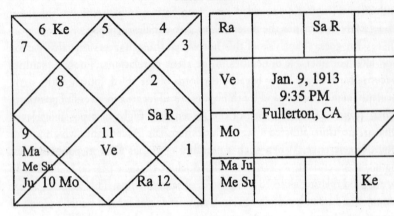

Navamsha Chart

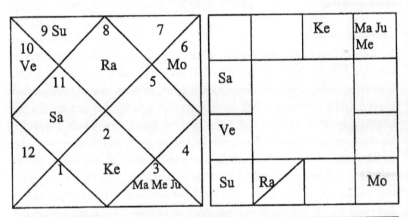

Planetary Positions		Vimshottari Dasha		
LG	24°LE40'	MA	7 Nov. 1910	Yogi Point CA 27-34'
SU	26°SA45'	RA	6 Nov. 1917	
MO	27°CP29'	JU	7 Nov. 1935	Yogi – MA
MA	07°SA06'	SA	7 Nov. 1951	
ME	07°SA23'	ME	7 Nov. 1970	Avayogi – KE
JU	09°SA02'	KE	7 Nov. 1987	
VE	10°AQ51'	VE	7 Nov. 1994	Duplicate Yogi – SA
SA	04°TA51'R	SU	7 Nov. 2014	
RA	14°PI 36'	MO	7 Nov. 2020	Daghda Rasis
KE	14°VI 36'			CP & LE

Chart 4. Richard Nixon.

Jimmy Carter's horoscope (see Chart 5, page 72) shows Ascendant lord Venus in a harmonizing Seven-Seven relationship with seventh lord Mars. Mars and Venus are neutrals to one another, and both occupy good bhavas from the Ascendant. The Seven-Seven mutual aspect itself impels lagnesha and this karyesha to actively relate. Moreover, by being Seven-Seven as lords of the first and seventh bhavas in this birth chart, they recapitulate their roles as lords of the first and seventh bhavas of the natural zodiac (which always begins with Aries in the first bhava, with Libra thus opposite it in the seventh bhava). This recapitulation reinforces the inclination of lagnesha and karyesha to be favorably disposed to one another. In doing so, it compensates somewhat for lagnesha's detriments (occupation of an enemy's rashi while being hemmed in between malefics in the adjacent rashis). Carter (lagnesha) has accordingly, throughout his career, relied on his wife (karyesha) for strength. Even now, this couple continues to work well together, both at home and on various humanitarian missions.

Fourth lord Saturn (mother) and first lord Venus are Three-Eleven to each other in Carter's birth chart, with Saturn exalted. Saturn's presence in the Ascendant as the karyesha of mother links it tightly to the Ascendant (which represents Carter), particularly since Saturn is exalted in this Ascendant. This linkage of Carter and mother is rendered even stronger because Moon (significator of mother) also sits in the lagna, conjoined with fourth lord Saturn and replicating the Three-Eleven relationship with lagnesha, Venus. In fact, Carter was exceptionally close to Miss Lillian, his mother. This would seem to be a case of good outcome (karaka and exalted karyesha in a good bhava) fueled by good skills (karaka and karyesha both participating in a harmonious Three-Eleven relationship with lagnesha, in which all grahas also enjoy beneficial placements relative to the Ascendant and to the fourth bhava).

And what of his younger brother, "Boozin' Billy"? The strong third lord Jupiter is Four-Ten to Venus, and Four-Ten arrangements can create disagreements between the partners about who will stay in the background. The question of who will be out in front sometimes becomes the relationship's central issue, and, in fact, here was a place where a portion of Carter's private life tried to intrude itself into his public life. (A very similar situation appears in Chart 13, that of Princess Diana, whose first and seventh lords stand Four-Ten to each other. See page 113.

People who are willing to work on their relationships can usually make Four-Ten relationships work, particularly if both lagnesha and

Rashi Chart

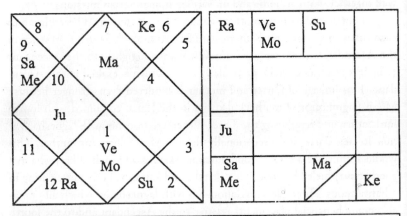

Navamsha Chart

Planetary Positions		Vimshottari Dasha		
LG	03LI 17'	JU	24 Jul. 1923	Yogi Point CA 9-35'
SU	15°VI 16'	SA	24 Jul. 1939	
MO	20°LI 60'	ME	24 Jul. 1958	Yogi – SA
MA	03°AQ02'	KE	25 Jul. 1975	
ME	28°LE24'	VE	24 Jul. 1982	Avayogi – MO
JU	21°SC38'	SU	24 Jul. 2002	
VE	00°LE32'	MO	24 Jul. 2008	Duplicate Yogi – MO
SA	09°LI 07'	MA	25 Jul. 2018	
RA	27°CA40'	RA	24 Jul. 2025	Daghda Rasis
KE	27°CP40'			CP & LE

Chart 5. Jimmy Carter.

karyesha occupy good bhavas, as counted from the Ascendant. The grahas involved in Four-Ten associations can transfer energy well, if not always harmoniously, by virtue of being in angular bhavas *(kendras)* from one another. This transfer of energy more readily becomes synergistic when the grahas are friendly or neutral to each other. It becomes antagonistic when the grahas are inimical to each other and subject to the stress of afflictions from malefics and poor placement by rashi and bhava. Moreover, since the fourth bhava represents the home, and, by extension, one's private life, and the tenth bhava signifies work, and, by extension, one's public life, there tends in Four-Ten relationships to be an issue around the natural "division of labor" in the pairing. Commonly (but not invariably), the partner indicated by the graha in the Four position is the private one, while the Ten person is the one who is most in the public eye. This happens to be true in Carter's chart, where his Jupiter (his brother) is in the fourth bhava, counted from Venus (Carter).

The sons of Mahatma Gandhi openly alleged that their father did not adequately support them. In Gandhi's horoscope (see Chart 6, page 75) Venus, the Ascendant lord, is in the twelfth bhava to Saturn, the fifth lord. Since it is frequently the case that the graha in the second position feels let down by the graha in the twelfth position, this situation induced the sons (Saturn) to feel disappointed in their father.

Gandhi's skills at relating to his associates (eleventh bhava) were likewise compromised, since lagnesha and karyesha (here, eleventh lord Sun) are also Two-Twelve to one another. Moreover, Sun and Venus are mutual enemies, and Sun occupies a bad bhava, as counted from the Ascendant. These positions promoted in Gandhi a feeling of being betrayed by his associates, particularly since the twelfth bhava indicates secret enemies. Note that here, the situation is the reverse of that with his sons: Gandhi felt disappointed with his associates because they (Sun) are in the twelfth to him (Venus).

When we consider Gandhi's relationship with his wife, we find that seventh lord Mars is conjoined with Ascendant lord Venus in the Ascendant. This suggests both a positive outcome (since the seventh bhava is occupied by benefic Jupiter and aspected by its lord, by marriage significator Venus, and by benefic Mercury) and good relating skills (since lagnesha and karyesha exist in a One-One relationship influenced by benefics and occurs in a good bhava). The couple did remain together for life (since the grahas are conjoined in a good bhava with benefic Mercury and are aspected by benefic Jupiter). Conflicts did arise, however (since the grahas are hemmed in between Saturn in the second bhava and Sun in the twelfth). Some of these conflicts were probably due to Mars (who occupies a rashi that is neutral to him) feeling overshadowed by the more powerful Venus (who occupies his own rashi).

Many of these disagreements (problems with relating skills) were probably settled (outcome) by Gandhi's willingness to "appear" to compromise. Venus in its own rashi in the Ascendant shows a strong desire for conciliation, but on one's own terms. Here Gandhi's skills at association were more apparent than real, for he achieved his goals, not by negotiation (which requires relating skill), but by coercion. Remember that the overall tone of One-One relationships depends on the general strength or weakness of the two grahas involved. The two parties will be impelled to relate, but may not relate on an equal footing. Gandhi's strong Venus backed by Mars enabled him to haggle his way gently but firmly toward his goal and usually to attain it, for a person with a powerful Ascendant lord is difficult to defeat. Gandhi's determined stand against the British, his resolve to practice celibacy in his marriage, come what may, and the general tenacity of his other convictions all reflect the tendency toward serene inflexibility that became a hallmark of his life.

Examples Using the Karaka

It is best to use the natural significations of the grahas for support and color rather than for primary analysis when using them as a source of information on an individual's relationship skills. Natural significators are less useful than bhava lords for analysis, because significators are factors of reduced differentiation. While Jupiter, for instance, occupies one rashi for about a year, everyone born during that year will not experience the same specific relationship experiences. Jupiter will, however, contribute an overall flavor to those experiences.

As an example, let us return to Jimmy Carter (see Chart 5, page 72) and his brother Billy. Mars, the sibling karaka, participates in a Seven-Seven relationship with Carter's Ascendant lord Venus. Had the karaka's Seven-Seven influence predominated over that of the Four-Ten placement of the bhava lords, we would have expected the brothers to relate more directly and clearly than they often did. Their style of relating would have reflected less of the Four-Ten nature that it displayed. A mutual aspect like Seven-Seven incessantly stimulates two people to become actively and reciprocally involved in that relationship. That the

Rashi Chart

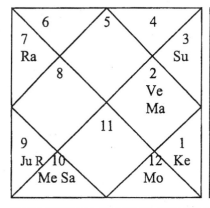

	Ju R		
	October 2, 1869 7:11:48 AM Porbandar, India		Mo Ra
Ke			
	Sa	Me Ve Ma	Su

Navamsha Chart

Mo	Ke	Ve Ma	Su
Me Sa			
Ju R		Ra	

Planetary Positions		Vimshottari Dasha		
LG	24°VI 46'	ME	7 Dec. 1855	Yogi Point AR 17-42'
SU	16°VI 52'	KE	6 Dec. 1872	
MO	27°CA30'	VE	7 Dec. 1879	Yogi – VE
MA	26°LI 21'	SU	7 Dec. 1899	
ME	11°LI 43'	MO	7 Dec. 1905	Avayogi – JU
JU	28°AR08'R	MA	8 Dec. 1915	
VE	24°LI 22'	RA	8 Dec. 1922	Duplicate Yogi – MA
SA	20°SC20'	JU	7 Dec. 1940	
RA	12°CA09'	SA	8 Dec. 1956	Daghda Rasis
KE	12°CP09'			SA & PI

Chart 6. Mahatma Gandhi.

significator occupied a positive position relative to the lord of the Ascendant facilitated an upgrade in their interaction from general annoyance with one another to a certain folksy cuteness. Had Mars and Venus been Six-Eight, however, the two might have permitted their disagreements to escalate (poor skills) and the situation might have become a serious embarrassment to the ex-President (poor outcome).

Karaka relationships can be used in combination with bhava-ruler relationships to enhance the certainty of the analysis by generating confluence. Figure 7 (page 66) shows both Venus (lord of the third bhava of siblings) and Mars (the natural significator of siblings) placed in the eighth bhava from the Ascendant, and in the twelfth bhava from Ascendant lord Sun. This confluence of troubling positions assures us that we concluded accurately that the person and his or her siblings will often disagree. In figure 4 (page 60), fourth lord Jupiter occupies the third bhava from first lord Mercury, and Moon (significator of mother) occupies the ninth bhava from Mercury. This reinforces our judgment that the individual possesses an intrinsic ability to relate well to his mother.

Mahatma Gandhi (see Chart 6, page 75) was a man who never shrank from questioning authority when he believed it to be acting unjustly. In his horoscope, the Moon (who acts as lord of his tenth bhava of government and authority) forms a Four-Ten relationship with lagnesha Venus. For Four-Ten relationships to work well, the people involved must be willing to put in the requisite effort to make them work. Here, both lagnesha and karyesha occupy good bhavas, as counted from the Ascendant, which promotes at least a potential for harmony. Also, both grahas are strong (since both occupy their own rashis). These astrological combinations testify to the ability that Gandhi and the British displayed to continue to negotiate through thick and thin.

We note, from the outcome of his relations with governments, however, that these mutual strengths encouraged the authorities and Gandhi to become deeply entrenched in their own separate points of view, instead of giving them a ready willingness to compromise from strength. Here, as in previous examples, this Four-Ten placement created a private/public focus—in this instance, one characterized by severe disputes over how to apportion administrative control between the homeland (India, as represented by Gandhi) and the outer world (England, as represented by the colonial power). What Gandhi effectively desired was to lead his country out of its domestic affiliation with England!

When we look at the placement of the Sun in Gandhi's chart relative to lagnesha, we discover that Sun (the karaka of authority) forms a Two-Twelve relationship with Venus. The malevolence of this placement is intensified, because the Sun sits in the evil twelfth bhava of Gandhi's chart. It was this Two-Twelve configuration that, by encouraging Gandhi to perceive that the British usually negotiated with him in bad faith, inhibited him from bringing more effective relating skills to bear on the situation, and inspired him to wrangle with them instead. As noted above, the Two-Twelve relationship between lagnesha Venus and the Sun, the karyesha for associates, promoted a feeling in Gandhi of being betrayed by his friends. The Seven-Seven relationship that the Ascendant lord makes with Jupiter, a karaka for friends and associates, had the effect of driving him to interact with them, even though such interactions were often rancorous because his skills at communicating with them were so compromised by the relative Sun-Venus placement.

Remember that a natural significator assumes great importance when a bhava significator disappears—i.e., when the lord of the Ascendant owns another bhava as well. In such cases, the relationship to be evaluated is the one that exists between the Ascendant lord and the significator for the bhava to be examined (instead of that bhava's lord). In figure 4 (page 60), Mercury is lord of both the first and the tenth bhavas, which means that there is no second graha with which to create a relationship vis-à-vis employers that is based on bhava lordship. We, therefore, use the Sun in its capacity as significator of employers to represent the tenth lord. Since Mercury and the Sun sit in a Two-Twelve relationship in this chart, we discover that this is the one area in which the individual may not possess noteworthy relationship skills—which may be precisely why he is in business for himself.

Interrelations Among Significant Others

The individual birth chart is such a mine of information that it can even be used to describe the relationships created between the various others in a person's life. One of the easiest ways to prospect for this sort of astrological ore is to rotate the horoscope to change the bhava that signifies the person into the Ascendant. To learn something of your mother's life, rotate your horoscope until your fourth bhava—the bhava of the mother—becomes the first, and read the horoscope from there, as if it were hers. The second bhava from this new Ascendant (the second bhava from your fourth bhava, or your fifth bhava) represents her undifferentiated family. That new Ascendant's third bhava (your sixth bhava) represents her siblings (your maternal uncles and aunts), the new fourth bhava (your seventh), her mother (your maternal grandmother), and so on. Similarly, the third bhava (siblings) from your ninth bhava (father) represents your paternal uncles and aunts, the fourth bhava from your ninth bhava represents your paternal grandmother, and so on.

Extending the principle of rotating a horoscope to the limit, we can, for instance, evaluate how John F. Kennedy's wife got along with her mother without even using Jackie Onassis's birth chart. We do this by rotating JFK's horoscope (see Chart 7, page 79) to make Pisces, his seventh bhava, into her Ascendant. The fourth bhava from this new Ascendant (his tenth bhava) now represents her mother. When we examine the disposition of the lords of these two bhavas—Jupiter for the new Ascendant and Mercury for the new fourth bhava—we find them in a Two-Twelve relationship. That Mercury (Jackie's mom) sits in the twelfth bhava to Jupiter (Jackie) permits us to conclude that Jackie tended to feel unsupported by her mother (whether or not her mother felt that she was being supportive of her daughter). Jackie was, moreover, perhaps insufficiently skilled to resolve this issue with her parent.

Interestingly enough, Jackie Onassis's difficulties in relating to her mother are confirmed by her own horoscope (see Chart 8, page 80) by the Six-Eight position of Venus (the Ascendant lord) with Saturn (the fourth lord). This Six-Eight relationship is particularly stressful, because Ascendant lord Venus occupies the eighth bhava from that Ascendant.

This method of rotational analysis works much of the time, but it is not, of course, infallible. One specific exception involves grandchildren, who can sometimes be read from the ninth bhava (the fifth bhava away from the fifth bhava of children), and sometimes from the fifth bhava itself, since they are the sort of children that most parents can expect to be blessed with in late adulthood. Also, do not extend these rotations too far away from the original horoscope. The fifth bhava (children) away from the fourth bhava (mother) is the eighth bhava—but in your birth chart, your mother's children are represented by your first (yourself), third (younger siblings), and eleventh (older siblings) bhavas, not exclusively by your eighth.

Rashi Chart

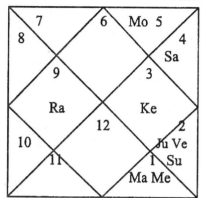

Navamsha Chart

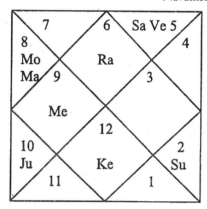

Planetary Positions		Vimshottari Dasha		
LG	27°VI 17'	VE	31 Aug. 1900	Yogi CP-12-58'
SU	15°TA08'	SU	31 Aug. 1920	
MO	24°LE30'	MO	31 Aug. 1926	Yogi – MO
MA	25°AR43'	MA	31 Aug. 1936	
ME	27°AR53'	RA	01 Aug. 1943	Avayogi – ME
JU	00°TA20'	JU	31 Aug. 1961	
VE	24°TA03'	SA	31 Aug. 1977	Duplicate Yogi – SA
SA	04°CA29'	ME	31 Aug. 1996	
RA	19°SA47'	KE	01 Aug. 2013	Daghda Rasis
KE	19°GE47'			LE & SC

Chart 7. John F. Kennedy.

Rashi Chart

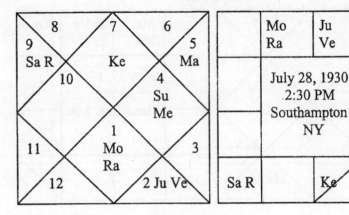

Navamsha Chart

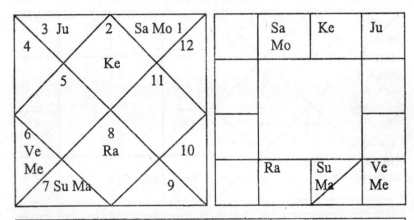

Planetary Positions		Vimshottari Dasha		
LG	25°LI 06'	KE	20 Feb. 1928	Yogi Point LI 18-21'
SU	12°CA17'	VE	20 Feb. 1935	
MO	02°AR44'	SU	20 Feb. 1955	Yogi – RA
MA	21°LE57'	MO	20 Feb. 1961	
ME	09°CA33'	MA	20 Feb. 1971	Avayogi – VE
JU	16°TA42'	RA	20 Feb. 1978	
VE	28°TA54'	JU	21 Feb. 1996	Duplicate Yogi – VE
SA	01°SA47'R	SA	21 Feb. 2012	
RA	24°AR20'	ME	21 Feb. 2031	Daghda Rasis
KE	24°LI 20'			CA & CP

Chart 8. Jacqueline Onassis.

THE FOUR
CORNERSTONES

$\mathcal{A}$ll humans bring to their relationships personal bundles of karma and vasana. Indeed, a sizable portion of the interaction between two people occurs via the medium of the auras created by their individual karmas and vasanas. Most relationships begin as delicate sprouts that require the sustained sustenance of the flavors (rasas) that are associated with them. We all know that only certain flavors combine well—that, while both asparagus and chocolate are wonderful on their own, few people find pleasure in steamed asparagus smothered in chocolate sauce. Thus, we sometimes observe that two people, admirable on their own, combine like garlic with peaches, while two who individually cope poorly with life may locate in one another the sort of complementary flavor that rhubarb finds in sugar.

Such people (or rather, their auras) support or obstruct one another. This interaction is absolutely essential in evaluating the viability of a relationship. Support in this context means rapport, which develops between humans when their circumstances, minds, and actions—their bhavas—are aligned. The more concord in each area of life, and the greater number of areas of life in which there is concord, the more likely it is that sufficient healthy mutual rasa will be created to make the pairing endure. From an astrological perspective, we search for evidence of such affinity in the pattern of auras that the individual grahas intimate for each of the horoscopes.

We accomplished this, in the previous chapter, by surveying a single birth chart to discover the rapport potential between a person and the significant others in his or her life. In this chapter, we compare two horoscopes—via the art of synastry alluded to earlier—to gain deeper insight into the prospects for the relationship rapport between two people. When a certain minimum of support is evident between two horoscopes, we gain the confidence needed to predict a greater likelihood of relationship success. Two people who lack that minimum level of support are unlikely to relate harmoniously, at least spontaneously, however well motivated they may be. That doesn't mean, however, that they shouldn't try! Relationships still develop between people whose synastry displays fundamentally unfavorable mutual dispositions. As long as such relationships persist, instinctive episodes of discord are likely to persist along with them. How long a relationship continues (i.e., its eventual outcome) is a job for seventh-bhava analysis. Synastry's task is to tell us how harmonious or inharmonious that relationship will be while it lasts (i.e., how skillfully the participants will relate).

THE FOUR CORNERSTONES

In Jyotisha, we measure alignments by establishing different *lagnas* that "tie down" the astrological positions of the grahas in horoscopes so we can compare them for meaningful relationship alignments. Maharshi Parashara, the father of Jyotisha, is prominent among the great jyotishis who teach the principle of *sudarshana* ("good sight"), a technique that ties down horoscopes from three angles: the Ascendant, the Moon as Ascendant, and the Sun as Ascendant. Jyotisha's standard jargon designates these three the *udaya lagna*, the *chandra lagna*, and the *surya lagna*, respectively. Each of these relates to a separate sheath (see chapter 1) in an embodied being: the Ascendant to the physical body, the Moon to the astral, or subtle, body, and the Sun to the causal body. Every embodied being is a body/mind/spirit composite. Sudarshana is "good sight," because it makes embodied life visible to us from its three most fundamental perspectives: the physical (Ascendant), the mental-emotional (Moon), and the spiritual (Sun). In the context of relationships, it is useful to tie down the grahas in each of the aforementioned principal ways, using the Ascendant, the Moon, and the Sun as focal points.

We then add a fourth angle from which to view the horoscopes: the Venusian angle. Venus, representing desire or strong personal yearning for what promises pleasure, is included in this group of factors because desire is one of the necessities of embodied existence. The *Sankhya* philosophy of India teaches that the ultimate cause of the entire universe is the desire of the absolute reality to experience itself. That desire causes a sense of separateness to arise. From this separateness, the manifested universe appears. Everything in our world arises from, exists in, and dissolves back into desire. The *Tantras* have, therefore, counseled everyone who wishes to comprehend the inherent nature of life to study thoroughly the nature of desire. Most people enter into relationships because, in some way or other, they desire one another, or desire something that the other has. This all-important ingredient of desire, is the domain of Venus, especially in romantic relationships.

Sankhya teaches that there is no end to desire. Cravings are numberless. Yet two people are often drawn to relate to one another when their physical, mental, or spiritual experiences (their hankerings) are complementary. In other words, two people are likely to be interested in relating when raga is substantial and dvesha minimal in their mutual physical, mental or emotional, philosophical or spiritual, or pleasure-seeking lives. We will call these four astrological focal points—the Ascendant, the Moon, the Sun, and Venus—the "four cornerstones" of compatibility analysis, because it is highly unlikely that two people will build the edifice of a harmonious relationship successfully unless at least one pair of these cornerstones provides a strong foundation by creating a supportive connection in their birthcharts.

THE INTERACTION OF TWO HOROSCOPES

The analyses you are about to read will be somewhat familiar to those who know how to compare the positions of a single graha in two horoscopes from the viewpoint of Western astrology. Though they are not specifically mentioned in the classical Sanskritic texts, these techniques broadly follow the traditions of Jyotisha, being derived from Jyotisha's more strictly lunar-based methods. The rasas that make our relationship lives most worth living are our emotions, which may have cued the ancient jyotishis to make the Moon the most important of the factors used to evaluate relationship success or failure. The Moon represents manas, the mental faculty that determines the life experiences to which our senses are attracted (which promote raga) and the ones that our senses try to avoid (which promote dvesha). While a strong, well-placed Moon in a horoscope tends to produce a stable, enjoyable sensory and emotional life, a disturbed Moon imbalances one's sensory and emotional existence.

The Moon's condition is so critical to an individual's welfare that much of Jyotisha has, since the days of its origins, been framed around it.

Jyotisha's most traditional methods of comparing two horoscopes for marriage are collectively termed the *kutams* (roughly, "a group with a purpose") or *poruttbams* (loosely, "a compatible union"). These methods of synastry determine the degree of a couple's compatibility by using a system of points derived solely from the interaction of the Moons in each birth chart. We have, in these analyses, dropped some of the wholly Moon-based criteria, and extended others to include the Ascendant, Sun, and Venus, as well as the Moon. We introduce these methods with the hope that jyotishis everywhere will investigate their value by applying them in practice, and hope that they may eventually be admitted to Jyotisha's official canon when they have passed the test of time.

The primary synastrical method of the ancient traditional poruttham marriage-compatibility analysis is to count from the Moon in one horoscope to the Moon in the other, and to interpret the result—a method we explain in detail later in chapter 5. As is typical of this type of counting in Jyotisha, the count from one rashi to the other is inclusive. For example, if one horoscope has the Moon in Aries, and the other has the Moon in Libra, the Moon in Libra is seven rashis away from the Moon in Aries, and vice versa. The key is to remember that the count is always inclusive: *Aries*, Taurus, Gemini, Cancer, Leo, Virgo, and *Libra*, for a total of seven rashis. Similarly, if the Moon in one chart is in Taurus and the Moon in the other is in Scorpio, they are again seven rashis apart. We count similarly for our other three cornerstones: from Ascendant to Ascendant, Sun to Sun, and Venus to Venus.

Interaction of the Ascendants of two birth charts is particularly significant in that each of the other bhavas in the two horoscopes will align in the same way that the two Ascendants align. If, for example, the Ascendants are Five-Nine, the second bhavas of family and finance will also be Five-Nine, the fifth bhavas of children will be Five-Nine, and so on. This suggests that a fundamental general harmony of bhavas will underpin the couple's experience of life together, an essential raga that will punctuate their lives.

If, however, the Ascendants in two charts are Six-Eight, the fourth bhavas of vehicle, property, and emotional stability will also be Six-Eight, as will the tenth bhavas of career, and so on. Here, it will be easy for the dvesha that the Six-Eight relationship develops to extend into all realms of their shared existence. While the degree of general alignment or misalignment remains subject to the planetary specifics of the two charts, given that the totality of the indications of the twelve bhavas equals the totality of one's experience of life in the external world alignment of the Ascendants is clearly of great consequence to a couple's future together.

PRIMARY AND SECONDARY LINKS OF THE FOUR CORNERSTONES

As we saw in the last chapter, seven fixed relationships can arise between any two grahas or points in a horoscope, according to the number of rashis that separate them. If we examine the permutations for the four cornerstones of relationship life from one horoscope to another, we discover that we can classify the cornerstone interrelationships into the same seven fixed relationships comprised of two distinct categories. We will call these two categories "primary links" and "secondary links."

Primary links arise through the contacts of the four cornerstones of relationship life as mutually exclusive pairs: Ascendant to Ascendant, Moon to Moon, Sun to Sun, and Venus to Venus. These contacts are exceptionally potent. The primary links forged by these mutually exclusive pairs often provide a snapshot of instant insight into relationship compatibility. In fact, the nature of the interactions of these four pairs of cornerstones are potent indicators of whether a healthy relationship will develop between two people, especially if they intend to marry. Even a cursory look at many sets of horoscopes confirms that two people will rarely enter into a lasting harmonious relationship unless some strongly positive primary link exists between their birth charts.

Cornerstone analysis interprets the nature of the interaction of the innate tendencies (vasanas) of two people. We do not suggest here that a lack of supportive primary links between two charts will prevent any relationship from developing between two people. Lasting inharmonious relationships do occur in life. Whether or not a relationship, such as a marriage, will persist is determined directly by karma and indirectly by vasanas. Marital karma is examined by scrutinizing a horoscope's seventh bhava, seventh lord, and the significator of marriage. It is only in the context of vasana contact that we, assert that harmony will flourish with difficulty in the lives of any couple that lacks at least one pair of cornerstones that are agreeably placed relative to one another.

Secondary links arise through the cross-contacts between two horoscopes of any two of the four cornerstones of relationship. An Ascendant of one chart may be in the seventh rashi from the Venus of the other, or the Moon of one may be in the same rashi as the Sun the other. In this way, six pairs of secondary links can arise between two horoscopes: Ascendant-Sun, Ascendant-Moon, Ascendant-Venus, Sun-Moon, Sun-Venus, and Moon-Venus. They are paired because they are calculated twice, from the first horoscope to the second, and then from the second back to the first.

The need to "double-reckon" the secondary links means that they can be "mutual" or "unilateral." Mutual links are those that appear in both directions—for example, a beneficial mutual secondary link between the Suns and Moons in two horoscopes is one in which there is any variety of beneficial link between his Sun and her Moon and a similar link between her Sun and his Moon. It is precisely because such links can be either mutual or only one-sided that they are termed secondary, as opposed to primary, links. Primary links are always mutual, identical links between two horoscopes. Unilateral secondary links are much less meaningful than primary or mutual secondary links, but they do add to the overall pattern of attraction, in a one-sided sort of way.

Although secondary links are not as potent as primary links, beneficial mutual secondary links among the four cornerstones often represent different areas of life in which attractions will overlap and be particularly rich and strong. Thus a strongly positive primary link between the Venuses in two charts will operate exclusively as a strong mutual desire for one another, because Venus simply indicates desire. But a supportive mutual secondary link between the Venus of one and the Ascendant of the other can indicate, instead, a profound desire (Venus) of the one for the body or material circumstances (Ascendant) of the other. Similarly, partners whose Moons and Suns are joined by a mutual secondary link are likely to find that each holds an emotional taste (Moon) for the philosophy of the other (Sun).

SEVEN TYPES OF GRAHA RELATIONSHIPS

Both primary and secondary links can arise between two horoscopes through the relative placement of the four cornerstones in any one of the seven fixed relationships that we described in chapter 2: One-One, Seven-Seven, Five-Nine, Three-Eleven, Four-Ten, Two-Twelve, and Six-Eight. Each of these relationships possesses its own assigned human qualities, its own personal "flavor." Jyotisha, to this day, is often taught in India in an anthropomorphic style. We believe there is both charm and practical utility in ascribing human attributes to the grahas and their relationships within the solar system, and we are convinced that these ascribed human attributes are particularly useful when applied to horoscope comparison for the purpose of relationship compatibility between two people.

The *Tajika* system of Jyotisha describes the grahas as capable of establishing four types of relationships with each other. According to Tajika, grahas can be open friends, secret friends, open enemies, or secret enemies. We have liberally expanded these four categories into the seven types of graha relationships shown in Table 2.

The extent of harmonious rapport between two people will depend on the type, the number, and the strength of the primary and secondary links among the four cornerstones across their horoscopes. A strong possibility for a harmonious relationship exists when a plurality of supportive connections exists among the relationship cornerstones. The greater the number of primary and mutual secondary associates, opposites, and active and secret supporters, and the stronger such activated cornerstones, the more supported the attraction between two people will be. Likewise, as the number of contrasts, secret adversaries, and active adversaries increases in a horoscope

Table 2. Relationship of the Grahas in Compatibility Analysis.

NAME	DEFINITION
Associates	Two grahas in the same rashi (One-One, as counted from each other)
Opposites	Two grahas in opposite rashis (Seven-Seven, as counted from each other)
Active Supporters	Two grahas in rashis that are Five-Nine, as counted from each other
Secret Supporters	Two grahas in rashis that are Three-Eleven, as counted from each other
Contrasts	Two grahas in rashis that are Four-Ten, as counted from each other
Active Adversaries	Two grahas in rashis that are Six-Eight, as counted from each other
Secret Adversaries	Two grahas in rashis that are Two-Twelve, as counted from each other

comparison, the likelihood for a congenial interaction decreases. Couples whose synastry displays all four of the cornerstones in desirable primary links, especially in the form of associates and opposites, are exceptionally likely to build a healthy relating foundation. A "vasana glue" binds them together. When, however, the plurality of interactions among the cornerstones of two horoscopes is obstructive, the vasana glue is unlikely to form any rapport strong enough to comfortably support the union through both thick and thin. The owners of such charts are much less likely to live together harmoniously over the long term.

The four cornerstones, however well aligned, should ideally be strong in and of themselves if they are to act effectively in any connection. Grahas can be weak or unstable when they occupy their debilitation rashi or the rashi of an enemy, when they are combust, defeated in a planetary war, exclusively associated with or aspected by natural malefics, and when they occupy bhavas six, eight, or twelve. In particular, cornerstones that inhabit the latter three bhavas of the originating horoscope will be much less effective in aligning the vasanas of a couple, unless such grahas happen to be very strong in those bhavas as a result of occupying their own or exaltation rashis.

A synergy connects the inherent skills and attitudes brought to a relationship (vasanas) and that relationship's outcome (karmas). You will recall that a vasana is a mental residue that inclines a person to act out a certain karma. A karma, in turn, encourages a person to fortify a certain vasana. Karmas and vasanas reinforce each other; as you strengthen one, the other is strengthened. Correlating karma with vasana creates four useful classes of relationship possibilities:

- Beneficial karmas + good vasanas = a smooth relationship that continues indefinitely;
- Detrimental karmas + good vasanas = good rapport between two well-meaning people who eventually part company, most likely amicably;
- Beneficial karmas + bad vasanas = two people who remain together while making life miserable for each other;
- Detrimental karmas + bad vasanas = two people who meet, mate, and, after a ghastly plunge, crash and burn.

The key to modifying untoward karmas (outcomes) is the generation of healthier vasanas, for healthy mental and emotional routines can help to rectify skewed relating patterns by evoking the synthesis of a more appealing mutual rasa. Many Indian jyotishis focus on pre-existing karmas alone, and thus concern themselves only with outcomes. "This marriage will end in divorce!" they thunder. In so proclaiming, they often forcefully bolster the client's ready-made fatalism. The prophecy gains momentum through a self-fulfilling dynamism. In contrast, we believe that vasanas must not be ignored, that they can be the key to transforming outcomes by kindling faith in and dedication to the prayers, rituals, or other traditional upaya (astrological remedy) that an individual may perform to effect that transformation.

Of the seven potential links between the cornerstones, the connections termed associates, opposites, active supporters, and secret supporters are factors that have long been recognized in Jyotisha as relationship builders. Poruttham evaluation recognizes as excellent a situation in which the man's Moon sits in the seventh rashi from the woman's, and states that situations in which his Moon occupies the ninth or eleventh rashi from hers are very good as well. Similarly, the tradition of Tajika Jyotisha states that grahas that are associates or opposites fully influence each other (and so are very powerful). Tajika also maintains that grahas that actively support each other exert three-fourths of their potential influence on each other, which makes their interaction only slightly less powerful than associates or opposites. Secret supporters are only mildly strong because, according to Tajika, the graha in Three exerts only two-fifths of its potential influence on the graha in Eleven, which exerts just one-tenth of its potential on the graha in Three. Do not be tempted to overvalue the numerical quantification here; these are relative numbers.

Please remember, however, that vasana attraction does not ensure harmony everywhere in life! Vasanas remain but one fundamental ingredient of life; karmas are their universal partners. Romeo and Juliet may have been soulmates, may have had a taste for each other, and may have seen in each other the perfect vehicle for marital enjoyment, but their union was the end of them. Their attraction was overwhelming, but, when it was juxtaposed with their external circumstances, the combination produced a lethal violence, which at least hints that their Ascendants did not agree. If attraction were enough to guarantee relationship success, Romeo and Juliet might have grown old together. Conversely, many couples live together efficiently for decades without any untoward material incidents, but also without passion, when their Ascendants agree. They may not, however, share tastes (Moon), enjoyments (Venus), or be soulmates (Sun).

It follows that karmic outcome must always be evaluated in conjunction with the degree of vasana rapport. Because vasanas have such an innate capacity to influence karmas, it remains equally important to understand in exactly what manner an attraction created by strong vasana interaction among the four cornerstones will be to the benefit or the detriment of the two people involved. A good place to begin this evaluation is to examine the nature of the seven fixed relationships.

Seven-Seven: Opposites

When one pair of the compatibility cornerstones occupies rashis that are seven places apart, they become opposites, forming a primary link. When, for example, the Ascendants of two horoscopes are mirror images of each other (for instance, Taurus rises in one birth chart and Scorpio in the other, or Gemini rises in one horoscope and Sagittarius in the other), the Ascendants are opposites. Should the two Moons of two horoscopes fall in rashis that are opposite each other in the sky, they become opposites. The two Suns or the two Venuses of two birth charts, when similarly positioned, also create a relation of opposites. All of these positions are examples of supportive primary links (see figure 8, page 91).

An "opposition," in the context of Jyotisha, is established by rashi position. Here, it is used in a sense different from how it is used in Western astrology, where an opposition is commonly defined by degree orb and is often deemed obstructive. In Jyotisha, opposition by rashi is thought to promote positive complementarity ("opposites attract"), because rashis that are opposite one another in the sky have complementary natures. As polar opposites, each of the rashis provides what its opposite needs or lacks. While most of us probably associate the term "opposites" with problematic contrasts—"John and Mary are so opposite to one another! How can it last?"—we here focus on the natural attraction that opposites like men and women have for each other, despite (or because of) their great differences. Opposition, in Jyotisha, indicates strong complementarity in the appropriate areas of life. In the relationship context, this facilitates the development of a powerful current of mutual raga. This complementarity customarily translates into a strong current of attraction, often generated by a fascination for the other's differences.

The relation of opposites is, in fact, the strongest of the potential jyotishical connections between any of the four cornerstones, especially when those opposites are primary or mutual secondary links. Nature provides us with many examples of the creative dynamism inherent in the union of opposites. Males and females are present everywhere in the biological world—positive and negative poles enable the dynamic flow of electricity and magnetism. Activity and effort alternate with rest and relaxation in a life lived fully as surely as winter follows summer. An awareness and acceptance of differences, by such means as observing nature's juxtapositions (a glorious sunset at the juncture of day and night, pounding surf at the seashore), can teach an "opposites" couple how to harmonize the energy that their coupling generates.

A word of warning: relationships that invoke the vasana interaction of opposites are prone to spells of volatility amid the harmony, even in the

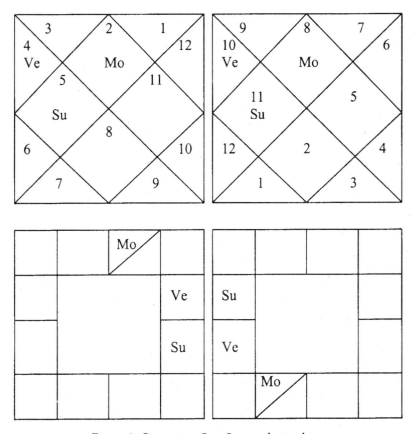

Figure 8. Opposites; One-Seven relationships
of the four cornerstones.

presence of powerful mutual fascination or distinct mutual need. Men say of women, as women do of men, "There's no living with them, and no living without them." This is because their mutual dissimilarity is simultaneously so enchanting and so bothersome. Though the volatility of opposites can become extreme when one party determines to remold the other in his or her own image, an "opposites" couple can still often de-escalate into harmonious relating, perhaps because their synergy is much deeper than their disagreements.

We may obtain considerable insight into the vasana interaction suggested by any of the seven cornerstone contacts if we consider the astrological themes associated with the bhavas that each planetary alignment invokes. Opposites, for instance, summon the themes of the seventh bhava by virtue of their Seven-Seven rashi relationship. Because the seventh bhava primarily symbolizes partnerships, the contact of the cornerstones as opposites is the most supportive and potent of our relationship compatibility links.

Visual metaphors—placing ourselves in the position of one of the grahas and examining the angle at which you see the other graha—can also assist us to illumine the significations of cornerstone placements. Opposites stare directly at one another as if entranced—the ancient Sanskritic tomes say they have "full sight" of each other—by virtue of their Seven-Seven position by rashi. Just as two people who meet head on will carefully assess each other and their respective trajectories, opposites are always "checking one another out." Compelled to interact constantly and spontaneously because the other is always "in your face," the interplay of opposites is never dull!

One-One: Associates

When any one of the four cornerstones occupies the same rashi across two horoscopes, they become associates and form either a primary or a secondary link. Associates are almost as strong as opposites, but associates are drawn to each other by their shared—rather than their opposite—experience of life. The associate relationship is more about sameness than it is about the complementarity of opposites. In the intimacy developed by associates it becomes easy to relax into habitual patterns of behavior that, since they are innately familiar, need not threaten the partner. The associate bond thus promotes comfortable, but not necessarily evolutionary, relationships. It's the stuff of the "men-only" club and the ladies' league. Oriental savants have long understood that it is the mating of beings who enjoy opposite natures, not the perpetual cloning of the same being, that best drives evolution. Carl Jung writes to emphasize this point, "The Chinese have never failed to recognize the paradoxes and the polarity inherent in what is alive. The opposites always balanced one another—a sign of high culture. One-sidedness, though it lends momentum, is a mark of barbarism."[1]

Here again, nature provides us with instructive examples. Many animals (teenagers included) prefer to move in packs. While the herd provides a certain safety born of the strength that is in numbers, the group dynamic concurrently breeds a closed, and often cruel, elitism that rejects others whose only misdeed is to be different. In tightly ordered groups, even occasional or harmless deviance is rejected. When you have witnessed the achievement of a noble goal through the coordinated efforts of a band of like-minded people, you have seen an example of the alignment of associates at its best. If you have ever experienced rejection because of your accent, your religious faith, or the color of your skin, you have experienced the small-minded smugness that typifies the principle of associates at its worst.

This diminished capacity for acceptance of differences makes couples who have a majority of associates as their primary and mutual secondary horoscopic links relate best when they can remind themselves that variety is the spice of life. The disinclination of the "associates" couple to rock their "love boat" produces a stability and predictability in the relationship that, if not periodically interrupted, can deteriorate into boredom or apathy. They must remember that, if one partner, after years of spiritual disinterest, decides to meditate for twenty minutes a day, it is not a sign of impending lunacy. Nor should a passing interest in gangster rap on the part of a normal teen persuade this couple that their son's future will be one of violence and crime!

One reason for this reluctance on the part of an "associates" couple to welcome variance is that the One-One relationship activates only the first bhava of self, implying that associates find more of themselves in the other, at times, perhaps, rather narcissistically. The visual metaphor of the horoscope supports this connotation as well. Grahas in the Ascendant all "see" the rest of the horoscope from the same platform. Associates seem to share the same angle of vision when looking at any of life's bhavas (finances, property, children, and all the rest). The very proximity of associates in the same

---

[1] David Rosen, *The Tao of Jung: The Way of Integrity* (New York: Viking/Arkana, 1996), p. 92.

astrological rashi tends to compel their interaction, much as two people confined to the same room are likely to interact. It is much harder to ignore someone who shares your space than someone who is out of your sight.

The strongest connections among the four cornerstones as primary or mutual secondary links are those of opposites and associates, because these links are akin to people who, being in each other's mutual field of vision, are hard to ignore. Adaptable people generally value a composite of the portraits of opposites and associates, for anyone who exclusively craves variety in experiences is as surely headed for trouble as is the rigid ultra-conservative who is overcommitted to conformity. Since most partners fare best when endowed with a spectrum of attitudes and behavior, the relationship compatibility analysis ideal is to have opposites and associates mixed together as primary and mutual secondary links across two charts (for example, three primary opposites links with one primary associates link, or vice versa). Such strong and ideal links are, admittedly, rare, which may be an astrological reflection of the fact that very few couples indeed enjoy a seamless vasana interface.

Five-Nine and Three-Eleven: Active and Secret Supporters

Next in importance are active and secret supporters. If we quantify opposites and associates as having roughly the same (full) value for promoting the smoothest vasana interface possible between two people, then active supporters have roughly a 75 percent relative value, and secret supporters have roughly a 50 percent value. We emphasize relativity here, because two horoscopes in which all four of the cornerstones create primary secret supporter links are still well matched, they are simply not as well matched as are two horoscopes whose primary cornerstone links are all of the associates or opposites variety.

When one of the four cornerstones of one horoscope occupies a rashi that is five or nine away from the rashi occupied by one of the four cornerstones of another horoscope, such grahas become active supporters. If these grahas are three or eleven rashis apart, they are secret supporters (see figure 9, page 95). Once again, such links may be either primary or secondary. Active supporters are stronger than secret supporters, but neither is as strong as opposites or associates.

Active supporters gravitate toward relationship, because the two rashis involved always belong to the same astrological element (fire, earth, air, or water), and thus possess many similar qualities. Both Taurus, which is nine rashis away from Virgo, and Virgo, which is five rashis away from Taurus, are, for example, earth rashis. Similarly, Aries and Sagittarius, two rashis the same distance from each other as Taurus and Virgo, belong to the fire element. Active supporters base their relationship on shared experience, rendering such unions somewhat akin to associates, but weaker. After all, in the visual metaphor of the horoscope, associates are much "closer" to each other than are active supporters. They occupy both the same rashi space and the same rashi element.

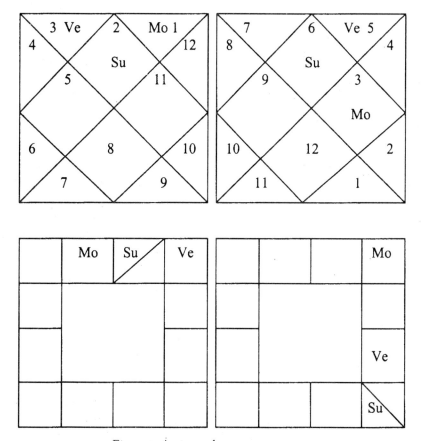

Figure 9. Active and secret supporters.
Five-Nine relationship; Ascendant and Sun.
Three-Eleven relationship; Moon and Venus.

The secret-supporters relationship is based on complementarity of experience, rendering such unions akin to those of opposites, but weaker. In
the horoscope as visual metaphor, opposites "look" at each other directly,
while secret supporters "look" at each other obliquely. This obliqueness is
perhaps why secret supporters often end up longing for each other secretly.
Tajika Jyotisha presumably regards the secret-supporters relationship as a
positive one, because the two rashis involved always belong to elements that
synergize well, such as air and fire, or water and earth. All other factors being equal, secret supporters tend to be the weakest of the harmonious links
between the four cornerstones.

Five-Nine "active friends" placements emphasize the fifth bhava–
ninth bhava dynamic that the teacher-student and father-child relationships
share. The relating of active friends is often driven by a desire to learn and
teach, to aspire and inspire, to charm and protect. Active friends pattern
their vasana interaction along the lines associated with these themes. Three-
Eleven secret-friends placements reflect both the third and the eleventh
bhava associations with siblings and friends. Very often, couples with a predominant pattern of secret friends between their cornerstones are very
brotherly/sisterly or friendly toward each other. These modes of relating are
two ingredients of a very good vasana glue, but such relationships often
show a marked diminishment of the stereotypical passion and intimacy associated with marriage. We have a large number of horoscopes of married
couples with an emphasized pattern of secret friends who have long lived together in friendship and who have confessed to living and feeling for many
years more like brother and sister than husband and wife.

Four-Ten: Contrasts

As it did in our examination of the single horoscope, a Four-Ten dynamic
tends to focus the couple's attention on their differences, probably because
the elements of the rashis involved do not synergize well (fire and water,
earth and fire, air and earth, water and fire). Unlike the synergistic differences that attract opposites, the dissonance among the elements invoked by
contrasts is often irreconcilable, especially in the matters represented by the
fourth and tenth bhavas, which are naturally evoked by this relationship.
The fourth and tenth bhavas represent the stark contrast between the
depths of night and the blazing light of midday, for a graha in the fourth
bhava is near the nadir of the birthplace, while a graha in the tenth is at its
zenith. The fourth bhava represents the privacy of home, while the tenth
represents the public arena of the rest of the world. The difference implied

here is the difference between introversion and extroversion, passivity and activity, privacy and publicity.

A relationship founded on contrasts will, thus, often focus on questions of who will tend to the couple's private life (usually running the home) and who will attend to its public aspect (typically the career). Since Ms. Ten is likely to be more career-oriented than Mr. Four, she may feel aggrieved that her partner wants her to desert her successful Manhattan law practice simply because they now have a child. Whereas relationships of opposites may occasionally deteriorate into power struggles, relationships of contrasts usually head down the road of who is right and who is wrong, or who is more important and who should sacrifice their self-importance in a given situation.

The visual metaphor of the horoscope for contrasts supports this style of interaction as well (see figure 10, page 98). Grahas in a Four-Ten relationship are organized around the angular, succedent, and cadent astrological houses, each of these groups forming a square. Squares are "unnatural" constructs—human inventions that rarely occur spontaneously in nature. However useful squares may be to architecture, they remain subject to tremendous stresses, precisely because they struggle against the spontaneous flow of nature's more curvilinear patterns. Relaters with cornerstones in a contrasts alignment are likely to suffer ongoing stress in their vasana encounters.

Six-Eight and Two-Twelve: Active and Secret Adversaries

Grahas that sit in Six-Eight relationships to one another usually display the sort of contentious interactions that elements in Six-Eight exhibit. Note that, in the case of both, the pairs of dissonant elements invoked are identical to those of the elements at play in the case of contrasts, namely fire and water, earth and fire, air and earth, and water and air. In considering bhava meanings for the Six-Eight relationship, we find that the sixth bhava represents disputes and the eighth intrigues, the sixth acute diseases and the eighth chronic ones. Moreover, both indicate enemies. A relationship of active adversaries may encourage pugnacity, promote enmity, foster arguments, and evoke themes of poor health. Ill will over perceived unfairness (as may occur if one partner feels that health-care obligations for the other, diseased partner form an unfairly heavy burden) may regularly rock the relationship boat. Still, if the outcome indications in both individual charts are positive, the relationship may endure—though the jagged vasana encounter will plague the relationship with eternal squabbles.

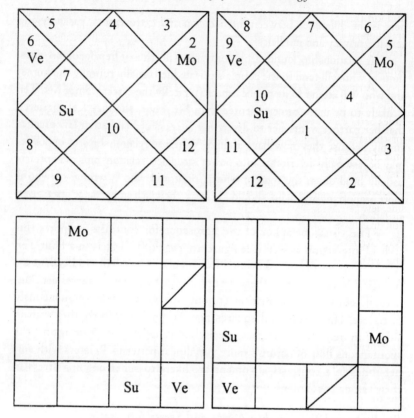

Figure 10. Contrasts.
Four-Ten relationship of the four cornerstones.

Visually, the Six-Eight relationship resembles the sort of fighter's stance that one sees at a boxing, wrestling, or martial arts match. The antagonists stand almost facing each other but slightly to one side, to enable each to keep the other in full view without directly exposing their vital organs to attack. Six-Eight anyone?

Two-Twelve relationships are those of secret adversaries. These involve discordant element patterns identical to those of contrasts and of active adversaries. From the bhava standpoint, while the second bhava represents liquid assets, the twelfth undermines those assets by its rulership of expenditures. While the second bhava indicates one's kith and kin, the twelfth represents immigration, isolation, and solitude. Mistress Two will tend to hold such second-bhava matters as interaction with family and the accumulation of cash dearer than will Master Twelve, who may feel sufficiently detached from kith and kin that he prefers prolonged travel that takes him away from the family, travel on which he spends Two's nest egg. Two will naturally tend to interpret Twelve's action as sabotaging (or at least not supporting) the relationship, while Twelve believes everything is proceeding just as it should.

A recurrent secret-adversaries theme is that the person with a cornerstone placed in the second rashi as counted from the other feels (and sometimes actually is) somehow let down by that other secret adversary. Support for this attitude can be found both in the antithetical meanings of the second and twelfth bhavas and the visual metaphor of the horoscope, for it is easy to imagine a graha in the twelfth rashi to another as being behind it, in the former's blind spot. With our ears and eyes oriented to our front and side, few can enjoy having someone behind them, in their blind spot, a position in which an opponent can operate clandestinely. Culture, East and West, reflects this preference: Hollywood Westerns portray the sheriff sitting with his back to the wall, while the Chinese art of Feng-Shui advises its adherents to position themselves in a room so that they face the chi (prana).

While it is usually easy to sequence the relative importance of opposites, associates, active friends, and secret friends, sequencing the relative strength of contrasts and adversaries is less straightforward. All these placements are disruptive, but contrasts can sometimes be more difficult to handle than active or secret adversary patterns. Contrasts operate mostly on a chess-game analogy, in which each player is openly vying to win the game, while active and secret adversaries more often operate subliminally rather than consciously. The sixth, eighth, and twelfth bhavas all represent loss, disease, and enemies, but the eighth and the twelfth specifically rule behind-the-scenes manipulations and secret enemies (see figure 11, page 100).

Let us emphasize strongly here that, while active and secret adversaries are difficult planetary relationships, they merely represent adversarial alignments. They do not necessarily indicate that the partner is an overt and malicious enemy. No conscious, active malevolence or "dvesha aforethought" is implied here, just a tendency for the relationship not to work out because of the interplay of the vasanas of the two people involved. When most or all of the four cornerstones of a relationship are contrasts, active adversaries, or secret adversaries the likelihood greatly increases that the relationship's harmony, and possibly its life span, will be limited, unless the karmic outcome analysis of the two individual charts is very promising. In such a case, the relationship will probably be punctuated by many recurrent, but remediable, tensions.

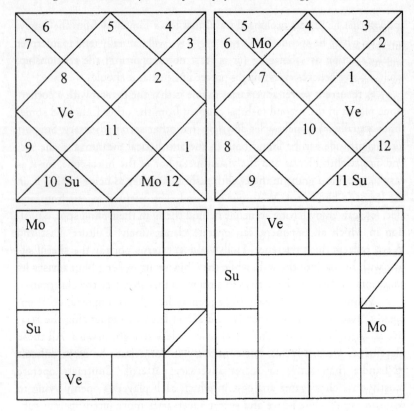

Figure 11. Active and secret adversaries.
Two-Twelve relationships of the Ascendant and Sun.
Six-Eight relationships of the Moon and Venus.

STRENGTH OF VASANA ALIGNMENTS

A strong possibility for harmony in a relationship exists when a plurality of beneficial connections exists among the four relationship cornerstones. Conversely, no lasting harmonious relationship is likely to develop when a plurality of detrimental connections exists among these cornerstones. Even a single strong favorable primary link (which, by default, makes the preponderance of primary links unfavorable) can be—but need not be—sufficient to produce compelling vasana alignment in a couple. What, then, of the many situations that occur between the extremes of attraction and repulsion vasanas? Evidently, the permutations of the seven planetary patterns will generate a vast number of potentials from which we must select a few likely interpretations. One way to differentiate between the prevalence of aligned and misaligned vasanas is to discern the difference between strong alignments and listless ones. Here is a useful rule for assessing the strength of any one of the favorable contacts between two cornerstones:

> There will be strong vasana alignments between those people whose four cornerstones have the well-disposed links of One-One, Seven-Seven, Five-Nine, or Three-Eleven. Such links are particularly potent when the degree positions of the two factors are within 7½° of each other, in the context of the connection they create.

Seven-and-a-half degrees forms one-fourth of a rashi. Two grahas affect each other most strongly when they sit exactly atop one another in conjunction. Even after they have moved one-fourth of a rashi apart, however, they can still exert about 75 percent of their potential influence on each other, a significant amount. To illustrate, let us assume that the Sun occupies 5° Scorpio in one birth chart, and 10° Capricorn in another (see figure 12, page 102). If we ignore the intervening slice of sky (which we have already signified by naming the relationship Three-Eleven, or secret supporters), we can treat the two Suns as if they occupied the same rashi, whereupon we discover that only 5° separate them. This makes their connection, which is a primary link, particularly strong.

Remember that it is rashi position that establishes these relative graha placements: we use the Rule of 7½° only in the context of rashi position. Even when two grahas occupy positions that are near to one another by degree, in this variety of analysis, the relative relationship of their rashis to one another is more important. Let one graha be at 29° Virgo and another appear at 1° Libra. Even though they are but 2° apart, as measured in the zodiac, they are still secret adversaries that fall well outside the range of the 7½° rule, as measured by rashi count, because Libra and Virgo are Two-Twelve to each other.

In relationship analysis, the principle of proportional strength, based on an inverse ratio to 30°, applies to all graha relationships. Two grahas that are 10° apart will exert about 67 percent of their potential force on each other. If they are 15° apart, they will exert about 50 percent. Beyond 15° this strength drops exponentially. Once they move 30° apart, their positive force for mutual attraction has dwindled to near zero. A Venus at 18° Aries in one horoscope and one at 12° Libra in the other produce a Seven-Seven relationship that, since their degree positions are but 6° apart, exert 80 percent of the potential mutual influence of this primary link. When, however, the Sun in one horoscope is at 5° Pisces and the Sun in another chart is at 28° Virgo, they sit 23° apart, which reduces the intensity of the connection to less than 24 percent of its potential.

Even with weak proportional strength among favorable links between cornerstones, there will still be some supportive vasana alignment, for mutual attraction will occur any time a positive primary or a mutual secondary link exists between any of the four cornerstones. The degree distance between those activated cornerstones merely measures the potency of that mutual

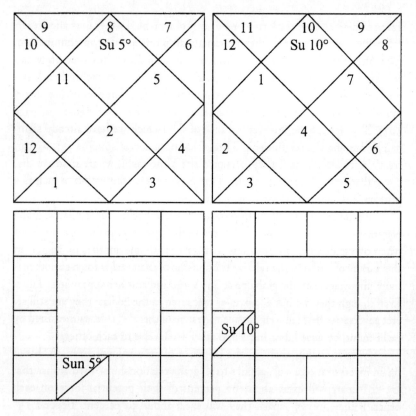

Figure 12. The Rule of 7½° between the two Suns.

vasana attraction or detraction, for where no positive relationship exists between two cornerstones, a negative one must be present. If raga does not develop between two people, dvesha will. It is only a saint of the highest caliber who can overcome all graha and auric influences, and who can thus relate to all beings with perfect equanimity. If the connections between the cornerstones, beneficial or detrimental, exist in wide orbs, the two people involved may not realize that they are particularly attracted or repulsed by one another, but, in some subtle manner, they will be. Raga or dvesha is bound to develop, its intensity determined by the closeness of the orb.

Given that influences in Jyotisha usually accumulate, rather than cancel one another out, another method with which to distinguish between strong and weak cornerstone attractions is to gauge the cumulative effect of the various cornerstone contacts. The weightiest of all connections are, of course, the primary links (Ascendant-Ascendant, Moon-Moon, Sun-Sun, and Venus-Venus). The owners of two horoscopes that have three out of these four in positive relation to each other will have a much stronger mutual attraction than two people who have only one such beneficial connection. If these primary connections are within the 7½° orb, so much the better. Moreover, if the secondary links (one Sun to the other's Moon, etc.) are mostly within close orbs, we can then boldly predict that a powerful vasana attraction will draw these two individuals together.

In every less-obvious situation—such as when there are many primary connections that are outside the 7½° orb and a paucity of cross-connections that are, however, very close to each other—judgment based on intuition and experience alone can astutely weigh each factor and sum them effectively. When unsure about which way to turn, you may choose to examine factors that are less commonly evaluated to try to discern the relationship pattern and make it cohere in an accurate image. You may inspect, for example, the mutual positions of the Ascendant lords or of the dispositors of the Moon, or use the cornerstone methodology to compare grahas other than the four cornerstones. Such additional methods are, however, best invoked only in cases of ambiguity or uncertainty, because, as more factors are included, the complexity of the analysis multiplies.

When a plurality of good, strong relationships exists between two horoscopes, the skills the two individuals bring to their interaction will be good. When the links are mainly nonsupportive, the skills that they bring are likely to be found wanting. Remember, however, that relationship links, however strongly supportive, whether primary or secondary, govern vasana attraction and not necessarily happiness! A relationship's karmic outcome is never necessarily limited to the skills that the partners bring to it. The force of vasana attraction will, however, often provide an evolutionary flavor to a relationship that will improve its chances of enduring its inevitable periodic fluctuations.

WHEN CORNERSTONE AGREEMENT MAY NOT BE REQUIRED

Cornerstone analysis is just one generally reliable method for determining the nature and strength of an interaction between two people. Other principles also influence compatibility, one of the most potent of these being a principle called *sama dasha*.[2] A dasha is a "planetary period," an interval during which a particular graha's influence on a person is paramount. *Sama* means "same." Sama dasha occurs whenever two people run parallel dashas over the course of a relationship. For instance, suppose two people get involved when both are in their Mars dashas. They need not have begun those dashas at precisely the same time; even a gap of several months or a year or two will suffice.

Sama dasha implies a strong attraction between two people because the tone of that dasha provides a fundamental ground of understanding of how to relate. During their Mars periods, for example, both partners will experience life on Mars, life from a Martian perspective. Mars indicates initiative, exploit, and intensity. It is very likely that both members of the couple will never deal with these and other Martian themes any more strongly in their lifetimes than they will during the Mars dasha. Through the practical experience of tasting Mars's essence in their daily lives, they will come to understand something of the nature of Mars, regardless of what Mars may indicate in their individual horoscopes. Such a sharing of the Mars adventure may be sufficient to create a supportive common ground for their relationship, even when none of their four cornerstones agree. This principle (which, of course, has its own exceptions) will be developed in chapter 10. We mention it for now as a good example of how mechanisms other than cornerstone alignment can pull a couple together.

---

[2] For an understanding of dashas, consult any Jyotisha primer, including our *Light on Life* (London: Penguin, 1996).

EXAMPLES OF CORNERSTONE ANALYSIS

The analysis that follows for the four famous couples will illustrate many of the principles presented in this chapter.

Paul Newman and Joanne Woodward

These two famous Hollywood stars both have Sagittarius Ascendants (see Chart 3 and 9, pages 51 and 106). The Ascendants are associates, because they are in a One-One relationship. Their Ascendants are within less than 1½° of each other, rendering them exceptionally potent by the principle of proportional strength. Their Moons are both in Aquarius, within 7° of each other—again, an exceptionally strong One-One link of associates. Their Venuses are Three-Eleven, placed within less than 1½° of each other. None of these cornerstones is in the vitiating sixth, eighth, or twelfth bhavas of their individual horoscopes. That three of the four cornerstones are in supportive primary links implies cumulative relationship strength, particularly since the Rule of 7½° applies to all three of these links. These three strong primary links form a clear, powerful combination for strong and enduring mutual vasana attraction and interaction, and the supportive relationship skills and attitudes that accompany it.

Several mutual links also exist in these two horoscopes. Note that the mutual secondary links need not be identical; they need only be similar—both must belong to the beneficial group or to the obstructive group. Among the mutual secondary links, Newman's Ascendant and Woodward's Venus are Three-Eleven (within 0°08') and her Ascendant is One-One to his Venus (within 3°). This secondary link is mutual, because both Ascendants and both Venuses are involved. Another mutual secondary link is formed by his Ascendant-her Moon and her Ascendant-his Moon, both pairs being Three-Eleven. Because his Moon-her Venus are One-One and her Moon-his Venus are Three-Eleven, the couple's mutual Moons and Venuses generate yet a third mutual secondary link.

Experience suggests that this is an inordinate number of very strong contacts between two horoscopes, a situation that predicts an almost effortless ability for mutual alignment. This intensely positive set of vasanas has surely encouraged the two to work out whatever differences might crop up between them. Couple these beneficial vasanas with the favorable relationship karmas in their charts (as attested by outcome analysis) and you have a recipe for relationship success. Indeed, this couple is famous in Hollywood for being able to remain married for so long.

Rashi Chart

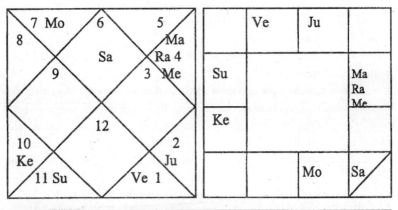

Navamsha Chart

Planetary Positions		Vimshottari Dasha		
LG	18°SA57'	MA	11 Aug. 1925	Yogi Point PI 20-30'
SU	15°AQ11'	RA	11 Aug. 1932	
MO	01°AQ60'	JU	12 Aug. 1950	Yogi – ME
MA	23°CP09'	SA	12 Aug. 1966	
ME	21°CP26'	ME	12 Aug. 1985	Avayogi – MA
JU	14°TA40'	KE	12 Aug. 2002	
VE	20°AQ12'	VE	12 Aug. 2009	Duplicate Yogi – JU
SA	16°SA47'	SU	12 Aug. 2029	
RA	13°AR 01'	MO	13 Aug. 2035	Daghda Rasis
KE	13°LI 01'			GE, VI, SA & PI

Chart 9. Joanne Woodward.

Queen Elizabeth II and Prince Philip

This famous royal couple (see Charts 10 and 11, pages 108 and 109) has three primary links: associates Sagittarius Ascendants (One-One within 8½°); associates Cancer Moons (One-One within 5½°); and secret supporters Venuses (Three-Eleven within 8½°). Although both cornerstone Moons are in the vitiating eighth bhava, both are strong, because they occupy Cancer, the Moon's own rashi. They also enjoy one mutual secondary link: her Ascendant-his Venus are active supporters (Five-Nine within 16°) and his Ascendant-her Venus are secret supporters (Three-Eleven within 0°40').

These three primary links are not quite as strong as those of Newman and Woodward, for two of the primary links (their Ascendants and Venuses) fall just outside the 7½° orb. Still, three beneficial primary links are sufficient to create a supportive and vital mutual vasana interaction, especially because two of them are the potent One-One connection of associates, and because their three primary links are supported by a beneficial mutual secondary link. Because the mutual link averages to an orb of 8°20' (16° + 0°40' = 16°40'/2 = 8°20'), all three of the primary links and the one mutual link fall either within or just outside of the powerful 7½° orb.

The mutual secondary link between their Ascendants and their Venuses are particularly notable, because both component parts of this mutual secondary link are already in a powerful beneficial primary link: their Ascendants are associates and their Venuses are secret supporters. This reciprocal relationship link is an example of confluence, which makes the influence of the primary links between these two cornerstones all the stronger. In turn, given that their Ascendants are already One-One and their Venuses Three-Eleven, by confluence, the mutual secondary link also gains in significance.

Confluence often involves recurrence of an astrological tendency through diverse, but related, horoscope patterns. Had their Ascendants and their Venuses not been in a beneficial primary link, the significance of the mutual secondary link would have been less prominent; the confluence would have been diminished. The confluence of strong beneficial links between their charts suggests some compelling linkage between them, and their marriage has, in fact, endured through thick and thin. If only their famous offspring, Prince Charles, had been so lucky.

Rashi Chart

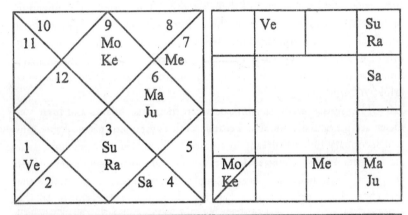

Navamsha Chart

Planetary Positions		Vimshottari Dasha		
LG	28°SA33'	ME	13 Dec. 1922	Yogi Point SC 0-01'
SU	07°AR23'	KE	14 Dec. 1939	
MO	19°CA18'	VE	13 Dec. 1946	Yogi – JU
MA	28°CP 03'	SU	13 Dec. 1966	
ME	11°PI 50'	MO	13 Dec. 1972	Avayogi – SU
JU	29°CP41'	MA	14 Dec. 1982	
VE	21°AQ08'	RA	13 Dec. 1989	Duplicate Yogi – MA
SA	01°SC38'R	JU	14 Dec. 2007	
RA	27°GE39'	SA	14 Dec. 2023	Daghda Rasis
KE	27°SA39'			SC & LE

Chart 10. Queen Elizabeth II.

Rashi Chart

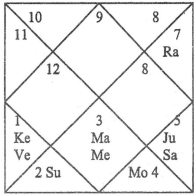

	Ke Ve	Su	Ma Me
	June 10, 1921 9:46 PM Corfu, Greece		Mo
			Ju Sa
		Ra	

Navamsha Chart

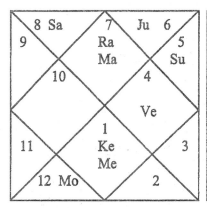

Mo	Ke Me		
			Ve
			Su
		Sa	Ra Ma	Ju

Planetary Positions		Vimshottari Dasha		
LG	20°SA48'	ME	2 Feb. 1905	Yogi Point SA 29-25'
SU	26°TA35'	KE	3 Feb. 1922	
MO	29°CA29'	VE	2 Feb. 1929	Yogi – SU
MA	01°GE50'	SU	2 Feb. 1949	
ME	20°GE46'	MO	3 Feb. 1955	Avayogi – SA
JU	18°LE 01'	MA	3 Feb. 1965	
VE	12°AR58'	RA	3 Feb. 1972	Duplicate Yogi – JU
SA	25°LE35'	JU	3 Feb. 1990	
RA	01°LI 43'	SA	3 Feb. 2006	Daghda Rasis
KE	01°AR43'			AR & LE

Chart 11. Prince Philip.

Prince Charles and Princess Diana [3]

This example (see Charts 12 and 13, pages 111 and 113) illustrates the importance of opposites and associates to enduring constructive vasana interplay in a relationship. The Ascendants, the Suns, and the Venuses of Prince Charles and Princess Diana, are all active supporters. Their Moons are secret supporters. This is clear astrological testimony to the vasana attraction between the two, an attraction that led to the world-famous fairytale wedding.

Why, then, their evident inability to communicate with one another, a failure that ultimately promoted separation and divorce? For one thing, the benefit of having all four cornerstones favorably aligned is reduced in intensity by the distance between these grahas. The pairs of their Ascendants and their Venuses are approximately 22° apart (quantifiable as only 27 percent powerful), a great gulf by the Rule of 7½°. The Suns sit within a more modest distance of 13° from each other. Significantly, Princess Diana's Sun occupies the vitiating eighth bhava, devoid of strength in her horoscope, which diminishes the cornerstone linkage of her Sun to that of Prince Charles. These substantial orbs of separation and the natal position of Diana's Sun, decrease the power of these three primary links, links whose value is already diminished, because they are only supporters instead of the more powerful and important opposites or associates. By degree distance, their strongest link exists between their Moons, separated by only 5°. Their Moons, however, are only secret supporters, which, unfortunately, is the weakest supportive graha relationship.

Prince Charles and Princess Diana have two mutual secondary links between their four cornerstones. These mutual secondary links are only supporters—instead of opposites or associates—in both directions. These are her Ascendant-his Venus (Three-Eleven, roughly 2° apart) and his Ascendant-her Venus (Three-Eleven, roughly 11° apart). The other mutual secondary link is formed by his Sun-her Moon (Five-Nine about 28° apart) and her Sun-his Moon (Three-Eleven within a 10° span). Contrast these two mutual secondary links with the three mutual secondary links of Newman-Woodward and the one mutual secondary link of Queen Elizabeth II-Prince Philip. Aside from being outnumbered in the case of Newman-Woodward and not having the same confluence in the case of the royal couple, note that not even one of the important opposites or associates

---

[3] We are aware that another horoscope for Princess Diana has surfaced, and that some astrologers are convinced that another birth time is accurate. We prefer, however, to use the birth time officially released by Buckingham Palace.

Rashi Chart

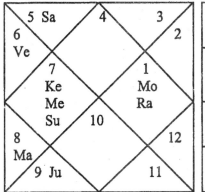

	Mo Ra		
	Nov. 14, 1948 9:14 PM London, England		Sa
Ju	Ma	Ke Me Su	Ve

Navamsha Chart

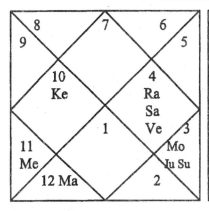

Ma			Mo Ju Su
Me			Ra Sa Ve
Ke			

Planetary Positions		Vimshottari Dasha		
LG	12°CA14'	KE	16 Jan. 1945	Yogi Point AQ 09-55'
SU	29°LI 17'	VE	17 Jan. 1952	
MO	07°AR 17'	SU	17 Jan. 1972	Yogi – RA
MA	27°SC48'	MO	17 Jan. 1978	
ME	13°LI 49'	MA	17 Jan. 1988	Avayogi – VE
JU	06°SA45'	RA	17 Jan. 1995	
VE	23°VI 15'	JU	17 Jan. 2013	Duplicate Yogi – SA
SA	12°LE 07'	SA	17 Jan. 2029	
RA	10°AR47'	ME	18 Jan. 2048	Daghda Rasis
KE	10°LI 47'			GE, VI, SA & PI

Chart 12. Prince Charles.

patterns appears as either a primary or a mutual secondary link for Charles and Diana. Moreover, those links that do occur do not enjoy the requisite closeness of orb that would make them consequential.

Still, many people whose cornerstones are far less well aligned than those of Charles and Diana enjoy happy, successful relationships. The problem here is one of karmic outcome; the results they experienced as a couple (as indicated by their karmas) did not reflect the good intentions that they very likely had (as indicated by their vasanas). We must here look further, beyond the trusty 20 percent of rules that answer 80 percent of our questions, to see why this marriage failed. Diana has an unafflicted Venus as lord of the seventh bhava tenanting its own rashi. This testifies to a certain good space (sukha) about her marriage (specifically, about her partner's position and fame). But Venus's strength here is deceptive, however, for it occupies the first two degrees of an even rashi, a position technically known as *mrita avastha* (a "dead state"). Venus is also weak in the harmonic subchart that relates to marriage (the *navamsha*, see chapter 9). Couple this with the debilitation of Jupiter, her marriage significator, and Jupiter's affliction by the natural malefic Saturn, and the weakness of her marriage karma becomes more evident.

Now, let us examine her personal vasanas for marriage by the methods introduced in the previous chapter. We see in her horoscope that lagnesha Mars and karyesha Venus (for marriage) create a Four-Ten relative planetary placement. By all accounts, Diana struggled with foreground-background, private life-public life issues throughout the duration of her relationship with Charles. Our evidence for concluding that her single-sided relationship skills were weak is reinforced by the Six-Eight alignment that marriage karaka Jupiter makes with lagnesha Mars.

Charles's chart also eludes our 80/20 rule, for his seventh bhava and its lord, Saturn, are unafflicted, though certainly not strong. Marriage karaka, Venus is, however, manifestly weak by our rules, being both debilitated and flanked by malefics. Also, seventh lord, Saturn, though occupying a neutral bhava, as counted from the lagna, occupies the eighth bhava, as counted from the seventh bhava—a position that is considerably to its detriment. Other reasons for the breakdown of this marriage appear in Charles's navamsha, which we will examine in a later chapter.

Charles's individual relationship skills appear to be somewhat better than Diana's, since his lagnesha, Moon, and his karyesha for marriage, Saturn, form a propitious Five-Nine relationship. Note, however, that the Moon is the enemy of Saturn, implying that Prince Charles may have a

Rashi Chart

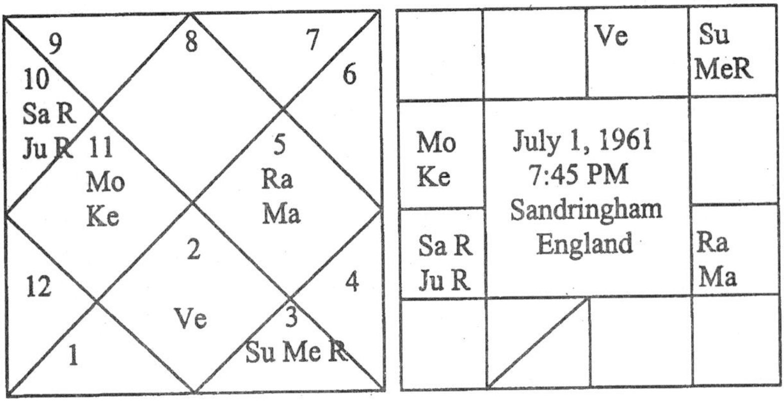
9
8
7
10
6
Sa R
Ju R 11
Mo
Ke
5
Ra
Ma
2
12
4
Ve
3
1
Su Me R
Ve
Su
MeR
Mo
Ke
July 1, 1961
7:45 PM
Sandringham
England
Sa R
Ju R
Ra
Ma

Navamsha Chart

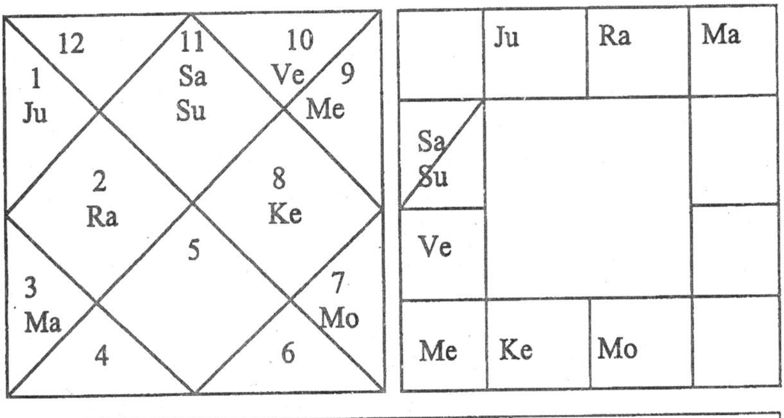
12
11
10
1
Sa
Ve
9
Ju
Su
Me
2
Ra
8
Ke
5
3
7
Ma
Mo
4
6
Ju
Ra
Ma
Sa
Su
Ve
Me
Ke
Mo

Planetary Positions		Vimshottari Dasha		
LG	25°SC 05'	MA	4 Feb. 1957	Yogi Point CA 21-24'
SU	16°GE21'	RA	4 Feb. 1964	
MO	01°AQ43'	JU	4 Feb. 1982	Yogi – ME
MA	08°LE20'	SA	4 Feb. 1998	
ME	09°GE53'R	ME	4 Feb. 2017	Avayogi – MA
JU	11°CP46'R	KE	4 Feb. 2034	
VE	01°TA 05'	VE	4 Feb. 2041	Duplicate Yogi – MO
SA	04°CP30'R	SU	4 Feb. 2061	
RA	06°LE24'	MO	5 Feb. 2067	Daghda Rasis
KE	06°AQ24'			SC & AQ

Chart 13. Princess Diana..

vasana to act inimically toward his spouse, particularly since Moon creates a stressful Six-Eight arrangement with his marriage karaka, Venus. Since the Ascendant is the epitome of the horoscope, the lagnesha is the epitome of the Ascendant. Someone whose lagnesha is afflicted often fails to do well when put under pressure, and the pressure of being heir to the world's most famous throne has certainly seemed to torment Charles from time to time.

The failed relationship of Charles and Diana thus serves as a conspicuous example of how good cornerstone placements alone may not suffice to prevent poor marriage outcomes when other factors in the horoscope do not cooperate. We offer it as a sobering illustration of the complexities that can appear within synastry, and of the importance of the navamsha in predicting marital outcomes.

Adolf Hitler and Winston Churchill

After eliminating Venus, who is used most appropriately in the context of marriages and marriage-like situations, we can use our remaining three relationship cornerstones, which are the three primary points of sudarshana, to analyze any type of relationship. We can even use cornerstone analysis to examine the interaction between two warlords, like Hitler and Churchill (see Charts 14 and 15, pages 115 and 116). Destructive though it may have been, their interaction was clearly a relationship, as their many biographies depict. It was, moreover, a relationship that was not wholly bereft of benefit, for Churchill, at least, became world-famous as a direct result of his refusal to capitulate to "Herr Hitler."

That any relationship between them would be rough is suggested by the fact that their Ascendants are Two-Twelve and their Suns Six-Eight. Their Ascendants are within 3½°, which makes this adversarial link particularly strong. Their Suns both occupy rashis of Mars and are within 7½° of one another, all of which fanned the flames of their adversarial relationship. That their Moons were Five-Nine suggests shared tastes in life, perhaps including their shared taste for war. It was likely this interaction of their Moons that gave them a relationship on the world stage, while the interaction of their Suns and Ascendants likely ensured that that relationship would be adversarial, despite the fact that Hitler tried assiduously to make peace with Britain after he had conquered France. Other factors escalated the predominant antagonism of their cornerstones into outright hostility: Churchill's Mars was in Two-Twelve relationship to Hitler's, his Ketu occupied, and his Saturn aspected, Hitler's Ascendant, and Hitler's Saturn aspected Churchill's Moon. We will take up such matters in detail in the next chapter.

Rashi Chart

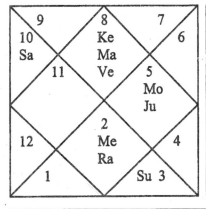

	Me Su Ma Ve R		Ra
		April 20, 1889 6:37:52 PM Braunau-Am-Inn Austria	Sa
Mo Ke Ju			

(North Indian style chart at left with houses numbered 1–12; planets: 9 Mo Ke Ju / 10; Sa in house 4; 1 Me Su Ma Ve R; 2; 3 Ra)

Navamsha Chart

(North Indian style chart at left: 10 Sa / 11; 8 Ke Ma Ve; 5 Mo Ju; 2 Me Ra; 3 Su)

		Me Ra	Su
Sa			Mo Ju
	Ke Ve Ma		

Planetary Positions		Vimshottari Dasha		
LG	04°LI 22'	VE	26 Oct. 1887	Yogi Point PI 26-09'
SU	08°AR30'	SU	28 Oct. 1907	
MO	14°SA19'	MO	27 Oct. 1913	Yogi – ME
MA	24°AR 05'	MA	28 Oct. 1923	
ME	03°AR22'	RA	27 Oct. 1930	Avayogi – MA
JU	15°SA56'	JU	27 Oct. 1948	
VE	24°AR23'R	SA	27 Oct. 1964	Duplicate Yogi – JU
SA	21°CA 08'	ME	28 Oct. 1983	
RA	23°GE45'	KE	27 Oct. 2000	Daghda Rasis
KE	23°SA45'			AR & LE

Chart 14. Adolf Hitler.

Rashi Chart

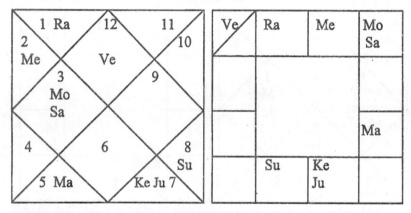

7 Ju Ke	6	Mo 5
8 Me		4
Ve R	Ma	
Su 9		3
	12	
10		2
Sa		
11		Ra 1

	Ra		
Sa	Nov. 30 1874 1:30 AM Woodstock England		Mo
	Su Ve R	Ju Ke Me	Ma

Navamsha Chart

1 Ra	12	11
2		10
Me	Ve	
3		9
Mo		
Sa		
4	6	8
		Su
5 Ma		Ke Ju 7

Ve	Ra	Me	Mo Sa
			Ma
	Su	Ke Ju	

Planetary Positions		Vimshottari Dasha		
LG	07°VI 49'	KE	22 Dec. 1870	Yogi Point GE 26-27'
SU	15°SC37'	VE	21 Dec. 1877	
MO	07°LE30'	SU	22 Dec. 1897	Yogi – JU
MA	24°VI 27'	MO	23 Dec. 1903	
ME	25°LI 29'	MA	23 Dec. 1913	Avayogi – SU
JU	01°LI 28'	RA	22 Dec. 1920	
VE	29°SC55'R	JU	23 Dec. 1938	Duplicate Yogi – ME
SA	17°CP29'	SA	23 Dec. 1954	
RA	02°AR15'	ME	23 Dec. 1973	Daghda Rasis
KE	02°LI 15'			CA & CP

Chart 15. Sir Winston Churchill.

BUILDING ON THE CORNERSTONES

Now that we have some idea of who may be inclined to interface smoothly with whom, and to what degree, we can penetrate more deeply into the potential for long-term vasana chemistry. Even the choicest of attractions is likely, at times, to be at odds with the deeper karmic nature of the attraction. Will a vasana allurement that is facilitated by strong links among the four relationship cornerstones mature into a mutually satisfying relationship? Or will that relationship, instead, develop major crises, despite, or even because of, the bonding that flows from a deeper and less conscious karmic attraction? Are we in fact not at all attracted to some of the potential people with whom, theoretically, we could relate very well? Do some of us not get involved with and remain with partners for whom we seem to possess no particular affinity, or with whom we sometimes vehemently disagree?

These and other issues can be addressed to a considerable degree through standard astrological analyses. A sophisticated unraveling of such relationship intricacies, however, requires some understanding of the principles of karma, principles that underlie every aspect of human existence. We have all found, on occasion, that our karmic experiences (our "fate") are not always aligned with our conscious preferences. One major human conundrum is how to reconcile the often-dramatic extent to which the experiences and desires of the soul vary from those of the conscious ego. How many truly heroic people become heroic through conscious design, and how many suddenly discover heroism within themselves when thrust into a crisis? Few are the vanquishers of deprivation, abuse, ill health, or war who deliberately create such hazards that they may overcome them.

An individual's conscious ego desires bliss in every relationship, yet few persist sufficiently to attain this bliss. Before bliss is served at the relationship banquet, we must each consume the often-bitter fruits of the relationship seeds we have sown in a past. Our pasts may include the experiences of past lives, as well as the formative psychological experiences we soak up between birth and age six. Mistakes are often the best grist for the mill of more accurate judgments, and many people become enmeshed in multifarious relationship dramas before wiser relationship skills and choices develop. Even with the right relationship choices, one lifetime may not be sufficient to create true harmony. In the words of our Jyotisha guru, "If a couple relates exceptionally well throughout their current life, know that they have practiced intensely in many previous lives."

The reverse may also be true. A couple that experiences nothing but misery and disappointment despite a mutually compelling attraction may also have had many a negative preamble in previous lives. The codependent who cannot leave an abusive partner may be gathering necessary experience from unwise karmic seeds sown in the past. Abuse is undeniably wrong, but the experience of abuse may serve to catalyze useful insights in the form of fledgling vasanas about fundamental relationship strategies that can eventually build bridges to other more satisfying relationships.

People are attracted to each other to work out their mutual karmas, their *manubandhanas* (bonds of karmic debt). A relationship that observers term dysfunctional may, for the protagonists, seem natural, or even unavoidable. So the masochist attracts the sadist, the teacher the student, the parent the child. The rasa you are "fated" to experience as a result of powerful relationship karma—bliss, strife, or some admixture of both—will unfold after you attract to you an appropriate partner to share your steps in the relationship dance. That dance, when performed well, can lead to a sublime experience whose flair may surpass whatever skills the dancers individually brought to the floor. When poorly executed, it can lead to a tangle, instead of a tango. How elegantly or crudely you consummate the relationship dance often depends largely on the insightful application of the human will, which is founded, in turn, on a correct understanding of the deeper karmic circumstances at play.

The Ascendant, the Moon, the Sun, and Venus are four building blocks of marriage. Their connection in opportune ways is what pulls people together. When well configured with one another, these four cornerstones "magnetize" the auras of the people involved in such a way as to invite them to interact. These cornerstones will, however, only deliver their full promise of marital bliss, no matter how potent that promise may seem, when the other grahas cooperate. The four cornerstones are but four threads on Jyotisha's loom. To weave the complete garment of a couple's relationship, we must also interlace the strands of Jupiter, Mercury, Mars, Saturn, Rahu, and Ketu.

Even when the foundation of a relationship is firmly based on good connections among the four cornerstones, the influence of natural malefics on these four building blocks can disturb the development of a satisfying relationship. Conversely, any natural benefics that enhance the indications of the four cornerstones will shore up development on that foundation. A compelling vasana attraction is indicated for two people when a majority of the four cornerstones create puissant primary links. Secondary links add flavor and definition to the primary attraction, but it is the influence of the natural benefics and malefics on these primary and secondary links that really helps to determine whether this attraction will ensure conscious harmony or conflict for the two people involved.

BENEFICS AND MALEFICS

Although Jyotisha recognizes six natural malefics—Saturn, Mars, Rahu, Ketu, Sun, and waning Moon—we will here consider the influences of only the first three. The Sun and Moon are excluded from the relationship parade of malefics because they are two of our four relationship cornerstones. Ketu is redundant, because, wherever Rahu influences, Ketu's influence must also appear, since in Jyotisha's mythology, they form two parts of the same entity. Similarly, we will consider only Jupiter, the first of the four natural benefics (Jupiter, Venus, waxing Moon, and unafflicted Mercury), because Venus and the Moon are relationship cornerstones, and because Mercury's influence, when benefic, is mostly minimal in this context.

Three powerful malefics quite obviously tip the scale in the direction of relationship challenges and difficulties when weighed against a sole benefic—but don't marriages and other partnerships require constant effort and attention even when they work well? It has often been said that a long-term intimate relationship can be one of the most difficult, but potentially rewarding, of spiritual practices. The reality is, however, that personal interactions have, over the expanse of human history, all too often reflected far more selfishness than altruism. Ethics, morals, and other positive controls on human nature can strip away like a veneer when the push of perceived personal needs or wants comes to a shove. Any serious relationship involves the mingling of the karmas of the parties involved, and the karmic account of the average human contains more selfish vasanas and karmas, which are reflected by malefics, than altruistic ones, attested to by Jupiter, the Great Benefic. It is selfishness that fuels the conflagrations that can and do occur during the vasanic and karmic commingling that human relationships personify.

Jyotisha strives to portray the reality of the vasanas and the karmas faithfully, rather than to sugarcoat a possibly bitter situation by airily declaring that all will somehow effortlessly be well. The astrological dynamic is not as grim as it may seem, however, because the noncontact of these malefics with the relationship cornerstones in a horoscope actually creates dynamically positive effects. In other words, each instance of noncontact of a cornerstone with a malefic acts as a contact by a benefic. In the same way that Rahu and Ketu are "shadow grahas" that exert malefic influence even though they have no physical existence, these "noncontacts" are "shadow benefics" that assist Jupiter in the task of balancing the circumstances of the relationship. Additional mitigating situations in which the malefic grahas do not disturb the four cornerstones are described later in this chapter. Alarm at having three potential malefics arrayed against one lonely benefic is thus largely unwarranted in many individual horoscopes.

The Great Benefic

Jupiter, whom Indian tradition calls the *mantri* ("counselor") and the *devaguru* ("teacher of the gods"), is unparalleled in his ability to give good advice and be impartial in judgment. This fact is reflected in Table 1 (page 44), which informs us that Jupiter is the enemy of no graha. This makes Jupiter astrology's ultimate advisor/adjudicator, for, even though he has enemies, he refuses to become inimical toward them. Jupiter desires to benefit all, regardless of what they desire for him. Jupiter's wisdom, inspiration, and intuition lay a soothing balm upon the rash of problems that so readily besiege relationships.

Consequently, when the respective Jupiters of two horoscopes influence the four cornerstones (and for marriage, if possible, also the seventh bhava and its lord), the two people involved will (all other things being equal) be inclined to influence each other favorably during their liaison. They will share common constructive values, offer one another good advice, treat each other with due respect, learn from each other, and otherwise ennoble the marriage—provided, of course, that Jupiter is strong and, prefer-ably, rules good bhavas. Given that Jupiter is also the indicator of *guru kripa* (divine grace), the contact of a strong Jupiter with all the primary factors may well indicate a marriage that has been made in heaven. Such positive contacts become particularly strong when Jupiter conjoins or aspects within an orb of $7\frac{1}{2}°$

One reason that connections between strong malefics and aligned re-lationship cornerstones may well indicate marriages that work overall, but appear to be made in hell, is that the malefies tend to be poor negotiators. Jupiter (and Venus), both of whom represent good advice, bargain by po-litely, directly, and honestly stating their requests and appealing to reason. The malefics, however, who hold the selfish view that the end justifies the means, resort to either persistent or peremptory demands backed up by threats of force or actual punishment (Mars and Ketu), or have recourse to deviousness, guile, and unscrupulous negotiations like blackmail (Saturn and Rahu), however subtle.

Jupiter creates in those he influences a desire to support the other through good counsel and advice, an aspiration to help the other's positive experiences of life expand, and other Jovan intentions. Where these influ-ences most play themselves out is in the arena of the cornerstone with which Jupiter links. For example, when one chart's Jupiter influences the other chart's Sun, he will promote support for the fundamental outlook, phi-losophy, integrity, and authority of the other. A Jupiter who influences the other's Moon stabilizes and calms the other emotionally, promoting an eq-uitable sharing of domestic responsibilities He nurtures, while supporting and embellishing, the other's emotions. When benevolent, Jupiter's influ-ence on the Moon facilitates the creation of a savory, satisfying life rasa. When Jupiter affects Venus, his guidance will help the partners harmonize with one another, and will offer suggestions on how best to enjoy their mu-tual desires.

Jupiter's influence on the Ascendant facilitates support of the other's environment by providing good counsel on where and how to live and work, how much money to spend and what to spend it on, and so on. In addition, remember that the relationship that exists between two Ascendants aligns each of the bhavas in those two horoscopes into a similar connection. A Ju-piter who influences the Ascendants of both charts will thus encourage an already harmonious set of shared life experiences to become better, and a problematical relationship to improve.

Jupiter, in his capacity as a benefic, can influence the Four Corner-stones by conjoining one of them in the same rashi to create a One-One relationship, by occupying the seventh bhava from one of them to create a Seven-Seven relationship, or by throwing his special aspects. Jupiter aspects those rashis (and any graha that tenants them) that are five and nine away from his position, an action that nicely parallels the Five-Nine primary link. In fact, a Jupiter who rules one of the trinal *(kona* or *trikona)* bhavas—the Ascendant and the fifth and ninth bhavas from the Ascendant—will become all the more powerful to create harmony. Rulership of a kona is important for Jupiter, for he cannot act as a pure *raja yoga karaka* (see page 125).

Remember that Jupiter is called a benefic because, through his influence, a nourishing rasa can be extracted from an otherwise forlorn bhava. When raga is weak, Jupiter enhances it; when dvesha threatens, he tries to avert it. In short, Jupiter guides and gives good counsel wherever he gazes, but his influence on a pair of cornerstones will be most pronounced when his influence extends across both horoscopes. As is the case with secondary links, which can be mutual or unilateral, Jupiter may influence one or several of the four cornerstones of relationship mutually or unilaterally.

For example, take a couple that has Libra and Aries Ascendants, with Jupiter occupying Libra in the Aries chart and Leo in the Libra chart (see figure 13, page 123). In this situation, a relation of opposites (Seven-Seven), the strongest of the potential connections between any of the four corner-stones, exists between the Ascendants of the two charts. Seven-Seven relationships usually indicate strong complementarity. In this case, the complementarity will develop in matters that the Ascendant rules (the couple's physical existence). The Jupiter who occupies Libra in the Aries chart throws its gaze on the Aries Ascendant of that chart. If we were to take that Libra Jupiter and place it in the other horoscope, we would find it positioned in that chart's Ascendant (which is Libra). We re-emphasize the important point that the Libra Jupiter of the Aries-Ascendant chart occupies the Ascendant of the Libra-rising chart when transported to it. Similarly, the Leo Jupiter of the Libra-rising chart will aspect the Ascendant of the Aries-rising chart when transported to it (by Jupiter's full, special ninth aspect). We thus have the mutual influence of Jupiter on the same pair of the four cornerstones, the Ascendants of the two charts in this example. We can thus be confident that this Jupiter, which influences the Ascendants of both charts, will encourage those involved to provide one another good counsel and positive attitude in matters relating to their physical existence.

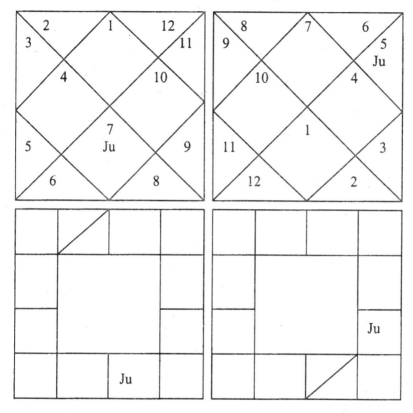

Figure 13. Jupiter influencing both Ascendants mutually.

Contrast this with the relationship shown in figure 14 (page 124), which shows a unilateral influence of Jupiter on one of a pair of well-aligned cornerstones. The Taurus and Scorpio Ascendants of the two charts shown create a desirable Seven-Seven relationship, a dynamic that is partially enhanced by Jupiter's unilateral contact. Note that, when transposed to the Scorpio-rising chart, the Cancer Jupiter of the Taurus-rising chart aspects that Scorpio Ascendant, but that the Pisces Jupiter of the Scorpio-rising chart does not aspect the Ascendant of the Taurus-rising chart when transposed to it. One implication of this one-way contact is that the Taurus-rising person will be motivated to intensify the enjoyment of the Scorpio-rising partner through the physical and environmental circumstances of their relationship (which the Ascendant represents).

Figure 14 also illustrates the total absence of Jupiter's influence on the pair of Moons as cornerstones (see page 124). Although the Moons form a

One-One relationship by occupying the rashi of Leo in both horoscopes, neither the Cancer Jupiter nor the Pisces Jupiter influence the pair of Leo Moons when those Jupiters are transported from one horoscope to the other. Such harmoniously configured Moons will encourage the couple to feel an instinctual emotional pull toward each other, but the lack of any enhancement from Jupiter means that there is less of a guarantee that the couple will be able to transform this harmonious primary link into enduringly pleasing emotional rasa.

Jupiter is such a benevolent graha that the very act of examining horoscopes for his influence on the cornerstones acts to improve our fluency in Jyotisha. It becomes a pattern recognition exercise that every student of Jyotisha should practice. Draw two horoscopes in which one of a pair of cor-

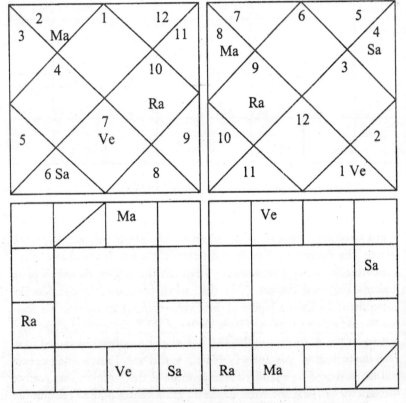

Figure 14. Jupiter influencing the Ascendants unilaterally.

nerstones (say, the pair of Moons) trines the other. For example, put Moon in Taurus in one chart, and Moon in Virgo in the other. Since Jupiter influences by trines, you can then be sure that, if Jupiter conjoins or aspects the Moon in one of these charts, he is bound to influence, by aspect or association, the Moon in the other. This will always be the case when two of the cornerstones are positioned vis-à-vis Jupiter in such a manner. You should not need to think; the realization should jump out at you. Similarly, you can be certain that a Jupiter who sits seven bhavas away from the Sun in one chart is bound to aspect the Sun in the other, if the two Suns happen to be Three-Eleven to one another. Jyotishical thinking is all about images. The more you encourage images to coalesce within you, the better your Jyotisha will become.

Venus

Jupiter's influence is always most valuable for marital harmony, since he is the only major benefic who is not one of the four cornerstones. This harmonizing principle also occasionally applies to Venus, however, especially when Venus acts as a raja yoga karaka for the horoscope. A raja yoga karaka is the graha that, in and of itself, fulfills the requirements for creating a dharma karma adhipati yoga in a horoscope. This yoga is formed when the lord of a trinal bhava (a dharma bhava—bhavas five and nine) combines in a horoscope, either by aspect or by association, with the lord of an angular (karma) bhava (bhavas four, seven, and eleven). A raja yoga karaka is any single graha in a horoscope that owns both a trinal and an angular bhava. Thus Mars is the raja yoga karaka for Cancer Ascendants (in which he owns bhavas five and ten) and Leo Ascendants (in which he owns bhavas four and nine); Saturn is the raja yoga karaka for Taurus (bhavas nine and ten) and Libra (bhavas four and five) Ascendants; and Venus is the raja yoga karaka for Capricorn (bhavas five and ten) and Aquarius (bhavas four and nine) Ascendants. (Note that neither Rahu or Ketu can be modified in this way, since neither owns any bhavas and so cannot serve as a raja yoga karaka.)

The cordiality that a Venus who acts as a raja yoga karaka can bring to a relationship provides yet one more reason why it is so essential to evaluate Venus's state when considering marriage. Remember, however, that, when one person's Venus associates with the Ascendant of the other (as with Charles and Diana), that Venus will act mainly as a primary factor of vasana attraction and not as an indicator of a smooth relationship.

Only when Jupiter associates in one horoscope with a Venus who associates with the Ascendant of the other can we confidently predict a smooth dynamic between the couple, for then Jupiter's involvement guides the Venus-Ascendant contact. Figure 15 illustrates such a situation. In this figure, Libra rises in the one chart and Venus occupies Libra in the other. Jupiter sits in Aries in the first chart, aspecting that chart's Ascendant as well as the other chart's Venus, which is superimposed therein.

Suppose, however, that we have two horoscopes with Capricorn Ascendants, one of which has Venus occupying Cancer and the other has Venus in Capricorn (see figure 16, page 127). In this instance, the two Venuses will act to form a Seven-Seven primary relationship as cornerstones, and each Venus will form a One-One and a Seven-Seven secondary

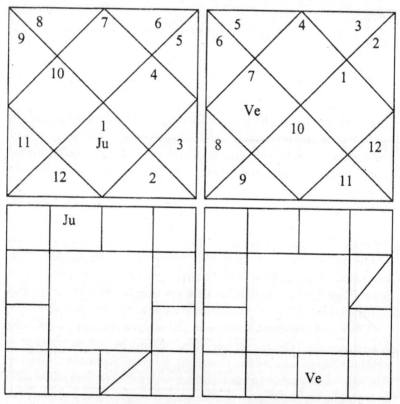

Figure 15. The Venus link to the Libra Ascendant,
enhanced by the aspect of Jupiter.

relationship with the Ascendant of the other chart. Each Venus can, how-ever, also be read as a smoothness factor, because each will act both as a natural benefic and as the raja yoga karaka in both birth charts.

Figure 15 and 16 emphasize the need to bring fluid judgment to bear on synastrical assessments of Venus, either as a benefic or merely as a pri-mary or secondary cornerstone link. Such judgment must be molded in the clay of the basic rules of Jyotisha and then baked in the kiln of practical expe-rience. Venus will also act as a benefic when it is the Ascendant lord in a horoscope. In most other instances, however, Venus will act primarily as one of the four cornerstones, and only secondarily as a benefic. When it does act as a benefic Venus's influence is strongly intensified when it con-joins or aspects within an orb of 7½°.

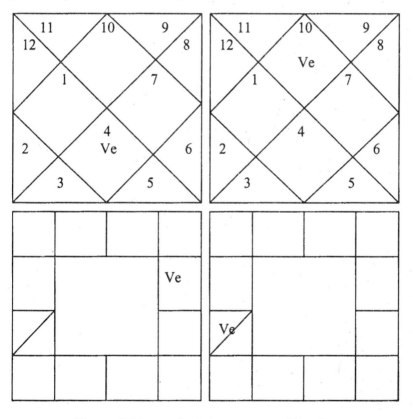

Figure 16. Venus as both cornerstone and benefic,
as the raja yoga karaka for both charts.

The Malefics

If benefics tend to add sweetness, then malefics add bitterness to the rasa of life. If the intensity of a match's potential sweetness depends on the strength of the harmonious links between the four cornerstones, the degree of bitterness that a malefic influence can create hangs on its strength to create virulent situations. Even when the four cornerstones are well aligned, certain issues that the couple will have to resolve may remain outstanding. Alternatively, it may happen that the couple generates by their interaction an imbalance that they must address. We can identify the life areas in which such dissonance will occur by evaluating the influence of the malefies in the one horoscope on the cornerstones of the other.

Each malefic will create tension according to its personal nature. Mars when well positioned can indicate strength, courage, passion, and the indomitable spirit and vigor needed to identify and pursue a desired goal. Marital pressures often goad Mars into irritability and inconsistency, however, when impatience to achieve his goals leads to an angry "all-or-nothing" attitude toward his partner. Saturn, who can, when positively placed, be the model of disciplined responsibility, practical realism, and dependability, too often descends into anxious rigidity, inhibited resignation, isolated melancholy, depression, and suspicion when he feels somehow threatened. The same Rahu who can be an insightful, imaginative, inspired original thinker can wilt under stress into a jumble of illusions, delusions, and confusions, escaping perhaps into the self-deception of neuroses or addictions. The universalist idealist Ketu, with his intuition, compassion, spirituality, and self-sacrifice, can give way to explosive violence, iconoclastic eccentricity, fanatical unconventionality, and emotional impulsiveness when he is strained.

The most ominous placements for the major malefics are those in which the malefic and one of the four cornerstones become associates, conjoined in the same rashi. Next in order of menace are situations in which a malefic occupies the seventh bhava from one of the four cornerstones, making the malefic and the relevant cornerstone opposites. Then come the special aspects that Mars, Saturn, and Rahu throw. These special aspects cause Mars to aspect those rashis (and any graha that tenants them) that are four and eight rashis away from its position, and Saturn to aspect all rashis and grahas that are three and ten rashis from its position. Cornerstone analysis is one of the few contexts in Jyotisha in which we consider Rahu to throw an aspect. For our purposes, we may deem Rahu to aspect the fifth and ninth rashis away from his natal position. We only consider Rahu's aspects in this context, not Ketu's, for Rahu is the head of that mythological cosmic serpent, and the head alone can see to cast a glance.

A malefic's influence is strongly intensified when it conjoins or aspects within an orb of 7½°. When a number of negative influences appear, they exert a cumulative effect. We search particularly for grahas that mutually influence the same cornerstone in both charts. For example, when a couple's Suns oppose each other to create a Seven-Seven relationship and the Saturn of the one chart occupies the same rashi as the Sun in that chart, that Saturn will quite clearly influence the other Sun as well. When a malefic's influence acts solely from one chart to another, the unilateral dynamic is not likely to be too bad. When that malefic affects the same cornerstone across both charts, however, the situation often becomes exponentially worse.

When Saturn interferes with a pair of cornerstones, one or both of the partners may perceive the other as being suffocatingly constrictive, distant, incommunicative, secret or manipulative, or acting in some other notably Saturnine fashion. These perceptions will focus primarily on the matters ruled by the affected cornerstone. Ordinarily, it will be the person in whose horoscope the influencing malefic sits who will be perceived by his or her partner as behaving unproductively or harmfully. If the malefic contact is a mutual one, the corresponding problematic themes will transfer in both directions.

Figure 17 shows of a couple whose Ascendants are Gemini and Scorpio (see page 131). Right away, we must expect vasana incompatibility in their mundane life, for their Ascendants form a Six-Eight relationship, one of active adversaries. Saturn, in the Scorpio chart, sits in Virgo. When we transpose this Saturn into the Gemini chart, we find that it aspects that Gemini Ascendant, by its special tenth aspect. Saturn in the Gemini chart sits in Taurus. When we transpose this Saturn into the Scorpio chart, we find that it sits opposite that Scorpio Ascendant. The charts in figure 17 thus have a mutual link of the Saturn in one horoscope to the Ascendant of the other.

This bilateral influence of Saturn on the Ascendant will intensify, in a Saturnian way, the imbalances that the Six-Eight relationship produces. The partners will share a strong tendency to consider the other's actions restrictive, and may also suspect one another of operating in secret, of failing to provide full information on matters ruled by the Ascendant. Perhaps he will become testy when she brings up business transactions to him, asking himself why she should be bothering him with such affairs. She, in turn, may feel that some of the tasks he requests her to do are creating unnecessary burdens for her.

The partners will have to actively try to resolve these tensions, but they will find their task complicated by the influence that the Saturn in the Scorpio-rising chart throws on that very Scorpio Ascendant, through its special third aspect from Virgo. Here, one naturally malefic graha thus influences *both* of a pair of primary links in *both* horoscopes. This, combined with the mutual link of the Saturn in one horoscope to the Ascendant of the other, creates a confluence of Saturnian influences that becomes a yet more powerful indicator of the Saturnine challenge to the relationship. Because the Gemini-rising chart's Ascendant is not influenced by its own Taurus Saturn, that person is less likely than the other to inaugurate the Saturn transference pattern between the couple, for such a person will have less of the Saturn aura stamped on his or her nature. The Scorpio Ascendant person is rather more likely to become the "pivot" for the interchange of the obstructive Saturn patterns that may mar the relationship, because of the heavier dose of Saturn in that birth chart.

The influence of Mars on cornerstones encourages a need for exhilaration that tends to lead to undue enthusiasms and hasty, exaggerated actions. The result of such ill-thought-out activity is often a confrontation that Mars's combative nature can quickly intensify. Suppose, for example, that John's Mars influences both his Ascendant and that of his wife, Mary. One day John, who is a true Martian at heart, comes home all excited to tell Mary, "Guess what, darling? We're moving to Alaska—tomorrow! Surprise! Isn't this going to be fun?" Unfortunately Mary, to whom a surprise is less enjoyable than a toothache, does not think that moving so far north will be much fun. She does think, however, that this is one more example of John's predilection for acting first and thinking later, without ever seeming to involve her in the decision-making process. The influence of Mars may now encourage a heated disagreement between these two otherwise well-intentioned people.

Rahu sows confusion, doubt, uncertainty, and lack of clarity wherever he goes, punctuating the vagueness that his shadow casts with sudden injections of the unexpected, the bizarre, or the occult. At best, the person with Rahu in a position to affect cornerstones in the charts of both partners will be perceived by the other partner as operating on a psychic, instead of a mundane, level. At worst, such people may be perceived as dragging their confusions, complexes, and phobias into the relationship dynamic. Another theme may be that the idiosyncratic Rahuvian behaviors are viewed as disruptive to the relationship.

It can be instructive to compare and contrast Rahu's aspects with those of Jupiter, since, in this context, both aspect the fifth and ninth rashis from their positions. In fact, we can usually make similar, but opposite, statements about a Rahu and a Jupiter who occupy similar positions and influence the same cornerstones. If Jupiter gives inspired, intuitive, conservative, rational, and modest counsel, we can often expect Rahu's counsel to be outlandish, idiosyncratic, and chimerical, even when it is insightful. If Rahu's hallmark is offbeat assessments and lack of convention, Jupiter blesses us with a more traditional clarity of thought and perception. Special care is required to interpret situations in which Rahu and Jupiter trine one another or occupy the same rashi, for then both influences will operate, in often-unpredictable ways.

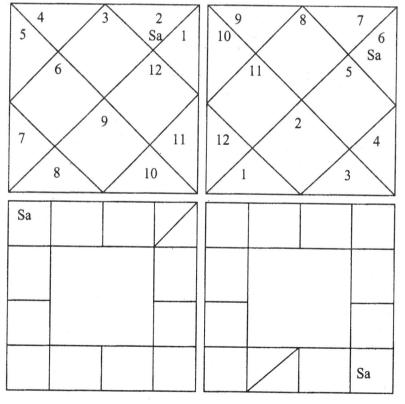

Figure 17. Saturn in both charts influences the
Ascendant in the opposite chart.

Exceptions to the Influence of Malefics on the Four Cornerstones

There are at least two conditions in which Mars and Saturn will not disturb the conscious experience of the foundations of a budding relationship. The first occurs when one of them rules the Ascendant in the originating chart. In classical Jyotisha, the lord of the first bhava is, by definition, always a good graha. Its influence on the four cornerstones in the other horoscope will, in this case, essentially supersede (in most cases, when Saturn is not exceptionally weak) its influence as a natural malefic. The second condition occurs when one of them is the raja yoga karaka for the horoscope.

When Mars or Saturn act as the raja yoga karaka, the contribution of these two grahas to the relationship will provide more benefit than damage, with just a few overtones of their naturally malefic persona. Contacts of even attenuated natural malefics usually indicate arenas in which the "work" of the relationship lies. Mitigated malefics, however, also bring forward their more noble qualities. Thus a Mars or Saturn as the lord of the Ascendant or as the raja yoga karaka of a chart (ideally in *both* charts) will emphasize Saturn's responsibility and depth, or the courage and initiative of Mars. Note that in figure 17, neither for the Gemini nor for the Scorpio Ascendant is Saturn attenuated by being either the lord of the Ascendant or a raja yoga karaka (see page 131). This backs a more challenging interpretation for the Saturn contact, at least in the context of such a relationship.

Figure 18 (page 133) illustrates some other examples of the contacts of malefics with the cornerstones of two charts. In this figure, the Ascendants again form an inharmonious Six-Eight primary link, but here a mutual Saturn and Rahu contact occurs to the pair of Ascendants. When transposed from one chart to the other, the Virgo Saturn of the Aries chart contacts the Virgo Ascendant of the other by association, and the Capricorn Rahu of the Aries chart influences that Virgo Ascendant by its special ninth aspect. The Cancer Saturn of the Virgo chart, when placed into the other chart, impacts, in turn, the Aries Ascendant by its tenth special aspect, and the Sagittarius Rahu colors the Aries Ascendant through its fifth special aspect.

Note that, in this simple illustration, the Venus cornerstone pair forms the desirable "opposites" primary link by virtue of being in a Seven-Seven relationship. Since, in neither case, is the Venus of one chart influenced by the Mars, Saturn, or Rahu of the other, we can conclude that the primary link created by the Venuses across the two charts is unblemished. Though the strength of this primary link is rather compromised (because occupation of the inauspicious eighth bhava while being aspected by Saturn substantially weakens the Venus in the Virgo chart), the link itself is still a positive one.

We must, however, also infer that the couple's environmental circumstances (as represented by their Ascendants) will be difficult to reconcile, since they are linked in the inharmonious Six-Eight relationship. This Six-Eight placement is likely to be exceptionally unwholesome because of the aggravating effects of the natural malefics Saturn and Rahu on both Ascendants across both charts. The unilateral influence of the Cancer Saturn of the Virgo chart on that very Virgo Ascendant further intensifies the innate negativity of the entire scenario. The disruptions that Saturn and Rahu promise here are unmitigated, because Saturn is neither the Ascendant lord nor the raja yoga karaka for either chart (and Rahu cannot act ei-

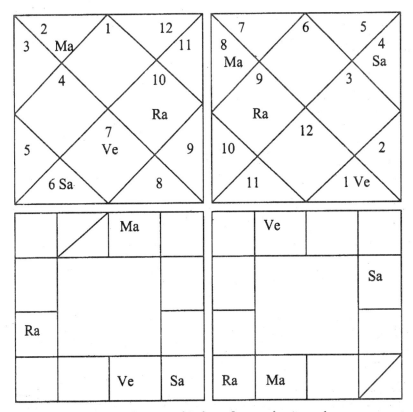

Figure 18. Saturn and Rahu influence the Ascendant
of the opposite chart.

ther as a lagna lord or a raja yoga karaka). All other factors being equal, this couple is likely to find such a relationship unsustainable, or, at the very least, chaotic. This, in spite of the promise of the positive Venusian link, whose vasana alignments may continually lead the partners to continue to desire something of (or in) the other in the midst of all the upheavals.

Factoring the influence of the natural benefics and malefics across two horoscopes injects complexity into relationship analysis. It is, however, a manageable complexity that repays the laborious scrutiny to detail that it demands with profound insight into relationship dynamics. Scanning two charts for a complete picture of the linkage among the four cornerstones will, with practice, eventually become an intuitive skill. Until that time, many students of these synastrical methods organize their information by manually transferring grahas of one chart into the other using a different color of ink. Try this yourself and you will be delighted with how readily the requisite patterns can be recognized.

KHANDANA AND MANDANA

Mandana represents creation in Sanskrit and *khandana*, destruction. In the context of a developing relationship, we can use mandana to indicate the positive interactions that promote the smooth intermingling of the auras of the two individuals involved, and khandana to represent the clashing that inevitably occurs from time to time. These two opposing principles need not be equally powerful, for sometimes, the negative factors that normally produce bitter rasa can be converted into positive, sweetness-producing influences that can assist us in our relationship-building program. As with opposing cornerstones, opposing factors can sometimes strongly complement one another.

In general, however, a predominance of benefic patterns in the horoscopes of two people whose four cornerstones are positively related will promote smoothness in the development (mandana) of their relationship. A predominance of malefic patterns between misaligned cornerstones will, instead, create obstacles that may promote an incipient relationship's destruction (khandana). When several benefic and malefic patterns each appear in two horoscopes, greater judgment is required.

Remember that Jyotisha analyzes destiny patterns with the intention of figuring out what to do about them, that we may "deal with our karma creatively" by enhancing, not diminishing, our free will. Each of us must play the cards that life deals out to us, and the more skillfully we play, the more successful we are likely to be. This is particularly true in relationship. When you find yourself in a position in which you are strongly attracted to someone (via positive relations among your four cornerstones), but discover a large number of negative overlays to those cornerstones from your malefics, you need to realize that such a relationship will likely be filled with tremendous hassles. You will probably be better off not taking on such a situation, since you will likely find it very difficult to digest the rasa that will develop. If the attraction is so exceptionally strong, however, that you do decide to take the relationship on, you should be prepared occasionally, to quaff a bitter draught. Acceptance of the implications of your decisions, however unsavory those implications may be, is the price of free will. Let us now turn to our example horoscopes to see how they are influenced by both benefics and malefics.

EXAMPLES

Prince Charles and Princess Diana

The horoscopes of this royal couple (see Charts 12 and 13, pages 111 and 113) elegantly illustrate what typically occurs when one malefic graha from one horoscope influences both members of a pair of primary links in *both* horoscopes. Let us first analyze the horoscopes singly, then sort out the overlap from chart to chart. You will probably find it useful to follow this sequence unvaryingly until it becomes habitual, for a haphazard approach to estimating degree of confluence can lead to much confusion.

The chart of Princess Diana shows a very dominant influence of the natural malefic Rahu, who occupies the tenth bhava near the zenith of the horoscope, whence it directly aspects the all-important Moon. This aspect of Rahu on the Moon gains great influence by falling within our $7\frac{1}{2}°$ orb, as does Rahu's influence on lagna lord Mars, with whom it is conjoined within $7\frac{1}{2}°$. Rahu thus exerts a double influence on Diana: on the Moon as the significator of the mind, and on Mars as the ruler of her body and her physical circumstances.

Transposing Diana's Leo Rahu to Charles's horoscope, we note that her Rahu aspects his Aries Moon by its ninth aspect. This fulfills our first condition for malefic modification, that one malefic graha from one horoscope influence both members of a pair of primary links in both charts.

Although their Moon cornerstones create the harmonious primary Five-Nine connection, the potent effect of her Rahu on both their Moons implies that a Rahuvian motif will become superimposed on the otherwise positive indications of the active-supporters relationship that their Moons share.

As stated earlier, the same Rahu that can be an insightful, imaginative, inspired original thinker can also wilt under stress into a jumble of illusions, delusions, and confusions, escaping, on occasion, into the self-deception of neuroses or addictions. This theme certainly displayed itself often in Princess Diana's marriage. She was characterized as a well-intentioned, but anxiety-ridden, individual, frequently unable to cope with the stresses her position thrust upon her. One way this lack of personal ease manifested was in eating disorders.

Rahu sows confusion, doubt, uncertainty, and lack of clarity wherever he goes, punctuating the vagueness that his shadow casts with sudden injections of the unexpected, the bizarre, or the occult. The person in whose chart Rahu sits in a position that affects cornerstones in the charts of both partners will often be perceived by the other partner as operating on a psychic, instead of a mundane, level. Such people may also be perceived as dragging their phobias into the relationship dynamic. The idiosyncratic Rahuvian behaviors may also be viewed as disruptive to the relationship. As more of Princess Diana's life is chronicled, these Rahu features will likely surface to a greater extent, especially in her marriage to Prince Charles.

The chart of Prince Charles also shows a dominant influence of Rahu, who sits within 25° of the zenith of the horoscope, also in the tenth bhava, also directly aspecting the Moon, also within 7½°. Rahu's influence on the Prince's aura is extensive, because that Rahu is conjoined within 7½° with the lord of the lagna (who happens to be the lord of the mind, the aforementioned Moon, as well). All these combinations are virtually identical to those of Princess Diana, the major difference being that, when we transpose his Aries Rahu into her horoscope, it fails to influence her Aquarius Moon. Thankfully, these two charts do not have the double challenge of Rahu in *both* charts influencing *both* members of a pair of primary links in *both* horoscopes.

The near-identical placement of the Rahus in these charts near the zenith while influencing the Moon (as the significator of the mind) and the lord of the Ascendant (as the indicator of the body) rendered both Charles and Diana votaries of the Rahu way of thinking described earlier. Rahu is likely to have encouraged them to perceive each other's ways and values as odd, impractical, and perhaps even phobia-ridden. Because of the one-sided manner in which Princess Diana's Rahu alone influenced both their Moons, she was the one characterized (accurately or not) as the prime mover of the Rahuvian themes in their life together.

John F. Kennedy and Jacqueline Onassis

We have seen what can happen when a malefic graha from one horoscope influences both members of a pair of primary links in both horoscopes. While this effect is very powerful, it is more powerful still when the same graha in *both* charts influences *both* members of a pair of primary links in *both* horoscopes. Such an influence may be overpowering. Double the trouble, so to speak!

For an example of the Rahus in two charts influencing both members of a pair of primary links in both horoscopes, we may examine the Kennedys (see Charts 7 and 8, pages 79 and 80). Kennedy's Moon and Onassis's Moon create a harmonious primary Five-Nine relationship, but his Rahu influences both of their Moons by its special fifth and ninth aspects, and her Rahu aspects his Moon, while being conjoined with her own. One result of this situation is that both partners are likely to have felt, from time to time, that the other's unconventional behavior was disrupting the relationship's harmony. This mutuality of Rahu-Moon interaction is likely to have caused Jacqueline Onassis to find a presidency filled with intrigues and many alleged affairs on the former president's part distasteful. JFK is equally likely to have found some of Jackie's quirks (like her enthusiasm for spending money) unpalatable.

The plot created by the transposition of grahas between their charts would be incomplete without considering the role of the natural benefic, Jupiter, in the synastrical patterns that their horoscopes generate. Kennedy's Taurus Venus and Onassis's Taurus Venus are associates. Both also have Jupiter in Taurus, which means that his Jupiter influences both his own and her Venus, just as her Jupiter influences both her own and his Venus. In this case, the same benefic graha in *both* charts thus influences *both* members of a pair of primary links in *both* horoscopes. Here, the benign reciprocal influence of Jupiter on a pair of the primary links presumably enabled the couple to support one another, through good counsel and advice, to help the other's positive experiences of life expand, and other similarly Jovan intentions.

The Jupiterian overlay on their marriage did not, however, cancel the Rahuvian theme; both Jupiter and Rahu concurrently had their say in the

marriage. The benign influence of Jupiter combined with the positive alignment of three of their four cornerstones to keep the marriage functional,
despite Rahu's mutually discomfiting affliction of both Moons. Rahu's confusions most likely operated chiefly on the plane of the astral body (associated with the Moon), while the blessings of Jupiter were most likely evident
primarily in the collaborative fulfillment of their desires (as represented by
Venus). The Moon represents manas, the mental faculty that determines
which life experiences you come to crave (raga) and which you come to ab-
hor (dvesha). By eclipsing the Moon, Rahu destabilizes your sensory and
emotional life, a destabilization that, here, works in both directions.

Jupiter's influence on their Venuses likely expanded their karma, their
mutual desire or strong mutual yearning for what promised pleasure for
them. She may have tolerated his affairs, and he her conspicuous consumption, because of the prestige, the prominence, and the success that their alliance created in the Camelot Era of American politics, a success that fulfilled
their mutual desires. Given the supreme importance of the health of the
Moon to a healthy long-term relationship, however, there is reason to doubt
whether Rahu would have permitted the marriage to endure in the long run,
had it not been so tragically cut short.

Queen Elizabeth II and Prince Philip

Whatever you may think of these two relics of a dying aristocracy (see
Charts 10 and 11, pages 108 and 109), they have something to offer to the
world in the enduring nature of their marriage. We have already described
the harmonious karmic links between their four cornerstones of relationship. Here we add the formidable overlay of benefic Jupiter contacts between
their charts. Queen Elizabeth's Capricorn Jupiter, which aspects her own
Cancer Moon, also aspects Prince Philip's Cancer Moon when it is transposed to his chart. Prince Philip, in turn, has his Leo Jupiter aspecting both
his Sagittarius Ascendant and his Aries Venus. Transporting his Jupiter to
Queen Elizabeth's horoscope, we find that it aspects both her Sagittarius
Ascendant and her Aquarius Venus. This is, thus, a reciprocal case of one
graha (Jupiter) from one horoscope influencing both members of a pair of
primary links in both horoscopes. Such a Jupiterian link to several of the primary pairs of cornerstones is extremely helpful to their marriage, in and of
itself. When we add a strong cornerstone alignment, we obtain a composite
pattern that suggests that such a union will likely endure.

Jupiter facilitates their union yet further by tempering the one pair of cornerstones that is out of sync (their Suns) bilaterally (her Jupiter aspects his Sun, and his Jupiter hers). To the question of how effective her debilitated Jupiter can be as a benefic, we offer a classical threefold *neecha bhanga*[1] (cancellation of debility):

- The graha (Mars) that is exalted in the rashi in whose Jupiter sits occupies a kendra from the Moon;
- Jupiter is aspected by the graha in whose rashi Jupiter is exalted (Moon);
- Jupiter is aspected by the graha in whose rashi Jupiter sits (Saturn).

Jupiter's influence assumes even greater importance when we perform outcome analysis on the Queen's seventh bhava. We discover a compromised seventh bhava (containing Rahu, bereft of benefic influence) and seventh lord (debilitated, with its dispositor debilitated, again without benefic influence). Even Jupiter, her significator, is debilitated (though with the cancellations detailed above). We suggest that marital success came to the Queen essentially due to a three-tiered tower of strength: strongly positive cornerstone relationships, good Jupiterian influence built on those cornerstones, and the middle-ground condition of the Prince's seventh bhava, seventh lord, and significator. The conclusion? Always apply careful judgment to tease out instances where vasana alignment, in the form of promising cornerstone affiliations, can modify the karmic outcome otherwise implied in the horoscope.

As an exercise, take the horoscopes of Paul Newman and Joanne Woodward and try to delineate which benefic and malefic influences they share.

---

[1] Under certain circumstances, a debilitated graha can have its weakness reduced by a method called neecha bhanga. For details see *Light on Life: An Introduction to Indian Astrology* (London: Penguin, 1996).

5

THE TEN
PORUTTHAMS

The ten principles called *porutthams*, or *kutams*, were developed and preserved over several centuries, primarily in southern India. These criteria, which form India's most popular method of synastry, evaluate compatibility by gauging the Moon position of the prospective groom in relation to the Moon of the bride. While there has long been dispute over which principles to include in the list, the generally accepted porutthams are: *Nakshatra, Gana, Mahendra, Stri Dirgha, Yoni, Rashi, Rashyadhipati, Vashya, Rajju,* and *Vedha* (or *Nadi*).

By counting from the position of the Moon in the female's chart to the position of the Moon in the male's chart, following the natural forward motion of the zodiac, poruttham evaluation provides yet further evidence that lunar astrology is fundamental to Jyotisha. All counting is, once again, inclusive (i.e., it must include both Moon positions). Thus, if her Moon is in Leo and his is in Scorpio, his Moon is four rashis away from hers (the first is Leo, the second Virgo, the third Libra, and the fourth Scorpio). Counting from one nakshatra to another is similarly inclusive.

The porutthams have traditionally been evaluated solely from the Moon. Considering the Ascendant's importance in today's world of Jyotisha, however, we have elected to stray from a strict Moon-based method to apply the synastry of the porutthams to the Ascendants, as well as to the Moons, of a couple. After all, many other ancient lunar-based factors have already been extended, over the centuries, to the Ascendant in modern Jyotisha. While this approach may raise the hackles on some hidebound traditionalists, we are confident that the value of analyzing the porutthams in this way will satisfy anyone who gives it a fair trial.

Those with a casual interest in Jyotisha who find the following discussion of the porutthams to be overwhelmingly technical and ethnocentric may skim it, or skip it entirely, without compromising their comprehension of the remainder of the book.

NAKSHATRA PORUTTHAM

This poruttham, which is known as *nakshatra poruttham* in northern India and as *dina poruttham* in southern India, evaluates the health and longevity of the partners with reference to one another. Its southern Indian name refers to the "nakshatra day," the day (*dina*) that is measured in some traditional Indian lunar calendars by the time it takes for the Moon to pass through one of the twenty-seven nakshatras.[1] For the purpose of this evaluation, the twenty-seven nakshatras are divided into three groups (*paryayas*) of nine nakshatras each. The first is called *janma paryaya* (birth group), the second is called *anujanma paryaya* (the group following birth), and the third is known as *trijanma paryaya* (third birth group). The first group consists of the nine nakshatras, counted inclusively from the nakshatra containing the bride's Moon at birth. The second group consists of the tenth to the eighteenth nakshatras, as counted from that Moon's nakshatra. The third group consists of the remaining nakshatras (numbers nineteen through twenty-seven), as counted from the original nakshatra. As is mostly the case with poruttham evaluation, all counting for Nakshatra Poruttham is from the woman's Moon to the man's—an old-fashioned astrological case of "ladies first."

Rules

1. Excellent alignment exists when, counting from the woman's Moon, the man's Moon falls in the fourth, sixth, or ninth nakshatra of any of the three groups.
2. Good harmony exists when the man's Moon falls in the second or eighth nakshatra of any of the three groups.
3. When the man's Moon falls in the first nakshatra of any of the three groups, there is average harmony.
4. Misalignment exists when the man's Moon falls in the third, fifth, or seventh nakshatra of any of the three groups.

---

[1] See Table 3, page 143.

As an example take Joanne Woodward (see Chart 9, page 106), whose Moon sits at 1° 59' of Aquarius in Dhanishtha nakshatra. Her sequence of nakshatras is shown in Table 3. Men born with the Moon in *Purva Bhadrapada*, *Punarvasu* or *Vishakha* *nakshatras*, which are the third nakshatras of each of the three Parayayas, respectively, would thus be incompatible with Joanne Woodward, as would men born with the Moon in *Revati*, *Ashlesha*, or *Jyeshtha nakshatras*, which are the fifth nakshatra of each of the three paryayas, or in *Bharani*, *Purva Phalguni*, or *Purva Ashadha nakshatras*, which are the seventh nakshatras in each parayaya. Woodward would have average harmony with men with Moons in *Dhanishtha*, *Mrigashirsha*, or *Chitra*, which are the first nakshatras of the three paryayas. The harmony would be good with a man whose Moon falls in the second or eighth nakshatra of any of the three groups (*Shatabhisha*, *Ardra*, or *Swati*, and *Krittika*, *Uttara Phalguni*, or *Uttara Ashadha*, respectively). Excellent alignment would exist between Woodward and a man whose Moon fell in the fourth, sixth, or ninth nakshatra of any of the three groups (*Uttara Bhadrapada*, *Pushya*, or *Anuradha*; *Ashvini*, *Magha*, or *Mula*; or *Rohini*, *Hasta*, or *Shravana*).

Table 3. Sequence of Nakshatras for Joanne Woodward.

JANMA PAYAYA	ANUJANMA PARYAYA	TRIJANMA PARYAYA
1. Dhanishtha	10. Mrigashirsha	19. Chitra
2. Shatabhisha	11. Ardra	20. Swati
3. Purva Bhadrapada	12. Punarvasu	21. Vishakha
4. Uttara Bhadrapada	13. Pushya	22. Anuradha
5. Revati	14. Ashlesha	23. Jyeshtha
6. Ashvini	15. Magha	24. Mula
7. Bharani	16. Purva Phalguni	25. Purva Ashadha
8. Krittika	17. Uttara Phalguni	26. Uttara Ashadha
9. Rohini	18. Hasta	27. Shravana

Joanne Woodward's husband is Paul Newman (see Chart 3, page 51), whose Moon sits at 8° 51' of Aquarius, in Shatabhisha nakshatra. Since this is the second nakshatra from Woodward's Moon in Dhanishtha, good harmony exists between them, based on nakshatra poruttham. When we extend this principle to their Ascendants as well, we find that Woodward and Newman have the same Ascendant nakshatra: Purva Ashadha. Since we count inclusively, Purva Ashadha is the first nakshatra from Purva Ashadha, which promises average harmony. Because indications from both the Moon and the Ascendant are positive, however, this average harmony from the Ascendant will act to enhance the already-good harmony from the Moon to yield excellent harmony, another case of astrological confluence.

Variants and Exceptions

1. Couples whose Moons occupy the same nakshatra have average agreement only if they were born in the nakshatras of Ashvini, Krittika, Mrigashirsha, Punarvasu, Pushya, Purva Phalguni, Uttara Phalguni, Chitra, Anuradha, Purva Ashadha, or Uttara Ashadha. Those born with the Moon in Rohini, Ardra, Magha, Hasta, Vishakha, Shravana, Uttara Bhadrapada, or Revati have good harmony, and those born with their Moons in Bharani, Ashlesha, Swati, Jyeshtha, Mula, Dhanishtha, Shatabhisha, or Purva Bhadrapada are inharmonious.

2. Rule 1 notwithstanding, couples who have the Moon both in the same nakshatra and the same rashi of the zodiac have excellent harmony. For example, a couple whose Moons each occupy Dhanishtha nakshatra would have excellent—instead of poor—harmony when both Moons sit in either Capricorn or Aquarius. When, however, one of their Dhanishtha Moons occupies Capricorn and the other Aquarius, they will lack harmony from the viewpoint of nakshatra poruttham.

     A real-life example of a couple whose Moons share both a nakshatra and a rashi is that of the late American civil rights leader, Martin Luther King (see Chart 16, page 146), and his wife, Coretta Scott King (see Chart 17, page 147). His Moon sits in Purva Bhadrapada at 26°47' of Aquarius and her Moon sits in Purva Bhadrapada at 23°07' of Aquarius. This gives them excellent harmony, based on this one poruttham. Had, however, one of their Moons been in Pisces instead of Aquarius (which is possible, since Purva Bhadrapada begins at 20°00' Aquarius and ends at 3°20' Pisces), that situation would have suggested incompatibility instead of excellent harmony.

3. Several other exceptions apply when both partners have their natal Moons in the same rashi. For example, the general rules above provide for excellent harmony when the nakshatra of the Moon of the man is the ninth of any of the paryayas, as counted from the woman's Moon. In the special case in which the man's nakshatra is the ninth of her trijamna

paryaya, the two nakshatras are adjacent, with hers following his. If the Moons of a couple occupy adjacent nakshatras, but his nakshatra follows hers, his nakshatra, will be the second of her jamna paryaya. By this exception to the general rules, both cases promise merely good harmony unless the two Moons occupy the same rashi and are either of the following: any of the pairs Bharani-Krittika, Pushya-Ashlesha, or Dhanishtha-Shatabhisha; or the man's Moon occupies Ashvini, Krittika, Mrigashirsha, Magha, Hasta, Swati, Purva Ashadha, or Shatabhisha. In these cases, the harmony becomes excellent.

When we refer again to Newman and Woodward, a Hollywood couple married for an improbable 30+ years in an environment that discourages marital stability, we see that both have their Moons in Aquarius in adjacent nakshatras, with his in Shatabhisha and hers in Dhanishtha. Since his Moon follows hers, the general rule would suggest merely good harmony. In their case, however, both their Moons tenant Aquarius and the two nakshatras are Dhanishtha-Shatabhisha. This also meets the second criterion above, since Newman's Moon occupies Shatabhisha. Any of these exceptions converts a combination that would normally give good harmony into one that bestows excellent harmony.

4. Another exception to the inharmonious placements of a couple's Moons in this poruttham is based on which of the *padas* of a nakshatra the male's Moon occupies. Each nakshatra, which spans 13°20' of the sky, is divided into four segments (*padas*) of 3°20' each. When the man's Moon occupies the last three padas of the twelfth nakshatra, counted inclusively from the woman's Moon, there is average agreement of the Moon placements. Under the general rules, this would create disharmony, because the twelfth nakshatra is the third nakshatra of the second paryaya. A similar rule applies to the fourteenth nakshatra from the woman's Moon, which would normally create disharmony, since it is the fifth nakshatra of the second paryaya. If, however, the man's Moon is in any of the first three padas of the fourteenth nakshatra counted from the woman's Moon, the disharmony is converted into average harmony.

5. One pada placement that converts harmony to conflict occurs when the Moon of the male occupies the fourth pada of the twenty-second nakshatra from the Moon of the female, a position that would ordinarily produce excellent harmony, since this twenty-second nakshatra is the fourth nakshatra of the third paryaya.

Rashi Chart

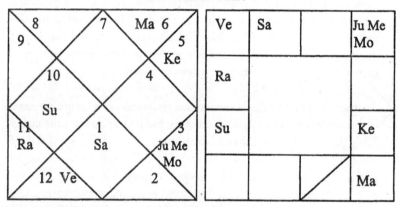

Navamsha Chart

Planetary Positions		Vimshottari Dasha		
LG	20°AR56'	JU	22 Dec. 1920	Yogi Point PI 2-20'
SU	02°CP16'	SA	22 Dec. 1936	
MO	26°AQ43'	ME	23 Dec. 1955	Yogi – JU
MA	29°TA 02'R	KE	23 Dec. 1972	
ME	18°CP54'	VE	24 Dec. 1979	Avayogi – SU
JU	08°AR19'	SU	24 Dec. 1999	
VE	17°AQ42'	MO	23 Dec. 2005	Duplicate Yogi – JU
SA	02°SA30'	MA	24 Dec. 2015	
RA	04°TA37'	RA	24 Dec. 2022	Daghda Rasis
KE	04°SC37'			GE & VI

Chart 16. Martin Luther King.

Rashi Chart

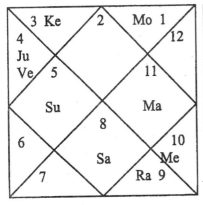

Ju Me	Su	Ve	Ra Ma
Mo	April 27, 1927 4:00 PM Marion, AL		
Ke	Sa R		

Navamsha Chart

	Mo		Ke
Ma	April 27, 1927 4:00 PM		Ju Ve
Me			Su
Ra	Sa		

Planetary Positions		Vimshottari Dasha		
LG	13°VI 37'	JU	3 Aug. 1923	Yogi Point GE 10-14'
SU	13°AR48'	SA	3 Aug. 1939	
MO	23°AQ07'	ME	3 Aug. 1958	Yogi – RA
MA	13°GE31'	KE	4 Aug. 1975	
ME	22°PI 15'	VE	4 Aug. 1982	Avayogi – VE
JU	00°PI 14'	SU	4 Aug. 2002	
VE	20°TA20'	MO	3 Aug. 2008	Duplicate Yogi – ME
SA	13°SC32'R	MA	4 Aug. 2018	
RA	07°GE56'	RA	4 Aug. 2025	Daghda Rasis
KE	07°SA56'			SA & PI

Chart 17. Coretta Scott King.

6. The most important transformer of harmony into disharmony in the matter of nakshatra poruttham occurs when the male's Moon occupies the eighth rashi, as counted inclusively from the female's Moon. In this case even excellent nakshatra placements (like the fourth, sixth, or ninth of any of the paryayas) are converted to disharmony.

This is the case with the Kings when we count nakshatra poruttham from their Ascendants, for his Aries Ascendant occupies the eighth rashi from her Virgo Ascendant. This implies a troubled prospect for their health and longevity quotient in a relationship. Because the porutthams are not primary methods of chart comparison, however, we must find supporting combinations in their individual charts in order for this disharmony to manifest as dramatically as it did for the Kings.

On inspection, we do find corroboration from both horoscopes. When we examine Coretta Scott King's chart, we find that her seventh bhava contains a debilitated Mercury, her seventh lord Jupiter occupies the very weak first degree of its rashi, and her seventh bhava and its lord are flanked by natural malefics (the waning Moon and the Sun). Her Venus, the significator for marriage, is flanked by malefics and is aspected by Saturn, even though it occupies its own rashi. This strong, but afflicted, Venus, when combined with her Jupiter in its own rashi as lord of the seventh, may simultaneously indicate both her husband's innate dignity and stature and her own ultimate bereavement.

Two vital and important combinations in Martin Luther King's chart threaten his longevity. The first is that Mars, the lord of the first and eighth bhavas—two bhavas whose strength is vital to longevity—occupies the very weak last degree of its rashi, a position that neatly parallels the weakness of her seventh lord in the first degree. The second combination also involves Mars, who sits on the Rahu-Ketu axis, participating in a *kala sarpa yoga* that will, thus, key its results to Mars, the lord of those two bhavas of longevity.[2] Did the Kings' shared karma (rnanubandhana) coordinate this drama by attracting these two to each other?

GANA

Gana (Class or Category) poruttham evaluates a couple's general sukha by classifying them according to three categories, as shown by the nakshatra positions of their Moons. A sort of natural rapport exists between people

[2] For information on kala sarpa yoga, see deFouw and Svoboda, *Light on Life*, chapter 10.

from the same gana, who can often adapt to one another more readily than can people of different ganas. Just as people with different cultural or ethnic groups are not always able to build bridges into each other's worlds, people with different ganas often have a challenging time of it when they marry. The nakshatras are classified into three ganas for the purpose of matching, based on this poruttham—*deva* (divine), *manushya* (human), and *rakahasa* (demonic)—but these classifications measure compatibility only, not innate character. The inhuman Adolf Hitler had his Moon in a human nakshatra, not a demonic one, and the Moon in the horoscope of the incomparable Indian saint, Ramakrishna Paramahamsa, occupied a rakshasa, not a deva, nakshatra.

Rules

1. Couples whose Moons occupy nakshatras in the same gana have excellent compatibility.
2. When the man's Moon occupies a deva gana nakshatra and the woman's Moon a manushya gana nakshatra, there is good compatibility.
3. When the woman's Moon occupies a deva gana nakshatra and the man's Moon a manushya gana nakshatra, the compatibility is average.
4. Incompatibility occurs when his Moon is in a rakshasa gana nakshatra, and hers is in a manushya gana nakshatra or if her Moon is in a rakshasa gana nakshatra and his is in a manushya gana nakshatra. Incompatibility also occurs when his Moon is in a deva gana nakshatra and hers is in a rakshasa gana nakshatra, or when her Moon is in a deva gana nakshatra and his is in a rakshasa gana nakshatra.

Table 4. Nakshatras of Gana Poruttham.

GANA	NAKSHATRA
Deva (Divine)	Ashvini, Mrigashirsha, Punarvasu, Pushya, Hasta, Swati, Anuradha, Sharavana, Revati
Manushya (Human)	Bharani, Rohini, Ardra, Purva Phalguni, Uttara Phalguni, Purva Ashadha, Uttara Ashadha, Purva Bhadrapada, Uttara Bhadrapada
Rakshasa or Asura (Demonic)	Krittika, Ashlesha, Magha, Chitra, Vishakha, Jyeshtha, Mula, Dhanishtha, Shatabhisha

Variants and Exceptions

1. When a couple's Moons occupy the same or the opposite rashis, their temperaments are said to match, whether or not their ganas do. For example, a couple's ganas will match if they both have Gemini Moons, or one has a Gemini Moon and the other a Sagittarius Moon, no matter what their gana nakshatras might be. However, in the special cases in which the couple's Moons sit in the seventh (samasaptami) position to each other in the opposite pairs of Cancer-Capricorn or Leo-Aquarius, the agreement of gana is not automatic. In both of the latter cases, we must apply the general rules of gana poruttham to determine agreement or disagreement.

2. If the dispositors of the Moons (lords of the rashis in which the Moons sit) of the couple's horoscope are either mutual friends or are both exalted or occupy their own rashis, any disharmony of this poruttham will be nullified.

3. If hers is a rakshasa nakshatra and his is a manushya nakshatra, disharmony is canceled if the nakshatra of the woman's Moon is more than fourteen nakshatras away from the nakshatra of the man's.

   When we apply gana poruttham to Woodward and Newman, we find an excellent match, for their nakshatras (Dhanishtha and Shatabhisha) are both of the rakshasa gana. Since, in any event, their Moons both tenant Aquarius, which gives them automatic gana agreement by virtue of samasaptami, this creates a sort of cumulative ideal gana poruttham, once by agreement of nakshatras and once by agreement of rashis. The same is true of Martin Luther King and Coretta Scott King, whose Moons both occupy Aquarius and Purva Bhadrapada.

   If we extend this principle to the Ascendant nakshatras for both couples, we find Dr. King's Ascendant nakshatra (Bharani) is manushya and Mrs. King's Ascendant nakshatra (Hasta) is deva, which produce average agreement. Woodward and Newman both have the same Ascendant nakshatra (Purva Ashadha), which again creates excellent agreement. Agreement from the Ascendants, thus, further enhances the already cumulative excellence of gana agreement for both couples.

MAHENDRA

Mahendra (Great Lord) poruttham evaluates both a couple's ability to have children (the "fruit" of coupling) and the happiness they will derive from their progeny. Mahendra poruttham thus reflects the value placed on children in classical Indian society. While mahendra poruttham provides general indications for the health, prosperity, and longevity of those offspring, the precise area of the child's life (health, career, etc.) that will be most affected must be determined by inspecting the couple's natal charts, as read from their Ascendants. Mahendra poruttham exists when the male's Moon occupies the fourth, seventh, tenth, thirteenth, sixteenth, nineteenth, twenty-second, or twenty-fifth nakshatras, as counted from the Moon in the female's horoscope. That this sequence ascends in increments of three starting from the fourth nakshatra makes it easy to remember.

Since the requirements for mahendra poruttham are so stringent that few couples qualify, it is usually evaluated in the context of rashyadhipati poruttham, the seventh poruttham in our sequence. When both mahendra and rashyadhipati agree or disagree, their confluence suggests pleasurable and painful results with children, respectively. Moderate agreement, which occurs when one of these porutthams agrees and the other does not, suggests that the couple's experience with offspring will sometimes veer toward the problematical. As is often the case with couples, neither Woodward/Newman nor the Kings qualify, either from their Moons or their Ascendants.

STRI DIRGHA

Stri dirgha (long woman) poruttham evaluates the partners' prosperity, of which wealth is the main, but not the sole, criterion. As with sukha, prosperity should be seen from general conditions, not specific, exclusive circumstances, for prosperity is just as absent from a life of affluence without magnanimity as it is in a life of abject poverty. The odd name "stri dirgha," which suggests an interest in promoting long-lasting prosperity, may refer to the ancient Indian identification of women with prosperity, as reflected in the person of Lakshmi, the goddess of plenty. A wife was—and often still is—traditionally referred to in India as the "Lakshmi of the house."

Rules

1. Stri dirgha exists for a couple when the nakshatra that contains the Moon of the male is more than thirteen nakshatras (some say more than ten nakshatras) ahead of the nakshatra that contains the Moon of the female.
2. Other authorities advocate a middle-of-the-road approach with a sliding scale. In this view, the match is poor when the male Moon is one to nine nakshatras away from the female Moon, good when the Moons are separated by ten to eighteen nakshatras; and excellent when the two Moons are nineteen to twenty-seven nakshatras apart.

The latter is the method we use in this book. When we apply it to the charts of Newman and Woodward, we find a double mismatch: his Moon is in the second nakshatra, as counted from her Moon, and their Ascendants occupy the same nakshatra. That this couple is indeed very prosperous is a timely reminder that the porutthams mainly provide color. They do not supersede the other combinations in the horoscope. More important primary combinations, like the many pancha maha purusha yogas, raja yogas, and dhana yogas (all of which augment prosperity and status) that crowd Newman's horoscope, provide better testimony to Newman's opulent existence than does stri dirgha. It is, however, interesting to speculate what such a double stri dirgha mismatch would have created in the absence of such superb yogas.

The Kings also have a mismatch for prosperity, albeit a single one, since only their Moons sit in the same nakshatra. Their Ascendants are excellently matched, his Ascendant nakshatra (Bharani) being seventeen nakshatras away from her Ascendant nakshatra (Hasta). One way we can resolve this apparent contradiction is to suggest that marriage probably improved the Kings' prosperity (because of their matched Ascendants). Their union may simultaneously have led, however, to the development of strong emotional differences pertaining to this enhanced wealth, in particular to their desires surrounding its use and acquisition, thanks to their mismatched Moons.

When stri dirgha matches, both members tend to contribute directly to the couple's financial prosperity. When it mismatches, however, only one member commonly shoulders this responsibility, be it by negotiation or simple evolution in the relationship. This situation applies both to Woodward/Newman and to the Kings, and most dramatically to Woodward, who gave up her own successful acting career after marrying Newman.

YONI

Yoni (Womb) Poruttham evaluates a couple's generative organs, with a view to ensuring successful mating. Though yoni poruttham is often taken—especially by Western students of Jyotisha—as a thumbnail evaluation of compatibility for sexual dalliance, it actually evaluates the more fundamental nature and degree of satisfaction and bonding that sexual contact will bring a couple. Good yoni compatibility suggests that the couple will be "karmically" aligned for sexual congress, even if challenges occur in that process at times. Two horoscopes with a misaligned yoni poruttham may imply that, although the partners enjoy "good" sex together, it is somehow less than satisfying. Moreover, this and all of the other poritthams are subsidiary to more primary evaluations derived from standard horoscope analysis.

Table 5 (see page 154), identifies each of the nakshatras as female or male, then symbolizes each by an animal's form, and finally assigns another creature or two as enemies.

Rules

1. Excellent yoni poruttham compatibility exists when the woman's Moon occupies a female nakshatra, and the male's Moon a male nakshatra, and their associated animals are compatible.
2. If both partners have their Moons in nakshatras that are either both female or male, and if the animals are compatible, then the agreement of yoni poruttham is good.
3. When the man belongs to a female nakshatra and the woman to a male nakshatra, the couple is at least not incompatible, provided that the animals are not incompatible.
4. Whenever the animal forms symbolizing the nakshatras are incompatible, there is no compatibility.

Woodward's Moon occupies Dhanishtha, a female nakshatra represented by a lion. Newman's Moon occupies Shatabhisha, a female nakshatra with the form of a horse. Because Dhanishtha's enemy is the elephant, not the horse, and Shatabhisha's enemy is the buffalo, not the lion, good yoni compatibility exists for them, as judged by the positions of their Moons. That both were born with their Ascendants in the same nakshatra (Purva Ashadha) also suggests good compatibility, for both automatically belong to the same gender (in this case, male), and are characterized by the same animal (monkey).

The Kings similarly enjoyed good yoni compatibility from their Moons, because both of them were born with the Moon in Purva Bhadrapada nakshatra. In addition, her Ascendant occupies the female buffalo, nakshatra (Hasta), and his occupies the male, elephant nakshatra (Bharani). Since the buffalo and the elephant are not incompatible, the Kings showed excellent yoni compatibility from their Ascendants. The compatible placements of both their Moons and Ascendants suggests confluent yoni poruttham compatibility, as was the case with Woodward/Newman as well.

Table 5. Yoni Poruttham.

NAKSHATRA NUMBER	NAKSHATRA NAME	GENDER	ANIMAL	INCOMPATIBLE YONI
1	Ashvini	Male	Horse	Buffalo
2	Bharani	Male	Elephant	Lion
3	Krittika	Female	Sheep	Monkey
4	Rohini	Male	Serpent	Mongoose
5	Mrigashirsha	Female	Serpent	Tiger, Dog
6	Ardra	Male	Dog	Dog, Rat
7	Punarvasu	Female	Cat	Monkey
8	Pushya	Male	Goat	Dog, Rat
9	Ashlesha	Male	Cat	Dog, Rat
10	Magha	Male	Rat	Cat
11	Purva Phalguni	Female	Rat	Cat
12	Uttara Phalguni	Male	Bull	Tiger
13	Hasta	Female	Buffalo	Horse
14	Chitra	Male	Tiger	Cow
15	Swati	Male	Buffalo	Horse
16	Vishakha	Female	Tiger	Cow
17	Anuradha	Female	Deer	Tiger, Dog
18	Jyeshtha	Male	Deer	Tiger, Dog

Table 5. Yoni Poruttham (continued).

Nakshatra Number	Nakshatra Name	Gender	Animal	Incompatible Yoni
19	Mula	Female	Dog	Tiger, Deer
20	Purva Ashadha	Male	Monkey	Dog, Goat
21	Uttara Ashadha	Female	Mongoose	Serpent
22	Shravana	Female	Monkey	Dog, Goat
23	Dhanishtha	Female	Lion	Elephant
24	Shatabhisha	Female	Horse	Buffalo
25	Purva Bhadrapada	Male	Lion	Elephant
26	Uttara Bhadrapada	Female	Cow	Tiger
27	Revati	Female	Elephant	Lion

RASHI

Rashi (Heap or Mass) poruttham evaluates the impact of a union on the overall prosperity of the social systems within which the couple exists, including their relationships with their extended families and in-laws, and perhaps even their impact on the prosperity of their society. Rashi poruttham gauges both the couple's impact on the public and personal society within which they must function and the extent to which the couple will be able to "fit in." As its name suggests, rashi poruttham uses rashis instead of nakshatras to evaluate compatibility. The count is still from the Moon of the female to the Moon of the male, always inclusive, and always forward in the zodiac.

Rules

1. When the male's Moon is two, five, or six rashis ahead of the female's Moon, there is no compatibility.
2. If it is three or four rashis ahead of the female's Moon the compatibility is good or average.
3. In the remaining positions (first, seventh, eighth, ninth, tenth, eleventh, or twelfth) the compatibility is excellent.

In this, and in several other cases, be careful not to confuse this poruttham method with the method of cornerstone analysis for the Moon, which draws on the more general principles of the compatibility of the four elements of Jyotisha. Porutthams are an older and different system than cornerstone analysis. Both methods have different rules to establish a distinct outcome. Rashi poruttham assesses the overall impact of prosperity on one's society, and vice versa; cornerstone analysis estimates the emotional vasana alignment of a couple. Each method is a different part of the elephant of Jyotisha to which we alluded in our Introduction.

In addition to a general enhancement or diminishment of the couple's extended family circumstances, each relative placement of the couple's Moons promises specific results. Among the incompatible placements, a male Moon in the second to the female Moon is said to harm the couple's longevity; in the fifth position, it harms marital happiness; in the sixth position, it creates difficulty with children. The third and the fourth placements, though good or average, are said by some to be linked to illness or hardship (the third) and to financial struggles (the fourth). In the excellent compatibility group, placement one promotes overall prosperity, seven enhances longevity, eight is good for children, nine indicates a strong marriage bond, ten suggests financial increase, eleven enhances enjoyment of pleasures, and twelve indicates good health and vitality.

Variants and Exceptions

1. The incompatibility of placements two, five, and six can sometimes be converted into good or average compatibility results. Exceptions for a two placement occur when the female's Moon occupies a feminine (even) rashi, for then the male's will occupy a masculine rashi. These exceptions include the following pairs of rashis: hers in Taurus, his in Gemini; hers in Cancer, his in Leo; hers in Virgo, his in Libra; hers in Scorpio, his in Sagittarius; hers in Capricorn, his in Aquarius; hers in Pisces, his in Aries. The exceptions for the placement of his Moon in the fifth to hers occur for two pairs of rashis: hers in Aries, his in Leo; and hers in Cancer, his in Scorpio.

2. When his Moon is in the sixth position, counted from hers, exceptions occur when the female's Moon occupies a masculine (odd) rashi, in which case the male's Moon will occupy a feminine rashi. These excep-

tions include the following pairs of rashis: hers in Aries, his in Virgo; hers in Gemini, his in Scorpio; hers in Leo, his in Capricorn; hers in Libra, his in Pisces; hers in Sagittarius, his in Taurus; and hers in Aquarius, his in Cancer.

3. The excellent compatibility promised when his Moon occupies the seventh rashi from hers is canceled in only two cases, for Moons that tenant Cancer-Capricorn or Leo-Aquarius. When we recall that this sort of compatibility cancellation also occurs for Gana Poruttham, we begin to suspect that matching a Cancer Moon with a Capricorn Moon, and a Leo Moon with an Aquarius Moon, is particularly difficult, all other factors being equal. This could perhaps be because the innate natures of the rulers of these pairs of rashis (Sun and Saturn-Moon and Saturn) are so thoroughly antithetical.

When we look at the charts of Woodward and Newman, we find the Moons of both occupy Aquarius, creating an excellent rashi poruttham agreement that is repeated from their Ascendants, which both appear in Sagittarius. The Kings also both have Moons in Aquarius. The excellent harmony that this poruttham produces is enhanced by the relationship between her Ascendant in Virgo and his in Aries, which is eight rashis away from hers, a position of excellent compatibility that is especially good for children.

RASHYADHIPATI

Like mahendra poruttham, rashyadhipati (rashi lord) poruttham evaluates the prospects for a couple to have strong children, and the prospects for prosperity in the lives of those offspring. The rules for rashyadhipati poruttham are broader than those of mahendra poruttham, for rashyadhipati poruttham is based on the natural relationship between the lords (*adhipati* = ruler, lord) of the rashis in which the Moons of the couple sit. The application of this straightforward rule becomes somewhat complex in practice, because grahas can display three sorts of relationship (friendly, neutral, or inimical), and some grahas do not reciprocate their relationship to others. For example, Mercury is a friend to Saturn, but Saturn is neutral to Mercury.

Rules

1. When the lords of the rashis of both partners are the same, or when they are mutually friendly (e.g., Sun-Jupiter), there is excellent compatibility for this poruttham.

2. When they are mutually neutral (e.g., Jupiter-Saturn), there is average agreement.

3. When they are mutual enemies (e.g. Sun-Venus), there is misalignment in the matter of children and those children's prosperity.

4. In the case of a one-sided relationship, the lord of the rashi of the female's Moon should be neutral to the lord of the rashi occupied by the male's Moon for agreement to occur. By way of example, if his Moon occupies Virgo (which is Mercury-ruled) and hers sits in Jupiter-ruled Sagittarius, there will be average agreement (for Jupiter is neutral to Mercury), even though, in the opposite direction (his to hers), Mercury is the enemy of Jupiter. If, in this case, hers were a Virgo Moon and his a Sagittarius Moon, there would be misalignment.

In our example charts, both the Kings and Woodward/Newman have their Moons in rashis ruled by Saturn, which creates good alignment for this poruttham. From their lagnas, Newman and Woodward also both have excellent rashyadhipati compatibility, since both have Jupiter-ruled Sagittarius Ascendants. For the Kings, his Aries Ascendant ruler Mars and her Virgo Ascendant ruler Mercury create a one-sided relationship, for Mercury is the enemy of Mars, but Mars is neutral to Mercury. Because agreement occurs only if her Moon is neutral to the rashi lord of his Moon, the Kings' Ascendants are misaligned for rashyadhipati poruttham, which vitiates their Moon alignments. Since the porutthams always are subsidiary to more fundamental methods of horoscope analysis, we once again have to assess these two horoscopes in other ways if we wish to resolve this poruttham conflict.

VASHYA

Vashya (obedient) poruttham, which evaluates the couple's mutual attraction and respect, contributes to the relationship's overall prospects, even though it is not of primary importance in this tenfold system. While gana poruttham, which plays a similar role, evaluates similarity of temperament, vashya poruttham comments on the couple's mutual harmony, which similarity of temperament does not, in and of itself, automatically guarantee.

Mutual attraction can powerfully join together the partners in a relationship, and can even potentially harmonize the differences they display in life's diverse arenas. Some believe that vashya poruttham also indicates the potential growth of the clan as a result of such a union, which would align this poruttham with mahendra and rashi porutthams.

Vashya poruttham is said to show excellent compatibility when the rashi that contains the male's Moon is attracted to the rashi that contains the female's Moon. According to most authorities, when the female's Moon rashi is attracted to that of the male, there is average agreement. Though a one-way attraction is sufficient for this poruttham, when the rare two-way attraction (Cancer-Scorpio) exists, it enhances the alignment. This poruttham is misaligned when there is no attraction in either direction. While tradition does not address the situation of two Moons in the same rashi, we can assume that such a situation creates desirable alignment for this poruttham, especially since Moons that occupy the same rashi are often deemed compatible. Table 6 lists the rashis to which each of the twelve rashis is attracted.

Table 6. Rashi Attraction for Vashya Poruttham.

ATTRACTING RASHI	ATTRACTED RASHIS
Aries	Leo, Scorpio
Taurus	Cancer, Libra
Gemini	Cancer
Cancer	Scorpio, Sagittarius
Leo	Libra
Virgo	Gemini, Pisces
Libra	Capricorn
Scorpio	Cancer, Virgo
Sagittarius	Pisces
Capricorn	Aries, Aquarius
Aquarius	Aries
Pisces	Capricorn

Both the Kings and Newman and Woodward show excellent compatibility in vashya poruttham, since their Moons all sit in Aquarius. Since Newman and Woodward also have their Ascendants in the same rashi (Sagittarius), they again have excellent agreement in this poruttham. The Kings, with his Aries Ascendant and her Virgo Ascendant, are poorly matched for vashya poruttham, as judged from their Ascendants, implying, perhaps, an enduring emotional attraction (Moon), but a diminishing long-term physical and life-style attraction (Ascendant).

RAJJU

Rajju (Rope) poruttham evaluates longevity, both of the spouse and the relationship, by measuring the *sumangali bhagyam. Mangala* commonly means "auspicious" in Sanskrit; most Indian women wear wedding necklaces called *mangala sutras* instead of wedding rings. Indians still (by and large) go into matrimony with the intention of making their first marriages endure. They put so much effort into properly matching horoscopes because they put so much value on the longevity of their relationships. One of the chief requirements for a long-term relationship is the well-being of the spouse, thus, rajju is one of the most important porutthams. Some, in fact, maintain that it is best not to proceed with a match if this poruttham is misaligned.

Rajju poruttham groups the nakshatras into five categories. Four of these—*pada* (foot), *uru* (thigh), *nabhi* (navel), and *kantha* (throat) rajjus— have an ascending *(aroha)* and a descending *(avaroha)* component, while the fifth, *shiro* (head) rajju has but one component. The twenty-seven nakshatras are assigned to the resultant nine categories of rajju as shown in Table 7.

Table 7. Nine Categories of Rajju and Corresponding Nakshatras.

Rajju	Nakshatras
Shiro rajju	Mrigashirsha, Chitra, Dhanishtha
Aroha Pada Rajju	Ashvini, Magha, Moola
Avaroha Pada Rajju	Ashlesha, Jyeshtha, Revati
Aroha Uru Rajju	Bharani, Purva Phalguni, Purva Ashadha
Avaroha Uru Rajju	Pushyami, Anuradha, Uttara Bhadrapada

Table 7. Nine Categories of Rajju and Corresponding Nakshatras (cont.)

Rajju	Nakshatras
Aroha Nabhi Rajju	Krittika, Uttara Phalguni, Uttara Ashadha
Avaroha Nabhi Rajju	Punarvasu, Vishakha, Purva Bhadrapada
Aroha Kantha Rajju	Rohini, Hasta, Shravana
Avaroha Kantha Rajju	Ardra, Swati, Shatabhisha

Rules

1. Excellent rajju agreement occurs when one partner's Moon nakshatra belongs to shiro rajju and the other partner's Moon belongs to a different category.

2. When both Moons belong to different rajju categories that have an ascending and a descending cycle, very good agreement occurs when both Moons are aroha; average when one is aroha and the other is avaroha; and barely acceptable when both are avaroha.

3. When both Moons belong to the same rajju category, there is misalignment, although certain authorities claim that Moons that share the same rajju category produce average agreement if one Moon is aroha and the other is avaroha. All sources agree, however, that misalignment occurs when both Moons are either aroha or avaroha within the same category.

Sometimes Moons that share the same nakshatra (which gives them rajju misalignment) show agreement in nakshatra poruttham. While it is best to have agreement in both nakshatra and rajju porutthams, nakshatra supercedes rajju poruttham in importance. For people with identical Moon nakshatras when nakshatra agrees but rajju does not, there is a risk that the alliance will be impermanent (perhaps, if the individual horoscopes suggest it, ending prematurely due to the spouse's death), even though the couple may make a successful match.

Newman's Shatabhisha Moon in avaroha kantha rajju and Woodward's Dhanishtha Moon in shiro rajju create excellent rajju agreement, because they are of different categories. Though their Ascendants both occupy Purva Ashadha nakshatra (aroha uru rajju), we have seen that this matches them for nakshatra poruttham, which supercedes rajju poruttham. This is particularly true because Newman's horoscope shows good longevity, both for his marriage and for his marriage partner, with all the benefics (Jupiter, Venus, and Mercury) occupying an angular bhava.[3] From one point of view, his seventh bhava of marriage partner is thus fully aspected by three natural benefics; from another, his seventh bhava lord Mercury sits in his first bhava, in the company of Jupiter and Venus, aspecting into its own bhava. Both are most desirable combinations for the well-being of the spouse.

The Ascendant nakshatras of the Kings are in aroha uru and aroha kantha rajju, which produces a very good match, but their Moons both occupy Purva Bhadrapada nakshatra in the same rajju (avaroha nabhi). Though nakshatra poruttham again prevails here, there is uncertainty around longevity, given the difficulties we have already chronicled in other porutthams for the Kings, and the confirmation we receive from other factors in their horoscopes. In Mrs. King's chart, two benefics, one of which is the seventh lord Jupiter, do tenant the seventh bhava, but that Jupiter is in a "dead" state, sitting atop the vitiating boundary between two rashis a position technically known as *rashi sandhi*. Moreover, Jupiter is conjoined by a debilitated Mercury. This is not a good combination, either for married life or for the marital partner's well-being. Once again, the porutthams provide the "color commentary," whereas the pre-eminent combinations in the natal chart provide the substance for the analysis of the karma-oriented outcome.

VEDHA

Vedha (Pious, Virtuous, Wise) poruttham evaluates the couple's resilience, their ability to ensure long-term happiness by driving away all misfortunes. Most couples qualify for this poruttham, because its stringent requirements for a mismatch make misalignment relatively rare. The following sets of nakshatras create mismatches when either partner's Moon occupies the one, and the other partner's Moon the other: Ashvini/Jyeshtha, Bharani/Anuradha, Krittika/Vishakha, Rohini/Swati, Ardra/Shravana, Punarvasu/Uttara Ashadha, Pushya/Purva Ashadha, Ashlesha/Mula, Magha/Revati, Purva Phalguni/Uttara Ashadha, Uttara Phalguni/Purva Bhadrapada, Hasta/Shatabhisha, and the trio of Mrigashirsha/Chitra/Dhanishtha. (Note that the triad of nakshatras that misalign one another—Mrigashirsha, Chitra, and Dhanishtha—are the obstreperous Mars-ruled nakshatras.) Both the Kings and Newman-Woodward match well in vedha poruttham, both from their Moons and their Ascendants.

---

[3] Maharishri Parashara, *Brihat Parashara Hora Shastra*, vol. II (Delhi: Ranjan, 1988), 45:60–61.

NADI

Many jyotishis substitute nadi (channel) for vedha as the tenth poruttham. In nadi poruttham the nakshatras are classified into three groups: *adi* (first) *nadi*, *madhya* (middle) *nadi*, and *antya* (final) *nadi*. These groups are also known as the kapha, pitta, and vata nadis, respectively, an obvious reference to the three principal constitutional types of Ayurveda, India's classical system of medicine. Table 8 shows these groups.

Table 8. Nadi Groups for Nadi Poruttham.

Adi, or Kapha, Nadi	Madhya, or Pitta, Nadi	Antya, or Vata, Nadi
Krittika	Bharani	Ashvini
Rohini	Mrigashirsha	Ardra
Ashlesha	Pushya	Punarvasu
Magha	Purva Phalguni	Uttara Phalguni
Swati	Chitra	Hasta
Vishakha	Anuradha	Jyeshtha
Uttara Ashadha	Purva Ashadha	Mula
Shravana	Dhanishtha	Shatabhisha
Revati	Uttara Bhadrapada	Purva Bhadrapada

The female's Moon nakshatra and the male's Moon nakshatra must belong to different groups if they are to have nadi poruttham agreement. Note that, while nadi poruttham agreement requires diversity, other porutthams, like gana, require similarity. In this respect, several of the other porutthams faithfully reflect life's general principle that like accommodates like. Nadi poruttham seems to approach relationships from the angle of the strength that lies in diversification.

Nadi poruttham requires us to turn to ayurvedic psychology, and the natures of kapha, pitta, and vata, the three *doshas*. These are forces that influence personality by influencing physiology. When the two members of a couple belong to the same category of dosha, there is a great tendency for them to reinforce one another's limitations (*dosha* = fault, mistake). Diversity of dosha is more likely to promote the kind of diverse behavior that will encourage these sorts of limitations to be minimized. We delve further into the doshas in chapter 8.

Woodward's and Newman's Moons match for nadi porattham, since their nakshatras of Dhanishtha and Shatabhisha belong to madhya nadi and antya nadi, respectively. They share the misaligned Purva Ashadha as their Ascendant nakshatra, however, which creates at least a neutral match for this couple, when compounded with their well-matched Moons. A similar situation prevails for the Kings, whose Moons both occupy Purva Bhadrapada. Since their Ascendant nakshatras (Bharani for him, Hasta for her) belong to madhya nadi and antya nadi respectively, however, their nadi agreement is at least average.

EVALUATION SUMMARY OF THE SAMPLE HOROSCOPES

The poruttham tradition asserts that the five most important of the ten criteria for matching charts are nakshatra, gana, yoni, rashi, and rajju porutthams. Moons that occupy opposite rashis are so highly valued that such a couple can be matched for matrimony even if they fail to score well on other porutthams, although if their Moons are Seven-Seven and they do score well on the porutthams, it is much better. Let us review how our examples fared in their evaluations for these five most important porutthams:

Nakshatra poruttham (evaluates the health and longevity of the partners with reference to one another): Woodward and Newman have good harmony from their Moons and average harmony from their Ascendants. The Kings have excellent harmony from their Moons, but disharmony from their Ascendants.

Gana poruttham (evaluates a couple's general happiness): Woodward and Newman are an excellent match, both from their Moons and Ascendants. The Kings show excellent agreement from their Moons and average agreement from their Ascendants.

Yoni poruttham (evaluates the contentment of their sexual contact): Woodward and Newman show good compatibility both from their Moons and their Ascendants. The Kings enjoyed good compatibility from their Moons and excellent compatibility from their Ascendants.

Rashi poruttham (evaluates the impact of a union on their extended families and social systems): Woodward and Newman and the Kings both show excellent rashi poruttham agreement from their Moons, which is repeated from their Ascendants.

Rajju poruttham (evaluates longevity, both of the spouse and the relation-ship): Newman's and Woodward's Moon nakshatras both create excellent rajju agreement, and, although their Ascendants do not match for rajju poruttham, they do match for nakshatra poruttham. Newman's horoscope, moreover, shows good longevity, both for his marriage and for his marriage partner. The Ascendant nakshatras produce a very good match for the Kings, but their Moons. although nakshatra poruttham again prevails here, Mrs. King's chart does not suggest longevity, either for the marriage or the marriage partner.

Our conclusions: Newman and Woodward show excellent agreement, both from the porutthams and from the combinations in their individual horo-scopes. This promises excellent compatibility and relationship longevity, which has been the case. The Kings show generally good poruttham agree-ment, but receive less positive reinforcement from their horoscopes. This situation for the Kings suggests good compatibility, but does not guarantee a lasting relationship, which, as we know, was true of their marriage.

COMMENTS AND CONCLUSIONS

A couple's compatibility increases with multiplying alignment of the various porutthams, which leads many jyotishis to seek to obtain a general agree-ment by averaging all ten poruttham criteria. While preprinted poruttham tables have been developed to make such evaluation-by-average easier, rely-ing on such seemingly clear-cut quantification can lure us into disregarding poruttham specifics. Take, for example, two couples who each show a favor-able overall poruttham score (say, seven out of ten). These couple are, de-spite their identical overall scores, still likely to encounter totally different life experiences if the first couple scores well in health and general compat-ibility, but poorly in the matter of children, and the second scores well for children, but poorly for health and general compatibility. Besides, the one couple may have scored well in each category of the five most important porutthams, while the second couple garnered the majority of their points in the least important of the ten categories.

Even more confusing is the fact that those who refer to poruttham tables are likely to find large scores listed (twenty-five out of thirty-six, for example, instead of seven out of ten). Such scores usually indicate that each poruttham was given a value that reflected its importance in the mind of the table's author. Another author, however, whose opinion of the relative importance of the porutthams differs and whose notion of what to include among the porutthams also differs, may assign each poruttham different values. A score of twenty-five on one table thus would mean something considerably different from a score of twenty-five on another table. Such variances, which are reason enough to be wary of the practice of averaging all ten criteria to obtain general poruttham agreement, also demonstrate how reliance on preprinted tables compromises the specific emphasis that the five main porutthams provide. It is due to these and other potentials for distortion of poruttham alignments that we have not included such tables in this book.

While the many jyotishis (particularly in southern India) who continue to use the porutthams extensively are generally convinced of their utility, another school of thought maintains that the porutthams do not "work." Such a blanket denunciation is, of course, as inaccurate as any blanket testimonial to the invariable validity of any of Jyotisha's principles. No principle of Jyotisha "works" for everyone all the time, but all its principles work for some people some of the time. Interesting questions can, and do, arise here. Do the porutthams work in places where they are used enduringly simply because they continue to be used thereby, heavily influencing the choice of bride and groom, or do they "work" because they actually work? Does poruttham analysis have more value as an Indian social ritual than as a precise astrological analysis, and is it that social value that makes the porutthams "work," or seem to work?

Whether or not the porutthams actually function as a primary method of chart comparison when used in the context of the society in which they arose is of little significance to us here. For us, the real utility of poruttham analysis lies in the ways in which it can enhance the specificity of compatibility analysis—how it can highlight particular areas of relationship strength and weakness. The porutthams are likely to provide little more than flavor to the ongoing relationship disappointment or satisfaction promised in those whose horoscopes display some more primary super-afflicted or ultra-favorable relationship dynamics. The value of the porutthams as indicators seems to increase substantially in those charts whose relationship karma is less fixed.

One reason why the porutthams may seem not to "work" is that they are traditionally measured exclusively from the Moon, the desire body (*manomayakosha*). Though, in past ages, the Moon's position was paramount in Jyotisha, it has been superseded in this Iron Age of Kali Yuga by the Ascendant, from which we read the physical realities of an individual and their world. Even if a good score on nakshatra poruttham, as read from their Moons, makes a couple agree on their approach to health, and disease, afflictions to their health as read individually from the Ascendants in their horoscopes, may be the actual reality of their lives together.

We see this in the charts of the Kings, for, though they match well in the poruttham of longevity when calculated from the positions of their Moons, he considerably predeceased her—something hinted at by the misaligned nakshatra poruttham based on the Ascendants. The emotional compatibility that this Moon-based poruttham agreement indicates may be the reason why Dr. King has been a continuing presence in Mrs. King's life, even after his physical death. Extending poruttham analysis to the Ascendant as well as the Moon reinforces the primacy of horoscopic combinations in the individual charts in determining the fate of a particular relationship.

When we combine the influence of the porutthams with the indications of the horoscope we come up with four groups of possible outcomes:

1. Poruttham match corroborated by horoscope combination match creates excellent compatibility and relationship longevity.
2. Poruttham match without horoscope combination match creates good compatibility, but does not guarantee a lasting relationship.
3. Poruttham disharmony when horoscope combinations are well-disposed may create a lasting relationship that is not likely to be particularly harmonious.
4. Poruttham disharmony combined with horoscope disharmony is unlikely to promote a successful relationship.

6

IS SHE A LAKSHMI?
IS HE A KUBERA?

The previous three chapters focus on assessing graha interactions between two charts. We now return to evaluating relationships mainly through a single horoscope, our purpose being to appraise the horoscopes of those who have become (or are about to become) new components of already existing relationship units. Jyotishis routinely scan the birth charts of newborns, recent spouses or spouses to be, partners to be absorbed into an established business, and other such clan entrants for information on how the karmas of such significant others will affect those of their new relatives.

India, as a nation, values emotional over mundane reality. Indian society continues to be acutely aware of relationship dynamics, in particular the energetics of what sociologists call the "extended family system." Absorbing new members into such a system reflects the subtle karmic truth that those important others whom you attract into your life (and who are attracted into it) are mirrors that reflect the condition of your bhavas. For those who know how to see, these salient others become useful signposts along the roads their own life journeys, and the moments of their induction into the family act as prashnas (inquiries) for that family system.

When a child is born in India, its parents often ask their jyotishi, "Will she be a Lakshmi? Will he be a Kubera?" Lakshmi being the goddess and Kubera the god of wealth, this question is really twofold: "Will this child be prosperous independently?" and "Will this child enhance its family's fortunes?" While many people ask such questions out of greed, the queries themselves are soundly motivated astrologically. Examining a child's chart gives a good general idea of what that child's lot in later life will be, how that lot will influence the conditions of any pre-existing relationship systems into which the child is born, and what can be done to ameliorate or enhance the situation. Similar questions are often put to the jyotishi regarding a prospective bride or bridegroom, or a proposed business partner or investor.

The answer to such an inquiry often throws light on the imminent destiny of the family (or other partnership) that has just taken on a new member. When a small child is fated to obtain something like money of which it has no knowledge and cannot handle because of its age, that something very often accrues to its *poshaka* (nourisher), the person who nourishes it and provides for it. When a baby is born with a silver spoon in its mouth, it is the poshaka who initially benefits from the prosperity yogas. These effects become evident during the child's first year in roughly two out of three cases, and within the second year in the remaining cases. How much poshakas benefit from the little Lakshmi or Kubera they nourish depends on the strength of their horoscopes. While a nourisher who is already rich will probably become richer, one who is poverty stricken may not be able to rise further than the middle class, unless he or she also has some powerful prosperity yogas that are ready to kick in. Bill Gates' parents, after all, didn't become millionaires immediately after his birth. It is quite likely, though, that they did experience a perceptible up-tick in their prosperity at that time.

It is also likely that the parents gave no thought to the possibility that their infant might deliver abundance into their home. On one occasion, our Jyotisha guru was consulting with a couple who started to crow about how well off they had become. They were doing so well, they reported, that they were now flying about the world in all directions instead of creeping along, earthbound, by auto and train. They had just had a child, and neither had connected their new-found prosperity with the child. After they left, our guruji spat out, "Did it ever occur to this couple that they may be sitting on these planes as a result of their little child? Do they bow down to it in thanks? No, their egos have become so inflated that they are too busy congratulating themselves for their good fortune to think about such things."

On the other hand, it is certainly fortunate for those children whose **births** promise misfortune that most people today have forgotten this principle. Some of the worst excesses ever performed in the name of Jyotisha have been committed on innocent children whose horoscopes appeared to predict tribulation for its parents or guardians. Parental egos should no more be cast down if a child is destined to impoverish them than they should be inflated if a child is born to pour gold into the family coffers. Relationship is a matter of karma and rnanubandhana (the bonds of karmic debt). A child who comes to you with a horoscope of destitution does so because your own destitution karmas have also ripened and are waiting for you to consume them. The child is as much an instrument of your karmic fulfillment as you are of its.

Similarly, a child who comes to you destined to enjoy prosperity has come to you because you, too, are destined to enjoy some prosperity. If you do right by that child, your mutual prosperity may develop yet further. If you mistreat it, you will be garroting the goose that is ready to lay your own golden eggs. Students of the law of karma marvel at the elegant sort of neutrality that involves both parties, often unconsciously, in creating their own situations. It is a dance, an oft-impassioned, but unconscious, ballet of bhava evolving into rasa. The more impassioned and heartfelt the steps, the more intense and satisfying the sukha that it spawns will be.

The information given in this chapter about new family members applies, in most cases, to contractual partnerships as well. For most people, the marriage partner is the only "chosen" family member; all other family members are acquired as karmic "accidents" of birth. When we have the opportunity "choose" a spouse, or for that matter a business partner, we must make very sure that we are mingling auras with people who will promote our mutual prosperity, not lead us into calamities like scandal or bankruptcy. Jyotisha can show us what sort of abundance dance will work best for us, and indicate with whom we should dance it. The techniques introduced in this chapter are just a beginning. But beware! This information is not to be used to create partiality or prejudice toward any of your extant dance partners. Do not twist the knowledge of Jyotisha. Use it instead to pry yourself out of the karmic ruts into which you have fallen.

GANDANTA

Gandanta is one of Jyotisha's frequently misused principles. It occurs when a child is born with its Moon (or sometimes its Ascendant) occupying the last 3°20' of Ashlesha, Jyeshtha, or Revati nakshatras, or the first 3°20' of Ashvini, Magha, or Mula nakshatras. Gandanta is but one variant of the more general phenomena of *sandhi* ("juncture," in Sanskrit). Just as in the natural world the junctures of dawn and twilight are the weakest manifestations of both day and night, the astrological gandanta is particularly inopportune, because it is a juncture of two rashis as well as two nakshatras. Classical tradition suggests that grahas located at these points are very weak, and indicate major problems in a person's life, unless appropriate remedies are used to mitigate the karmic implications of such placements, particularly when the Moon or the Ascendant is in gandanta.

Birth in these portions of these nakshatras also promises disturbances to one or another member of the family into which the child is born. Birth in the first quarter of Ashvini or Magha, for instance, is said to be bad for the father, especially for the first three months after birth. Children born in Mula are said to create trouble for their older brothers. Similar results are also traditionally attributed to other nakshatras that do not technically create a gandanta, including portions of Bharani, Rohini, Pushya, Uttara Phalguni, Chitra, and Vishakha.

Gandanta is a good example of the sort of principle that should be used to help forecast what lies ahead, not to encumber someone else with blame for one's own karmic burdens. Considering that portions of almost half the nakshatras in the sky promise some desolation to the family that has a child born in them, the potential for gandanta to be used for emotional blackmail is immense. Gandanta, which has great potential for being misunderstood, should never be the sole point of judgment in predicting of gloom for kindred. Dire portents must always be supported by confluence elsewhere in the horoscope. It is prudent, for example, to look for confirmation of damage to a father in an afflicted ninth bhava or ninth lord or Sun, trouble to a sibling in distress to the eleventh or third bhavas, or their lords or significators.

We must also let us be sufficiently creative in our interpretations to fit the dicta of Jyotisha to the world in which we live. Take the case of a father and son whose Moons both occupy Hasta nakshatra. One classical interpretation is that they will have difficulty living under the same roof. This could mean that the child's parents will divorce, with the mother gaining custody of her son; or it could mean that father and son will never see eye-to-eye. In one particular instance of this combination, father and son get along exceptionally well on those occasions when they are together, which are infrequent, since the father is often away on business. The letter of the prediction is thus fulfilled, with no particular anguish on either part—in good measure because the natal horoscopes of the father and son promise a good outcome to their relationships from several other angles of interpretation.

Principles like gandanta tend to work in such tidy, benign ways in horoscopes whose foundations (built of Ascendant, Moon, and Sun) are strong. Significant afflictions that promise results akin to those gandanta threatens may make it more difficult for two people to create agreeable solutions. Additional malefic influences may, in fact, encourage them to become enmeshed with one another, often without consciously intending to do so, whether or not such entanglement is productive. For example, Saturn, when positioned in Cancer in a child's chart, may indicate a very difficult pregnancy for the mother, especially when sufficient confluence exists to provide confirmation. If the experiences of pregnancy and birth are particularly extreme, the mother may develop such a strong attachment to the child that, with every new challenge, she may allow herself to be taken over by the hopes and fears that she feels for it. By thus succumbing, she may create within herself some of what Saturn, in Cancer, promises for a child: that its mother (Cancer is ruled by Moon, the significator of mother) may regularly be dominated by anxiety (the province of Saturn).

PREDICTING FOR THE FAMILY FROM THE HOROSCOPE OF THE CHILD

A child's birth chart can be the source of a wide variety of useful information. Suppose, for example, that an infant's horoscope indicates that it will leave its home soon after birth. One likely implication is that the child's entire family will move, since the baby will not be able to decamp on its own. Such a prompt move might occur after the birth of a child in whose horoscope most of the grahas occupy cardinal rashis (Aries, Cancer, Libra, Capricorn), rashis that promise movement. This is particularly true if one of these rashis is the child's Ascendant. In cases like these, the child's karma acts as a sort of catalyst to activate the pre-existing karmas of the other family members.

When jyotishis in India examine a newborn's chart, they commonly make predictions for the whole family according to the baby's dashas, yogas, and so on. If the infant's ninth bhava and Sun are well placed, the jyotishi will take it as a sign that the father will do well; if the fourth bhava is strong, the child's mother will do well, particularly if the Moon is also comfortably situated. A child whose chart brims with yogas for wealth and power is likely to find its family's fortunes improving to permit it to enjoy the juicy fruits of some of its karmas at a tender age.

Figure 19 shows the chart of the first of two brothers who are most assuredly Kuberas, for their births paralleled dramatic improvements in their parents' affluence. This horoscope, which has a Leo Ascendant, contains two dharma karma adhipati yogas (first lord Sun combined with seventh lord Saturn, and Sun combined with tenth lord Venus). There is also a major *dhana* ("riches") yoga: the combination of second and eleventh lord Mercury with the first and tenth lords, aspected by fifth lord Jupiter. In addition, raja yoga karaka Mars is exalted, and aspects the Ascendant lord. Moreover, lagnesha (which occupies the nakshatra of the raja yoga karaka) aspects the lagna, and the exalted Moon occupies the tenth bhava. As if this were not enough, this boy's horoscope also displays the lesser-known, but very noteworthy, *vasumati* yoga, which is formed when natural benefics alone occupy the *upachaya* bhavas (bhavas three, six, ten, and eleven) as counted from a strong Moon.

This horoscope is clearly brimming with prosperity. We can confidently predict that this prosperity will accrue to his parents, both because they are his poshakas and because his ninth lord of father and fourth lord of mother are exalted, which promises that the parents will prosper immensely. In fact, within one year of this child's birth, his family's income tripled; within five years, it was six times greater than it had been at his birth. In addition, the family acquired a huge property within a year of the birth.

Major yogas in the horoscope of a child indicate positive changes in its family's fortunes, whether or not the appropriate dashas are operating, but a favorable series of dashas will significantly magnify such effects. Here the

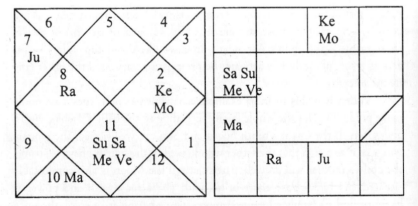

Figure 19. Chart of older Kubera brother.

child was born at the tail end of the dasha of his Sun, the graha that is involved in so many of his beneficent yogas. The dasha of the Moon, which is
exalted, anchors a vasumati yoga, and occupies the nakshatra of an Ascendant lord that is potent because it occupies an angular bhava and thus creates raja and dhana yogas. Moreover, the dasha of his Mars, his exalted raja
yoga karaka, occupies an upachaya bhava, further reflecting this prosperity
back to his mother and father (since Mars rules the ninth and fourth
bhavas). All of this implies that both the child and his poshakas are likely to
benefit from the good combinations in his horoscope.

Figure 20 gives the chart of the younger brother, who, curiously
enough, also enjoys a Leo Ascendant, and also has Ascendant lord Sun
aspecting his Ascendant. The Sun also occupies a beneficial nakshatra, in
this case, that of strong fifth lord Jupiter. Here again, the second and eleventh lords are the same graha, a Mercury that conjoins both the ninth lord
Mars—also the raja yoga karaka—and first lord Sun. This combination
gives both raja yogas (Ascendant lord plus fourth lord, and Ascendant lord
plus ninth lord) and dhana yogas of a potency similar to that which exists in
his brother's chart. In addition, there is a very potent *gaja kesari-yoga* and a
super-potent *hamsa yoga*, which occurs both from the Ascendant and the
Moon, with Jupiter strong by virtue of occupying the middle of his own
rashi. Furthermore, the tenth lord occupies the ninth bhava, supported by
the aspect of a yoga-causing Jupiter.

The strengths that exist in this birth chart caused yet another wave of
prosperity to roll over the family with the birth of this second child. This
wave's crests were amplified by a series of desirable dashas, for the boy

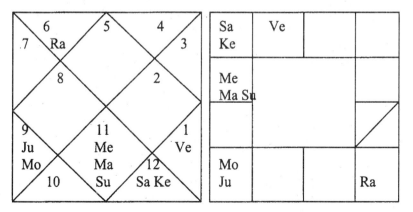

Figure 20. Chart of younger Kubera brother.

began his life in the dasha of tenth lord Venus, which sits in the ninth bhava as a participant of a raja yoga, because it is aspected by powerful fifth lord Jupiter. Venus is followed by the dasha of Ascendant lord Sun, after which this boy's dasha sequence follows that of his equally fortunate elder brother.

YOGIS, AVAYOGIS, AND DUPLICATE YOGIS

Another concept that we may profitably apply to the birthcharts of prospective new family members is described by the late brilliant jyotishi, S. Iyer of Bangalore, who maintained that he developed his system from seeds present in works on Nadi Jyotisha.[1] We have, for several years, used an expanded version of Iyer's system, which our Jyotisha guru taught to us. We find it to be reasonably accurate. Several parts of the system are too complex to describe here, but a few lend themselves to the analysis of all sorts of human relationships. One portion of the method that is of great utility in investigating relationship interactions is that of the yogi, avayogi and duplicate yogi. The *yogi* is the graha that provides prosperity to the native, while the *avayogi* obstructs prosperity. The *duplicate yogi* enhances (under certain conditions) the prosperity promised by the yogi, and reduces any destitution that the avayogi might forebode.

Calculating the Yogi, the Avayogi, and the Duplicate Yogi

This calculation is governed by the following rules:

1. Derive the longitude of the yoga point using this formula: longitude of the Sun + longitude of the Moon + 93°20', all longitudes being measured from 0° Aries.
2. The graha in the Vimshottari dasha system that rules the nakshatra containing the longitude of the yoga point is the yogi of the horoscope. This nakshatra is known as the yoga nakshatra.
3. The two nakshatras that trine the yoga nakshatra share the quality of the latter, to a reduced degree. These two nakshatras, which are also ruled by the yogi, are always ten and nineteen nakshatras distant from the yoga nakshatra.
4. The graha that rules the rashi containing the longitude of the yoga point is the duplicate yogi of the horoscope.

---

[1] H. R. Seshadri Ayer, *New Techniques of Prediction,* 2d ed., vols. I and II (Bangalore, India: Rohini, 1970).

5. Derive the longitude of the avayoga point with this formula: longitude of the yoga point + 186°40'.
6. The graha in the Vimshottari dasha system that rules the nakshatra containing the longitude of the avayoga point is the *avayogi* of the horoscope. This nakshatra is known as the *avayoga nakshatra*.
7. The two nakshatras that trine the avayoga nakshatra share the quality of the latter, but to a lesser degree. These two nakshatras, which are ruled by the avayogi, are always ten and nineteen nakshatras distant from the avayoga nakshatra.
8. Note that, in five of the thirty-six possible combinations of rashi ruler and nakshatra ruler, the duplicate yogi and the avayogi can be the same graha.
9. Note that, in two of the thirty-six possible combinations of rashi ruler and nakshatra ruler, the duplicate yogi and the yogi can be the same graha.

A couple of examples will help clarify these calculations and concepts. Joanne Woodward's Sun sits at 15°11' of Aquarius, which is 315°11' from 0° Aries, the beginning of the zodiac. Her Moon sits at 2°00' Aquarius (which is 302°00' from 0° Aries). The sum of these two longitudes is 617°11', to which we add 93°20', for a total of 710°31'. Since this total is greater than 360°, we subtract 360° from it, which gives us 350°31', which gives 20°31' of Pisces, as her yoga point. This point appears in Revati nakshatra, which is therefore her yoga nakshatra. Revati's ruler is Mercury, who becomes her yogi. The two nakshatras that trine Revati are Ashlesha (the tenth nakshatra from Revati) and Jyeshtha (the nineteenth nakshatra from Revati). Both of these Mercury-ruled nakshatras are also prosperity nakshatras, though to a lesser extent than is Revati. Jupiter, the lord of Pisces, is Woodward's duplicate yogi.

When we add 186°40' to Woodward's yoga point of 350°31', we get 537°11', from which we again subtract 360° to get 177°11', or 27°11' of Virgo, as her avayoga point. This point appears in Chitra nakshatra, which is thus her avayoga nakshatra. Chitra's lord is Mars, who becomes Woodward's avayogi. Chitra's two trinal nakshatras are Dhanishta (tenth from Chitra) and Mrigashirsha (nineteenth from Chitra). Both of these Mars-ruled nakshatras are also prosperity-obstructing nakshatras, though to a lesser extent than Chitra.

To determine Paul Newman's yogi, we add his Sun's longitude (283°14') to that of his Moon (308°51') and then add 93°20'. From the grand total of these longitudes (685°25'), we subtract 360°, for a total of 325°25'. This point (25°25' of Aquarius) is his yoga point, which appears in Purva Bhadrapada nakshatra, whose ruler is Jupiter, who is thus Newman's yogi. Purva Bhadrapada's trinal nakshatras are Punarvasu and Vishakha, both ruled by Jupiter. Newman's duplicate yogi is Saturn, the lord of Aquarius, and his avayoga nakshatra is Uttara Phalguni, making the Sun his avayogi. His avayoga nakshatra's trinal nakshatras are Uttara Ashadha and Krittika, both also ruled by the Sun.

Using the Yogi, the Avayogi, and the Duplicate Yogi

When a bhava lord is the yogi, or conjoins the yogi, or occupies the yoga nakshatra or its trines, the individual signified by that bhava is very likely to assist the owner of that horoscope somehow to become more prosperous, directly or indirectly. We use "prosperity" here in a liberal sense, for while your yogi often measurably impacts your material prosperity, sometimes your relationship with the person that the yogi indicates will do no more than enhance your sense of emotional stability. That emotional support, however, may be just the thing that you need at that moment to proceed forward with those actions that will advance your prosperity.

The opposite is true of the avayogi. When a bhava lord is the avayogi, or conjoins the avayogi, or occupies the avayoga nakshatra or its trines, the individual signified by that bhava is very likely to inhibit, obstruct, or destroy an individual's prosperity. Judge how much that prosperity will be benefited or detrimented by the strength of the bhava involved, and contrast it with the strength of the yogi or avayogi. In addition to the typical factors of strength, the bhava position of the yogi and the avayogi is very important. Both the yogi and avayogi are well placed if they occupy angular or trinal bhavas, and are ill placed if in bad bhavas. They are usually neutral if they sit in bhavas two or eleven. A yogi who occupies a good bhava will provide greater abundance than will a yogi who occupies the sixth, eighth, or twelfth bhavas. A debilitated avayogi that occupies a bad bhava will disturb affluence far less than an exalted avayogi who occupies the Ascendant or some other desirable bhava. If a strong yogi is an indicator of prosperity, a weak avayogi represents absence of obstruction to prosperity, which becomes a sort of backhanded prosperity.

We can apply this principle to any of our "partners" in life. If your fifth lord, for example, is the yogi, or if it conjoins the yogi or occupies the yoga nakshatra (or, to a lesser extent, its trines) your children, whether already born or yet to be born, are likely to be Lakshmis or Kuberas for you. We can make similar predictions for the fourth lord (the mother, ancestors), ninth lord (father, guru), third lord (younger siblings, neighbors), eleventh lord (friends, older siblings), sixth lord (maternal uncles, and even enemies), and tenth lord (government, employer). Even the twelfth lord or bhava can be influenced positively by the yogi, causing us, perhaps, to prosper through our "relationship" with foreign countries.

We will focus here on the seventh bhava in the context of marital or business partnerships (though we could just as well use a person's seventh bhava to evaluate his or her lawyer, or, for that matter, anyone with whom that individual relates who does not fall into a readily identifiable relationship). The basic principle for use of the yogi, avayogi, and duplicate yogi is quite simple when we confine relationship assessment to a single horoscope. Prosperity through marriage or business partnership is implied when the yogi of a chart links potently to its seventh bhava. If, however, instead the avayogi combines with the seventh bhava, prosperity through marriage or business partnership is imperiled. Keen judgment must be applied when both the yogi and avayogi link to the factors of the seventh bhava. In such mixed cases, one must assess the innate strength in the chart of both yogi and avayogi, and their involvement in yogas for either wealth or poverty, to determine which will overpower the other. The extent of the results that the yogi or the avayogi can provide will be in direct proportion to their strength.

A link between the yogi or the avayogi and the seventh bhava can occur in any one of the following ways (listed in descending order of importance):

1. The degree of the cusp of the seventh bhava occupies the yoga or avayoga nakshatra;[2]
2. The lord of the seventh bhava occupies the yoga or avayoga nakshatra;
3. The lord of the seventh bhava is the yogi or avayogi;
4. The seventh bhava is occupied or aspected by the yogi or avayogi;
5. The lord of the seventh bhava is in association with or aspected by the yogi or avayogi.

---

[2] The cusp of the seventh bhava is the precise degree of the seventh bhava, which is precisely 180° from the degree of the Ascendant.

The duplicate yogi's uses are few but powerful. In those two instances where the duplicate yogi and the yogi of the horoscope become the same graha, and that graha links to the seventh bhava in one of these five prescribed ways, prosperity through the partner becomes doubly assured. On the five occasions when the duplicate yogi and the avayogi become the same graha, which happens to link to the seventh bhava in one of the ordained ways, the prosperity-obstructing dynamic of the avayogi will be favorably modified after some time. This often means that the relationship will be punctuated by prosperity "ups and downs" that will usually fluctuate over the life of the relationship, moving more toward the plus side.

When the yogi and the duplicate yogi are two distinctly different grahas, and the duplicate yogi influences the yogi, the confluence generated renders prosperity through the partner yet more assured, provided that the yogi connects to the seventh bhava or its lord in the required manner. In this context of prosperity, the duplicate yogi influences the yogi either when the yogi occupies one of the three nakshatras that the duplicate yogi rules, or when the duplicate yogi associates with or aspects the yogi.

The same interpretation is warranted, even when a duplicate yogi that also happens to be the avayogi contacts the yogi, except that, in such an instance, the prosperity acquired through the partner will usually be accompanied by some significant trauma, or a great struggle at the very least. When a duplicate yogi links to a distinctly different avayogi, and that avayogi is connected to the seventh bhava in the requisite manner, obstruction to prosperity will result, in a degree that will depend on which of the two grahas is stronger.

The implications of these several principles are wide and varied, but a basic grasp of their spirit will enable intuitive students to synthesize the impact of combinations of the yogi, the avayogi, and the duplicate yogi on the seventh bhava, either singly or severally. Some illustrative examples will help to point the way to such integrated interpretation.

Joanne Woodward's chart shows Mercury, her yogi, ruling the seventh bhava. This suggests that her spouse, who is represented by her seventh lord, will improve her prosperity. Mercury is, however, both conjoined with an exalted Mars, her avayogi, and aspected by Jupiter, her duplicate yogi. Though this state of affairs is exceptionally mixed, it is likely that, while her powerful avayogi will create some problems, an overall experience of improved prosperity through her partner will prevail in her life. We conclude this on the basis of the enhancement that her duplicate yogi Jupiter provides to her yogi, Mercury, and the way in which that duplicate yogi modifies her avayogi. The raja yoga that Mercury and Mars create in the second bhava of liquid assets, which itself greatly promotes prosperity, strongly reinforces this conclusion. The influence of the yogi, the duplicate yogi, and the raja yoga on the avayogi here renders Mars a manageable annoyance in the otherwise very favorable scenario of gaining financial benefit through the husband. Perhaps it was this manageable avayogi, Mars, that inspired her to leave her career subsequent to her marriage to Newman.

The fact that Paul Newman's yogi, Jupiter, both aspects his seventh bhava and conjoins his seventh lord, and is aspected by his duplicate yogi, suggest that his spouse will greatly enhance his prosperity. The case for this in Newman's chart is clean and straightforward, because the Sun, his avayogi, does not influence the seventh bhava or its lord in any of the ways noted above. It seems, therefore, that we have, in the case of Newman and Woodward, a case of karmically appropriate partners for prosperity, since the yogis in both charts strongly promise the same affluent outcome through the partner. Not every case of prosperity through the partner will have this happy reciprocal situation, of course, or this connection of yogi and duplicate yogi to the seventh bhava or its lord. The odds are high, however, that prosperity will indeed flow through the partner in horoscopes where the yogi influences the seventh bhava and/or its lord, particularly when such a yogi is strong. The projected prosperity level will magnify when the duplicate yogi supports the yogi, all the more so if the yogi already participates in raja or dhana yogas.

An extremely complicated situation occurs in the horoscope of Jacqueline Onassis, whose financial prosperity benefited extraordinarily through her two marriages, especially through inheritance subsequent to the death of both partners. Her yogi, Rahu, occupies the seventh bhava of her chart, and is supported by occupying Bharani, one of the three nakshatras of Venus, her duplicate yogi. Although Venus is both duplicate yogi and avayogi, the contact that Venus enjoys with the yogi provides a prosperity confluence that permits us to view Venus more as duplicate yogi than as avayogi.

Moreover, the degree of Onassis's seventh bhava falls in Bharani, her avayoga nakshatra, and her seventh lord Mars occupies Purva Phalguni, one of nakshatras that trines Bharani. This triple confluence of partnership prosperity-obstructing placements (yogi occupying avayoga nakshatra, seventh bhava cusp falling in avayoga nakshatra, and seventh lord occupying avayoga nakshatra trine) would have totally submerged the benefit of the yogi's occupation of the seventh bhava had not the influence of Venus as avayogi been modified. This is a good example of how important a role the duplicate yogi can play in a chart.

Material abundance alone does not yield sukha, however, and Rahu's occupation of that seventh bhava in combination with mind-significator Moon did nothing to encourage happiness in her married life. This is particularly true since a malefic, when it becomes the yogi of a horoscope, tends to promise material prosperity, even while it denies emotional satisfaction. At least her relationship with JFK worked; while they had their share of problems together, they also greatly enhanced one another, and somehow pulled through till the end with the help of their strong multiple cornerstone alignments.

Using the Yogi in Chart Comparison

We have, thus far, considered the yogis and avayogis of individual horoscopes. Now we will examine where the yoga nakshatra or the avayoga nakshatra of one chart falls in the horoscope of another. In general, when a person with whom you want to establish a relationship has Ascendant or Moon occupying your yoga or avayoga nakshatra, that person is very likely to support or obstruct your prosperity, respectively. Such results will be particularly marked if the concerned yogi or avayogi is both well placed and strong.

This principle, which also applies, to a lesser degree, to the trinal nakshatras of the yoga or avayoga nakshatras, is but one portion of a complex system. Though it is a piece that will often work very well, it will occasionally fail, because it has been removed from the fuller context of Iyer's grander system. In this spirit, note that one possible exception to the foregoing occurs when the avayogi is both poorly placed and weak in a birthchart. In such cases, another whose Ascendant and/or Moon occupies the nakshatra of that weak avayogi may well promote prosperity, though perhaps only after some obstacles and setbacks between the relaters are overcome.

For a stunning example of the method described in the preceding paragraphs we need look no further than the horoscopes of Queen Elizabeth II and her consort, Prince Philip. Prince Philip's yoga nakshatra is Uttara Ashadha, for his yoga point falls at precisely 29°25' of Sagittarius. He will, consequently, tend to prosper through people born with their Ascendant or their Moon in the nakshatra of Uttara Ashadha. Queen Elizabeth II is born with her Ascendant in Uttara Ashadha, within about 1° of Prince Philip's yoga point! Is there any doubt that he has measurably and materially benefited through their alliance?

Using yogis and avayogis in a similar, but more specifically synastrical, vein, we can look into the birth chart of a prospective spouse and examine both the lord of the seventh bhava and the lord of the nakshatra in which the cusp of the seventh bhava falls. To illustrate, let us look into the charts of Jack and Jill, our nursery-rhyme couple who are contemplating going up the hill of marriage. We begin by examining both the lo..! of Jill's seventh bhava and the lord of the nakshatra occupied by the cusp of her seventh bhava. If either of these grahas is the yogi of Jack's chart, or occupies, in Jill's own chart, the nakshatra that is the yoga nakshatra of Jack's horoscope, this indicates a strong potential for a prosperous marital match. By implication, if either of these grahas is the avayogi or occupies the avayoga nakshatra of Jack's chart, the match may encourage Jacks's prosperity to fall down, and Jill's to come tumbling after. The same principles apply (albeit to a lesser degree) to the trinal nakshatras of the yoga and the avayoga nakshatras.

If we continue with our prior example of Queen Elizabeth II and Prince Philip, we discover that the cusp of his seventh bhava falls at 20°48' of Gemini, which puts that seventh cusp in the Jupiter-ruled nakshatra of Punarvasu. Since Jupiter is the yogi of the Queen's chart, this combination supports the previously described prosperity-enhancing dynamic that Prince Charles and Queen Elizabeth II share. Nor does the synastry of their yogis stop here. Mercury, the lord of his seventh bhava occupies Punarvasu, a trinal nakshatra to Vishakha, her Jupiter-ruled yoga nakshatra. In other words, the rashi lord of his seventh cusp occupies a nakshatra ruled by her yogi. Anyone who cares to work through the charts of another mutually prosperous couple will quickly note that Newman's seventh bhava is ruled by Mercury, Woodward's yogi.

Both of the foregoing examples are instances of one-sided relationships, of one individual's seventh bhava creating a relationship to the yogi of the other that is not present in the opposite direction. When the relationship between the seventh bhava of one chart with the yogi of another be reciprocal, it creates an exceptionally strong indication for viable, workable compatibility. When such a relationship of double activation exists with the avayogi, a signal lack of prosperity compatibility is likely. If both seventh bhavas of the horoscopes are connected to the yogi of the other, a cornucopia of prosperity is implied; both seventh cusps connected to the avayogi of the other may reinforce a lack of prosperity. If the seventh bhava of the one is linked to the yogi of the other, and the seventh bhava of the second connects to the avayogi of the first, a convoluted dynamic obtains in which one partner perceives prosperity and the other feels that prosperity is being obstructed by the first.

One-sided relationships always demand insightful interpretation. Suppose the nakshatra or rashi lord of Jack's seventh bhava is Jill's yogi, but neither the nakshatra lord nor the rashi lord of Jill's seventh bhava is Jack's yogi or avayogi. In such a case, the relationship prosperity is still likely to be very good, but it will be skewed in Jill's favor; she will be more likely to find herself benefited by the prosperity dynamics of their relationship than will Jack. Should the nakshatra or rashi lord of Jill's seventh bhava also simultaneously be Jack's avayogi, a complex relationship arises that will definitely be skewed to benefit Jill and to obstruct Jack's prosperity through their marital alliance. In such an instance, Jack is not likely to profit through their alliance to any reasonable degree. This neat package of emphasis often applies in the case of one-sided relationships, though it does occasionally break down. One thing that usually holds true in the case of one-sided relationships of a yogi or avayogi with the seventh bhava of another is that one or the other of the partners noticeably enhances or obstructs the prosperity of the other. This situation is the case with the one-sided contacts between both Prince Philip and Queen Elizabeth II, and between Newman and Woodward.

Examining yogis and avayogis across two charts can be used to evaluate synastry in any number of other significant relationships. For example, the person that the tenth bhava of a horoscope represents is a potential employer, in the form of a company or boss. Should your tenth lord also be your yogi, you may generally expect a prosperous business relationship with such a partner. A situation in which the lord of the tenth bhava of the horoscope of such a company or boss occupies your yoga nakshatra will also be felicitous. Your prosperity may even, on occasion, be benefited should your employer's yogi or yoga nakshatra link to your tenth bhava. In either case, there is a noticeable tendency for one or the other party to be highly benefited by the association. Ideally, the contacts between the yogis and yoga nakshatras with the tenth bhava should be reciprocal, leading to reciprocal prosperity.

Contacts of the tenth bhava with the avayogi and the avayoga nakshatra have the opposite implication: a lack of prosperity. More complex situations will require greater analysis, with both the general tone of the horoscopes and the strength and placement of the yogis or avayogis helping to determine how intense the effect will be in such instances.

A similar sequence of principles can be used for familial relationships that involve blood ties, where choice is usually much less of a factor than it is in romantic or business liaisons. Your mother is your mother, after all, and nothing can change that relationship. Should the appropriate corner-stones—Ascendants, Suns, and Moons—in your birth chart and that of your mother create good mutual alignments, your overall relationship vasana with her is likely to be one of mutual support. If concurrently, how-ever, the cusp of her fifth bhava falls in your avayoga nakshatra, you would be unwise to go into business with her, because some undesirable residual karmic knot, some obstructive prosperity tension, likely exists between the two of you in the context of commerce. Similarly, the fact that the cusp of your mother's fifth bhava falls in your yoga nakshatra is not sufficient cause to go into business with her, even though that business may make money, if the cornerstones of your horoscopes do not otherwise harmonize. The busi-ness success with your mother anticipated by such combinations may worsen other areas of your overall relationship. At the very least, it will probably make you ask yourself this futile question: "With such good indi-cations for prosperity between us, why can't my mother and I get along?"

The primary determinant of relationship success is its functionality: does it or does it not work reasonably well? The yogi and avayogi do not in-variably yield black or white analysis (either no obstacles, or insurmount-able ones, respectively). All they suggest is whether or not the relationship will promote prosperity overall. If a business executive who joins a firm for which one of these relationships exists between his yogi and the firm's tenth bhava, he may develop a prosperous relationship with that firm. Even though this relationship may cause ample cash to flow in his direction, how-ever, his experience there may be so problem-filled due to other astrological indications that sukha will completely elude him. Likewise, a manager who works for a company that links his or her avayogi to the company's tenth bhava may love the job, even though it pays poorly.

The yogi and avayogi provide guidelines for determining which actors in your life drama are likely to promote or detract from your prosperity. Employ-ing them can greatly enhance the sophistication of compatibility analysis, but you will need practice, patience, experience, and skilled intuition to learn how to use them effectively.

7

POISON DAMSELS AND MARTIAN BLEMISHES

If some people live the lives of Lakshmis and Kuberas, others seem destined to experience relationship outcomes that are more difficult to enjoy. Over the many centuries that Jyotisha has been used to deliberate the purpose and effect of relationships, certain pointers toward less-than-desirable relationship experiences have been identified. We here introduce four of these, three of which are judged typically from a single horoscope and a fourth, which, judged initially from a single horoscope, is then compared to the chart of a prospective spouse. While the first of these focuses on the two luminaries, being based on combinations of the day of the week, the nakshatra, and the phase of the Moon at birth, the others each center on one of the major malefics: Mars, Rahu/Ketu, and Saturn.

VISHA KANYA

The title *visha kanya* (literally, "poison maiden") comes from a reprehensible practice of yesteryear in which kings located girls whose horoscopes promised widowhood. These girls were sequestered at an early age and fed many types of poisons in gradually increasing doses to make them immune to their deleterious effects. By the time they reached puberty, these girls were thoroughly toxic and ready for use. The king who had directed the process was then ready to present one of these visha kanyas to anyone whom he wanted to kill, for any man who embraced such a lady would die after a very short time. One legend holds that Aristotle warned Alexander the Great about the dangers of such "venomous virgins"; another suggests that

Alexander died as a result of the embrace of a visha kanya who was awarded to him as tribute by the defeated King Porus.

Obviously no one would want to marry a poison damsel, for she would be widowed almost as soon as her husband first caressed her. Even after the process of "toxifying" such girls had died away, the fear of marrying women with what are reputed to be visha kanya combinations in their charts remained alive. As with *kuja dosha* (see page 190), part of the effect that the legend of a visha kanya produces is likely due to cultural and psychological factors, with fear of the deleterious influence of such astrological visha kanyas tending to produce a self-fulfilling prophecy of marital doom. Unfortunately, in some quarters, this visha kanya designation is still used indiscriminately to brand certain women as unfit for marriage. One still occasionally reads in books from India that women having visha kanya combinations should be avoided as marriage partners. Some claim that males who are born during these combinations will destroy their families and their clan, and that females will destroy their husbands. We comment on the visha kanya phenomenon in the hope that this esoteric curiosity of Jyotisha finds a useful place in the modern context, and that its potential for unfounded grief and superstition is diminished.

Visha kanya is defined by some classical authorities as a birth that occurs:

- On a Saturday, Sunday, or Tuesday which is a *dvitiya* (the second *tithi*, or day of the lunar fortnight), when the Moon occupies Ashlesha, Shatabhisha, or Krittika nakshatras;
- On a Sunday which is a *dvadashi* (twelfth tithi), when the Moon occupies Shatabhisha;
- On a Tuesday which is a *saptami* (seventh tithi), when the Moon occupies Vishakha;
- When the Moon in Bharani falls on a Sunday, Moon in Chitra on a Monday, in Mula on a Tuesday, in Dhanishtha on a Wednesday, in Jyeshtha on a Thursday, in Purva Ashadha on a Friday, or in Revati on a Saturday;
- When Saturn occupies the Ascendant, the Sun is in the fifth bhava, and Mars tenants the ninth bhava.

Maharshi Parashara, who obviously preferred more stringent conditions for this combination, defines visha kanya any birth that occurs:

* On a Sunday which is a dvitiya (the second tithi, or day of the lunar fort-night), when the Moon occupies Ashlesha;
* On a Saturday which is a saptami (seventh tithi), when the Moon occu-pies Krittika;
* On a Tuesday which is a dvadashi (twelfth tithi), when the Moon occu-pies Shatabhisha;
* In an Ascendant occupied by a benefic and by a malefic, both of which occupy the rashi of an enemy. (Others interpret this aphorism to mean that a benefic and a malefic must occupy the Ascendant and two malefics must appear in the seventh bhava.)

Parashara also adds two very important cancellations for visha kanya combi-nations that are too often overlooked. They occur:

* When the lord of the seventh bhava occupies its own bhava, as counted from either the Ascendant or from the Moon;
* When a benefic occupies the seventh bhava, counted from either the As-cendant or from the Moon.[1]

Other situations that preclude predictions of total doom for a visha kanya exist, the most notable being that the danger of destruction is said to be averted if benefics aspect the Moon. It is thus probably better to view these visha kanya combinations mainly as historical curiosities, unless strong confluence for widowhood appears elsewhere in the chart. Sadly, some In-dian ultra-traditionalists within orthodox Indian communities continue to "slander" their clients by literalizing combinations like visha kanya or kuja dosha (see page 190), effectively destroying their marital prospects in cer-tain cases. Such "pundits" often employ the strong Indian belief in horoscopy to spawn socially imposed "truths" that are as fallacious as the perverse portrayal of AIDS as a viral agent of moral retribution.

Although true visha kanya combinations are quite rare, one modern interpolation that readers may wish to test is our observation that the few people who do have them are often prone to addiction, allergy, or some other variety of hypersensitivity. Visha kanya combinations can, for both males and females, foster heightened susceptibility to alcohol, drugs, or

---

[1] Maharishi Parashara, *Brihat Parashara Hora Shastra,* vol. 2 (New Delhi, India: Ranjan, 1988, ch. 80.

tobacco, lactose intolerance, environmental and emotional sensitivities, food abuse, and other such over-reactive states.

Even when they are present, however, visha kanya combinations should not be used as the sole criteria for assuming addictive or unduly sensitive metabolic or behavioral patterns. Corroboration must be present, as it is when a visha kanya combination appears in conjunction with the "poison line" (*visha rekha*) of hand analysis. In such a situation, these tendencies amplify dramatically, especially in a very long and narrow hand. The "poison line" is a horizontal line on the ulnar side of the palm, about one inch above the main crease mark at the wrist. The line, which is typically about one inch long, runs from the outside of the hand towards its center, parallel to the wrist. When present, it is usually quite visible, though it is typically much fainter than the main flexion lines of the hand. Caution about addiction or hypersensitivity is likely to be warranted if you find a visha kanya combination in the horoscope of a potential relationship partner who has such a palm.

Kuja Dosha

Kuja dosha is, like the porutthams, a fine example of Jyotisha's approach to combining single-sided and "cross" comparisons of horoscopes in compatibility evaluations. Kuja dosha ("The Blemish of Mars") is defined as a birth that occurs whenever Mars occupies bhavas one, two, four, seven, eight, or twelve in a horoscope, as counted from the Ascendant, from the Moon, or from Venus. This is a planetary combination that is easy to spot. It is widely known, and inspires (frequently unnecessary) concern among astrologers and their clients alike. These factors make it very popular with immature jyotishis of limited knowledge, which may be why the notion of kuja dosha is now gaining such wide circulation in the West.

More than half the world's population must suffer from kuja dosha, since it occurs in half of all horoscopes when reckoned from the Ascendant, also in half of those computed from the Moon, and again in half of all charts figured from Venus. Its exaggerated dire results, however, which include the early death of the life partner, clearly do not occur in the substantial majority of the population that kuja dosha should theoretically afflict.

There must, therefore, be quite a number of mitigating circumstances (*dosha parihara*) for kuja dosha that modify it in the majority of horoscopes in which it appears. In fact, many such modifications are recognized in the traditions of Jyotisha, especially those of southern India. Unfortunately, these modifications have not been widely disseminated among jyotishis, because they, like kuja dosha itself, are fully described mostly in southern Indian texts on Jyotisha that, written in Tamil and other southern Indian languages, have remained inaccessible to casual students. Those who study Jyotisha's Sanskrit texts and their English or Hindi translations alone often overlook these works.

Central to the issue of understanding the kuja dosha tradition is an awareness of canons of Jyotisha in languages other than Sanskrit. To the best of our knowledge, only a very few classical Sanskrit works very briefly refer to the positions of Mars that obstruct marriage, one being Vaidyanatha Dikshita's relatively recent *Jataka Parijata*, another being the older *Brihat Parashara Hora* of Parashara. *Jataka Parijata* mentions it in but one of its thousands of verses. The first verse of a section called "Combinations for Excellent Brides" says: "Mars occupying the second, twelfth, seventh, the fourth, or the eighth bhava in the horoscope may cause the death of the wife. If Mars is in one of these positions in the chart of the wife to be selected, Mars will be harmful to the husband."[2]

Toward the end of his section on female horoscopy, and immediately on the heels of his definitions for visha kanyas, Parashara describes the marital affliction created by Mars, though he does not openly identify the combination as kuja dosha. He says "There is no doubt that the husband will die when in a woman's horoscope Mars occupies the lagna or the twelfth, fourth, seventh or eighth bhavas from the Ascendant, and is not associated with or aspected by a benefic. The same combination that makes a woman a widow also renders a man a widower. But when a man and a woman who both have this placement (of Mars) join in marriage, the effects of the combination cancel."[3]

As with other statements in Jyotisha's traditional texts, this verse's hyperbolic language should be taken literally only in those situations that show well-defined confluence. In any event, Parashara has included here two situations in which the combination will not operate: when there is benefic influence on Mars, and when two people with these placements of Mars marry. These two sketchy exceptions prefigure the long list of modifications to kuja dosha that have accumulated in Jyotisha over the centuries since Parashara.

---

[2] Vaidyanatha Dikshita, *Jataka Parijat* (New Dehli, India: Ranjan Publications, n.d.), 14:34.

[3] Maharishi Parashara, *Brihat Parashara Hora Shastra*, vol. 2, 82:47–49.

Kuja dosha is usually referred to in North and West India as "being mangalik." The word "mangala," which usually means "auspicious," is also a name for Mars. Some jyotishis believe that Mars is called mangala less because it is innately auspicious than because a native must perform many penances, sacrifices, and other auspicious actions to avert its evil effects.

While Mars does sometimes become auspicious for a lucky individual, it is still a violent and argumentative graha that does not promote marital harmony when configured with one of the bhavas of relationship. Since Mars has a strong influence on the happiness or lack thereof in a person's life, particularly regarding matrimony, the position of Mars becomes a prime indicator of marital happiness, both in the single horoscope and as part of the process of chart comparison. Though kuja dosha originally implied death of spouse, it was later modified to mean marital misery, and many Indians still carefully avoid marrying anyone with kuja dosha. It is certainly true that, whether or not a true kuja dosha exists in a horoscope, when Mars appears in bhavas one, two, four, seven, eight, or twelve, it brings its aggressive, disruptive aura to bear by occupation or aspect from each of these positions onto either the seventh bhava (of marriage), the eighth bhava (the mangala sutra), or both.

Many southern Indian pundits regard the kuja dosha that is counted from Venus as the most distressing combination, presumably because Venus is the significator of married life. Several Jyotisha texts advise examination of one's relatives through examination of the horoscope drawn with the significator of that relative in the Ascendant. A Mars that is prominently detrimental in a "Venus lagna" chart acts as if it were forming a direct combination with Venus, and combinations of Mars and Venus are known to inflame passions to the detriment of judgment. A kuja dosha placement of Mars from Venus will undoubtedly fail to promote marital happiness, though the placement must be supported by additional indications of confluence if the marriage obstruction is to become truly virulent. Venus and Mars move so much more slowly through the rashis than do the Moon and the Ascendant that masses of people are regularly born with this combination, only a few of whom will experience extreme marital tension.

The kuja dosha combination from the Moon is the next in strength. The combination from the Ascendant is the least disturbing (according to some). Given kuja dosha's frequent occurrence, one way to diminish the potential for misinterpretation is to recognize that it becomes stronger (and hence more relevant) when it appears in two of these three positions. It is particularly malignant when it recurs from all three positions. Even when such an ominous triple kuja dosha occurs, however, you should only predict abject marital misery where there is no mitigation! Kuja dosha's many modifications make it unwise to exaggerate its importance in a horoscope, particularly when other salient relationship combinations may be more meaningful in a particular situation.

Yet another way to differentiate a blood-red kuja dosha from an anemic one is to apply our Rule of $7\frac{1}{2}°$. A more ferocious kuja dosha exists when Mars occupies one of the relevant bhavas within $7\frac{1}{2}°$ of the degree positions of Venus, the Moon, and/or the lagna. (Remember to ignore the degree span of any intervening rashis when applying the Rule of $7\frac{1}{2}°$.) If Mars is more than $22\frac{1}{2}°$ distant from the positions of Venus, the Moon, or the Ascendant, the kuja dosha becomes very anemic indeed. Any positions in between can be gauged by proportion.

When assessing modification of a kuja dosha, it is important that each instance in a horoscope (from the Ascendant, the Moon, and/or Venus) be modified if the full kuja dosha for the whole chart is to be mitigated. You must, therefore, carefully evaluate each of the exceptions listed below from Venus, the Moon, and the Ascendant. For example, if kuja dosha appears from Venus and from the Moon, and a modification occurs only for the kuja dosha counted from the Moon, the horoscope still is afflicted by kuja dosha. However, a Mars that influences the seventh or eighth bhavas of a chart may disrupt marriage in other ways, even when it does not create kuja dosha. How it will obstruct will be guided by the nature of Mars as a powerful natural malefic, and by its role as a bhava ruler. Kuja dosha is a far stronger indication of danger to a relationship's longevity than is the mere influence of Mars acting in its capacity as a natural malefic on the seventh bhava. What makes it so is its propensity to inflate Mars's innate capability to disturb a marriage. A kuja dosha with modification deflates this to a significant degree, leaving Mars to act more in consonance with its innate nature, unmagnified by the kuja dosha.

Modifications to Kuja Dosha

There is considerable controversy in India as to what constitutes a legitimate modification to kuja dosha. We list here some of the modifications that have frequently been cited in texts and have been found to be generally valid. None, however, are automatically valid, for Mars must be essentially strong for a modification to function. All bets are off when Mars is heavily afflicted in a horoscope that harbors kuja dosha.

Kuja Dosha is modified for:

+ Mars in the second or the seventh bhava in female horoscopes, and Mars in the first, fourth, or eighth bhavas in male horoscopes;
+ Mars in Libra while occupying bhavas one, two, or eight;
+ Mars conjoined with, or aspected by, either Jupiter or Mercury, provided that Jupiter or Mercury is strong by both bhava and rashi position;
+ Mars in the rashis of Aries, Cancer, Leo, Scorpio, Sagittarius, Capricorn, or Pisces, in any applicable bhava;
+ Mars in the second bhava, while in Gemini or Virgo;
+ Mars in the fourth bhava, while in Taurus or Libra;
+ Mars in the twelfth bhava, while in Taurus, Gemini, Virgo, or Libra;
+ Mars and the Moon together in the same bhava, creating a wealth-producing combination called *chandra mangala yoga*. Mars and Moon also create chandra mangala yoga when they aspect each other, but the aspect yoga does not modify any kuja dosha that may be present.

There is also a tradition, followed mainly near Delhi and rarely in southern India, that claims that even the strongest kuja dosha ends once a person reaches age ·30. Mars "matures" at age 28, after which most uncomplicated kuja doshas expire. In worst-case scenarios, it may take until age 30. Marriages contracted by kuja dosha people prior to age 28 usually end unhappily, though they need not necessarily end prior to age 28. According to this tradition, any marital mishap that occurs to people with this combination who marry after age 28 will be due to harmful combinations in the horoscope other than kuja dosha. One rationale for this principle is that Mars indicates hastiness, and people with kuja dosha tend to proceed hastily into matrimony without adequately considering all the implications of that step. This native hastiness presumably mellows somewhat by the time people complete their third decade.

Cancellations of kuja dosha are so many that at least one will operate for the majority of those afflicted by the combination. Perhaps the main lesson to be gained by the whole cancellation exercise is to get us out of the mindset of thinking of kuja dosha as something set in stone. We are better off regarding it more as an important factor in marital happiness that must, however, be read in the context of the horoscope as a whole.

Generally speaking, Indian astrological tradition teaches that anyone who has kuja dosha can safely marry anyone else who has a kuja dosha of approximately equal strength, because the kuja doshas are said to cancel each other. Exactly what the original implications of the cancellation were is now a moot point, but we can wonder if both partners were regarded as evenly matched because both were expected to die early. Or was it that both partners would be feisty enough to deal with one another's Martian qualities?

We believe that the "fit competitor" theory is more likely to be the truth operating behind the matching of kuja dosha, rather than its traditionally ascribed purpose of preventing loss of partner. Mars, at his best, is a feisty and free-spirited graha that expresses his opinions forcefully; at worst, this forcefulness becomes aggression. If one member of a couple has a Mars that is markedly stronger than the other's is, the one will tend to dominate the other—which is no prescription for a healthy relationship. When both people have Mars positions of relatively equal strength, their assertiveness is relatively equal, and each can efficiently hold up his or her side of an argument without having to resort either to abject submission or to violence.

Comparison of kuja doshas hinges on the position of Mars in the two horoscopes. Within the realm of compatibility analysis, kuja dosha divides all horoscopes into three categories:

- Those that have no kuja dosha at all (*shuddha patrika*, or "pure chart");
- Those that have kuja dosha and also contain modifications to it;
- Those that have unmodified kuja dosha.

The kuja dosha compatibility rule is that the horoscopes of the two people who wish to marry should both belong to the same category. Those who are not affected by kuja dosha should marry similarly unaffected people; modified kuja doshas should marry other modified kuja doshas; and the unmodified should pair with the unmodified. The few positive exceptions to this rule occur only when the horoscopes otherwise intermesh extremely well. The negative exceptions occur when the kuja dosha in one birth chart is disproportionately strong when compared to the kuja dosha in the other.

Anais Nin

Nin (see Chart 2, page 49) has kuja dosha from two positions (Venus and the Ascendant), neither of which is modified. Mars in Virgo modifies only when in the second bhava; here Mars occupies Virgo as the lagna of her Ascendant chart and as the eighth bhava when counted from Venus. Mars is exactly 9°26′ distant from her lagna, placing Mars less than 2° beyond our rule of 7½°. In relation to Venus, Mars is precisely 6°03′ away, well within the requisite degree orb for a blood-red kuja dosha. The known facts of her married life imply strongly indeed that her kuja dosha was potent enough to disturb her romantic relationships. She married at age 20 (well before her 28th year). Although she never officially divorced, her great unhappiness in the marriage and prolonged separations from her husband were tantamount to a partition.

Outcome analysis establishes that Nin has an afflicted seventh bhava, lord, and significator, as the seventh bhava is aspected by malefics, and seventh lord Jupiter, who also happens to be the significator of marriage (this being a woman's chart), is severely combust in the sixth bhava. Kuja dosha here resolutely compounds the challenges of her married life.

Marilyn Monroe

Monroe's Mars (see Chart 18, page 197) occupies Aquarius in the second bhava from the Moon and the eighth bhava from the Ascendant. This double kuja dosha is technically altered because Jupiter conjoins Mars. For a true modification, however, Jupiter should be strong by rashi and bhava. Here, Jupiter occupies a weak rashi (Aquarius, owned by Saturn, who is neutral to Jupiter) and a weak bhava (the eighth). Monroe's kuja dosha thus remains unmodified. Moreover, Mars is 7°39' away from the degree of her Ascendant and only 1°38' away from her Moon, positions that enhance the potency of her two kuja doshas. Most would agree that her marriages and her love life were unstable.

Jacqueline Onassis

Jackie Onassis's kuja dosha (see Chart 8, page 80) appears only when counted from Venus (Mars in the fourth bhava), but it is modified because Mars occupies Leo. Although Mars is within the 7½° orb, her kuja dosha does not recur, either from the Moon or from the lagna. That she became a widow twice can be attributed less to this kuja dosha than to other factors, the most obvious being the conjunction of Moon and Rahu in her seventh bhava.

Paul Newman and Joanne Woodward

Newman (see Chart 3, page 51) has a "pure chart" in which there is not only no kuja dosha but also no negative influence of any sort to the seventh bhava. Only Saturn's aspect on the seventh lord and the significator of the seventh bhava taints an otherwise perfect seventh-bhava situation. According to the rules of horoscope comparison, based on kuja dosha, this horoscope should be matched only with another horoscope in which there is no kuja dosha.

Rashi Chart

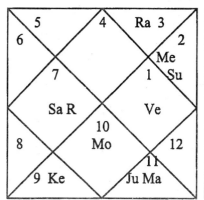

Navamsha Chart

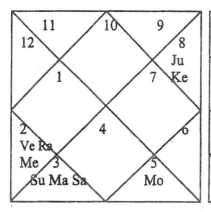

Planetary Positions		Vimshottari Dasha		
LG	20°CA15'	MA	15 Nov. 1924	Yogi Point GE 17-13'
SU	17°TA37'	RA	16 Nov. 1931	
MO	26°CP16'	JU	15 Nov. 1949	Yogi – RA
MA	27°AQ53'	SA	15 Nov. 1965	
ME	13°TA58'	ME	15 Nov. 1984	Avayogi – Ve
JU	03°AQ60'	KE	16 Nov. 2001	
VE	05°AR55'	VE	15 Nov. 2008	Duplicate Yogi – ME
SA	28°LI 37'R	SU	15 Nov. 2028	
RA	25°GE26'	MO	16 Nov. 2034	Daghda Rasis
KE	25°SA26'			AR & LE

Chart 18. Marilyn Monroe.

Newman has, in fact, been married for many years to Joanne Woodward (see Chart 9, page 106), who has a triple kuja dosha, by virtue of Mars occupying the twelfth bhava from both Venus and the Moon, and sitting in the second bhava from the Ascendant. These three doshas are, however, well modified, because Mars occupies Capricorn, conjoined with Mercury and aspected by Jupiter (who admittedly could be stronger). Moreover, Woodward was 27 years and 11 months old when she married Newman. This acts as a further cancellation, since Mars "matures" during one's twenty-eighth year (which began, according to Indian reckoning, when she turned 27).

Still, the stressful placement of her Mars will encourage potential disturbances to arise in her marriage. Perhaps the testimony of extraordinary cornerstone alignment—the fact that both have a Sagittarius Ascendant and both of their Moons occupy Aquarius—and Newman's own extraordinarily strong seventh bhava prevented any noteworthy marital imbalance. This may be a positive exception to the rule that people with kuja dosha should only marry other people with kuja dosha.

Queen Elizabeth II and Prince Philip

The Queen's kuja dosha (see Chart 10, page 108) appears in all three positions: Mars in the twelfth from Venus, in the seventh from the Moon, and in the second from the Ascendant. The dosha is however modified in all three cases. Prince Philip's kuja dosha (see Chart 11, page 109) occurs from the Moon (Mars in the twelfth) and from the Ascendant (Mars in the seventh). Both are modified because Mars is conjoined with Mercury. Though the Queen's kuja dosha is, therefore, stronger than the Prince's, the royal couple both have Sagittarius as Ascendant and their Moons are both in Cancer. These positive influences have allowed them a relatively incident-free marital life together.

One inescapable conclusion that we can draw from our limited examples, as well as from our broader experience in Jyotisha, is that kuja dosha is not likely to wreak havoc, in and of itself. For it to cause true misery, it must be supported by other combinations for marital tensions. Even when kuja dosha does exist, it will remain largely inoffensive if it is canceled and modified by good combinations for marriage.

RAHU/KETU'S EFFECT ON MARRIAGE

While the "true" grahas provide light to our awarenesses, Rahu and Ketu, the Moon's nodes, are *chaya grahas* ("shadow planets") that have position but no substance. They cannot shine light on us; instead they project life's "shadows," the fears, phobias, hang-ups, and secret lives that many of us lead or dream of leading. This section describes some of the astrological combinations through which Rahu or Ketu can apply these secret fears or tendencies to the aura of a marriage. How strongly these fears express themselves depends on the strength of the combinations and on the marital vasanas and karmas that the horoscopes otherwise exhibit.

There is no escape from the nodes, for Rahu and Ketu are bound to sit somewhere in everybody's horoscope. None of the observations that follow should, thus, be applied literally to a horoscope, unless that horoscope displays the type of clear confluence that will enhance and enliven them. In such cases, the predicted effects may show up less in the life of the individual in whose horoscope the Moon's node is activated and more in that of the partner. The power of the nodes to confuse can transfer influences from the one consort to the other, who, in effect, becomes the one's shadow.

Moreover, as with kuja dosha, these combinations apply most literally to situations in which there is no modification. The aspect (aspect only, not association) of a prominent Jupiter on the relevant node can modify the situation, as can other powerful influences that strengthen the bhavas and the lords of the bhavas involved. A benefic aspect from Jupiter on the pertinent node can sometimes (but not always) save marriages that Rahu or Ketu has made almost unsalvageable. We illustrate such nuances in the examples below.

Here is one essential rule of interpretation: If Rahu or Ketu occupies a rashi and that node is conjoined with the lord of that rashi, or if Rahu or Ketu sits in a rashi and that node aspects that rashi's lord, the shadowy influence of the nodes on that lord is intensified. (For this purpose, we take into account, as we did in cornerstone analysis, the fifth and ninth aspects of the nodes, along with their normal seventh aspects.) This nodal influence will be even more intensified if the dispositor of the relevant node occupies bhavas six, eight, or twelve, as counted from the lagna. The degree to which the following observations actually appear in someone's life of course depends on additional horoscopic factors, including the magnitude of afflictions or harmonious connections to the individual's seventh bhava and (to some extent) the dashas that they run.

Moreover, although the natural malefic nature of the nodes makes each of the following combinations challenging, these difficult themes will display their full degree of detriment to marriage only when the relevant node somehow influences the seventh bhava or its lord. That influence may be one of occupation, association, and/or aspect, and the offending node may affect the seventh bhava alone, the lord of the seventh bhava alone, or, in severe cases, both of them. Only such dire circumstances will permit the auras of Rahu and Ketu to take full hold over the marital bhavas and cause them to secrete into the relationship nothing but the rasa of dvesha.

Some people will have no node influencing its dispositor. Others will have a node that, though influencing its dispositor, has no link to any of the factors of marriage. These people are likely to have pleasanter marriages than those whom the nodes afflict on both counts. However, even when the nodes do beset both a graha and its rashi, along with the marriage bhava or its lord, there is no certainty that the person will experience all the consequences that we describe. Some will never marry, perhaps in unconscious anticipation of these very issues. For those whose horoscopes promise the karmic outcome of marital bliss, these afflictions may appear as fleeting thoughts that have little substance in reality. These inclinations usually become imposingly evident only in those horoscopes that indicate exceptionally difficult marital karma. In such circumstances, they are most likely to emerge during the dashas or bhuktis of the nodes, or during transits of the nodes that somehow activate these combinations.

The Influence of the Nodes on the Various Rashis

When Rahu or Ketu occupies a rashi of Mars (Aries or Scorpio) and that node is conjoined with or aspects Mars, it tends to inflame passions, which can lead to an unwise early marriage. This placement of Rahu and Mars also encourages the person to seek out a partner with fixed or dogmatic views. Such inflexible tendencies can, should Mars and the Node be particularly poorly placed, make adjusting to one another so difficult that separation may be the only practical solution. The person (or the partner, given the potential for transference that the nodes evoke) may also form a false opinion about the other's courage, which may lead to overcompensation, aggressive stances, and escalating displays of temper. The contact of the nodes can exaggerate Mars's native tendencies to act hastily and independently. When a partner points out these tendencies, it may lead to endless cycles of anger or attempts to dominate. Mismatches in the couple's interest in physical activities (leisure-time sports, sense of adventure, need for adrenaline experiences) may develop. Brothers- or sisters-in-law can become a source of problems that are difficult to resolve, or they may be the source of imagined problems that influence the relationship in a very real manner.

When Rahu or Ketu occupies a rashi of Venus (Taurus or Libra) and that node is conjoined with or aspects Venus, it lends a self-reflexive color to one's sexuality, which can promote an unhealthy preoccupation with narcissistic sexual responses (like masturbation). When further afflicted, the Venus-influenced node can lead outright immorality. The nodes may create excessive desire for the perfect sexual experience, perfect relationship harmony, or some similarly unattainable perfection, a craving that can enhance the need for sensuality and for harmony that Venus represents. In a fit of excess, this can lead the person away from the very sensuality and harmony sought. Such people sometimes develop the idea that they cannot satisfy their spouses sexually, and they may try to hide what they believe to be their own sexual defects. Or, they may accuse their spouses of being sexually inadequate. Taken to the extreme, this can lead to separation and divorce, or, if they remain married, to frustration and discontentment. The joint social life of the couple with friends and the shared expression of both partners in the arena of cultured and aesthetic tastes, entertainment, and food may be disrupted by idiosyncratic predilections. One belief says that this placement of a node can widow a woman (or cause a divorce) if she happens to run that node's dasha during her marriage, while, during other dashas, it can provoke separation, particularly during the dasha of that node's dispositor.

Mercury is a planet of intellectuality, communication, and youthfulness, which, when afflicted, can foment a perpetual lack of maturity. When Rahu or Ketu occupies a rashi of Mercury (Gemini or Virgo), and that node is conjoined with or aspects Mercury, one of the partners may be (or may believe themselves to be) incapable of satisfying the intellectual needs of the other. This state can so excite the desire for perfect communication that it can encourage discussion when words are unnecessary. This may actually lead such people away from the very communication they seek, by inviting petty gossip, frequent quarrels, or insecurity about the general state of communication in their married lives. This can, in turn, foment severe misunderstandings, including, perhaps, misconceptions about the spouse's faithfulness. Such a puerile and destabilizing suspicion of infidelity may tempt the person (or the partner) to look for other consorts (since Mercury also represents multiplicity). Mercury being a *napumsaka graha*, a planet of ill-defined or "unfinished" sexual maturity, the person may also be unable (in actuality or imagination) to satisfy the spouse sexually, or to relate maturely to the partner. This may inspire a "Peter Pan" or "Lolita" complex to surface and destabilize the marriage.

Moon represents manas, the recording, emotional, and sensory mind, which is, by nature, insecure, uncertain. When Rahu or Ketu occupies Cancer and that node is conjoined with or aspects the Moon, the resulting natural confusion and self-doubt greatly enhance the mind's insecurities. In our solar system, the nodes' task is to eclipse the Moon. This can create repeated doubts regarding choice of spouse ("Is this person right for me? Am I making a big mistake?") by inflating desire for the "perfect" domestic life. It may also facilitate doubts about relatives (how to relate to the in-laws). A node in these positions promotes a lack of focused action that often stems from indecision. This can kindle frustration and disappointment in married life. Guilt and regret may become a big part of the marital experience if an individual tries to hide some real or imagined misdeed from the partner. The couple may become pessimistic over their prospects, particularly if emotional problems prevent mutual understanding from developing. They may share a phobia, or may find casual mingling with members of the opposite sex to be more satisfying than trying to interact intensely with the spouse. One member of the couple may end up blaming the other for personal inadequacies, or the one may conclude, even without proof, that the other is psychologically or circumstantially unavailable.

When Rahu or Ketu occupies Leo and that node is conjoined with or aspects the Sun, it promotes rigid, fixed ideas of marital normality, and may make it difficult for the native to give up pre-existing ideas of what married life should be. Inability to cope with disagreements over beliefs may make the person ignore family life by taking solace in a religion, or in some otherwise admirable cause, to remedy a perceived lack of love and affection in their nuptials. Alternatively, it may be the partner who perceives a lack of love and affection from the node-afflicted person. Rahu and Ketu eclipse the Sun, so there may be some power struggles around the relative importance of individual careers, about who is to be the central authority (or how to share authority) in the relationship. One or both partners may feel that the other obstructs the ability to shine forth and achieve goals. The partners are likely to be easily excitable, arrogant, or irritable, and may become aggressive in their passions. This combination can result in widowhood or separation, particularly if the Sun is debilitated. In this latter case, there is danger that the marriage may dissolve during the dasha of either Sun or Venus.

When Rahu or Ketu occupies a rashi of Jupiter (Sagittarius or Pisces) and that node is conjoined with or aspects Jupiter, the couple will strive to maintain a conciliatory attitude in their union. They will, typically, continue to live together, being unlikely to separate, even if one of them develops a chronic disease, or if some other crisis burdens their marriage. Even if they cannot get along, they will try to compromise on the basis of religion, spirituality, fate, or karma. They are likely to have a preceptor, or to resort to counselors to guide them into sharing a similar approach to life. Neither husband nor wife is likely to be unduly demanding of the other. The biggest defect in such a match is a potential difficulty arriving at agreement about having and raising children, for the node may magnify questions of whether, when, and/or why to have children. There may also be distinct spiritual and religious differences, which may perhaps even come to a focus in how to raise the children. There may be tension over the preferred philosophical, moral, and ethical precepts that Jupiter represents. Such spiritual and religious diversity is unlikely to escalate into unproductive and divisive conflict, but it may stimulate a clear-sighted assessment of how tenable the philosophical and religious views are that each partner holds.

When Rahu or Ketu occupies a rashi of Saturn (Capricorn or Aquarius) and that node is conjoined with or aspects Saturn, it is a strong pointer toward separation or divorce if there is no favorable aspect of Jupiter. Here, the node's capacity to augment increases Saturn's normally pessimistic side, and intensifies Saturn's indications of separation, dissatisfaction, and isolation. The node, here, encourages the relationship to operate mostly on the grounds of work, responsibilities, and struggle, which can cause the relationship's *joie de vivre* to evaporate. There can also be the reality of (or the fear of) dealing with a partner who is needy in some ongoing way, a neediness that comes from some ongoing physical, financial, or emotional condition. Such couples may have arguments or chronic issues, of a variety that would seem likely to lead to a split. Yet, often, out of an exaggerated and almost perverse sense of responsibility, they are mutually stubborn enough to refuse to break their unproductive relationship, even when tempted to become involved in other relationships. Usually, neither the nodes nor Saturn encourage spontaneous compassion, or even a reflective turn of mind, and one partner may eventually desert the other if chronic challenges seriously afflict the union. It is frequently the unafflicted partner who develops momentum for separation, which he or she sees as a solution to the stresses that a severe relationship dynamic foments.

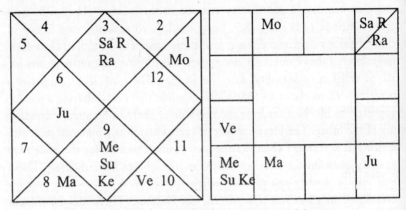

Figure 21. Rahu in Gemini lagna, aspecting Mercury.

An Anonymous Example

Figure 21 shows a chart in which Rahu occupies a Gemini lagna, from which it aspects Mercury with its full seventh aspect, thereby fulfilling the conditions required for Rahu to influence its dispositor. This combination will detrimentally enliven this marriage along the lines previously adduced for a node in a Mercurial rashi. Such effects will be copious in this life, because Rahu aspects the seventh bhava, which meets our corollary stipulation that the relevant node must influence the seventh bhava or its lord in order to orchestrate Rahu's anti-marital cacophony to a fever pitch. We find confluence to this situation that already indicates marital misery in the weakness of seventh lord Jupiter, who occupies an enemy's rashi in a weak degree position. Marriage significator Venus, furthermore, occupies the ominous eighth bhava, and natural malefic Saturn fully aspects the seventh bhava.

When a node fulfills both the essential and corollary conditions of our rule, particularly when additional malefic influence is present from the viewpoint of detrimental marital karmic outcomes, you can be sure that at least some of the above-mentioned principles will operate. In fact, this person was married twice. His first wife, considerably younger than he, died under mysterious circumstances within a year or so of the wedding. The second marriage, to a woman much his junior, lasted a mere six years and ended with his own death. Both relationships were marred by consistent miscommunications and arguments. The person had difficulties satisfying his second and much younger partner physically because of his advanced diabetes. The influence of Saturn and Rahu, in their capacity as significators for foreigners, facilitated his choice of wives, both of whom were foreign to his culture. This was a source of great unrest, dispute, and gossip in his family. As soon as he married for the second time, during his Rahu-Rahu bhukti, marital problems began and continued until his own demise, during his Rahu-Saturn bhukti. "Peter Pan" patterns were strongly present throughout his life, evidenced most clearly in his perpetual evasion of responsibility and his native adolescent optimism.

Anais Nin

The horoscope of Anais Nin is quite similar to the above man's Rahu position. Nin had Rahu in Virgo aspecting both its dispositor Mercury and the seventh bhava of marriage (see Chart 2, page 49). This obstructive influence is further compounded by the aspect of natural malefic Mars on the seventh bhava, and because the seventh bhava karyesha (who is also her marriage karaka) occupies the obstructive sixth bhava in a thoroughly combust state.

A Rahu who influences Mercury from a Mercurial rashi can generate phobic concerns regarding sexuality, fidelity, and the need to verbalize excessively. It is a matter of record that Nin displayed a marked tendency to overanalyze. She consulted many of the renowned psychoanalysts of her day and wrote voluminously in her diaries about herself and her (sexual) experiences, including her many affairs with prominent personalities of her day. Ironically, for all her promiscuity, the influence of Rahu on Mercury suggests that she may have been unable to satisfy either her partners or herself sexually.

Henry VIII

The traditionally accepted birth chart of the infamous Henry VIII (see Chart 19, page 207) shows a Ketu that fulfills both the essential and the corollary conditions for nodal marital affliction. Though both the dispositing graha involved (Venus) and Saturn (the Ketu-aspected lord of the seventh bhava) are strong by virtue of occupying their own rashis, the anticipated shadowy themes asserted themselves in his life. This is partly due to the rule of 7½°, for Ketu enhanced its sway significantly by sitting within an orb of 7½° to Venus and Saturn.

When a node dominates Venus, it may create an abnormal interest in searching for the perfectly harmonious relationship experience (which, in this king's context, perhaps included a partner who would produce an heir to the throne). In fact, this combination seems to have repeatedly enticed Henry into frustration and discontent with his wives, leading eventually to bloody separation and divorce.

King Henry entered the dasha of this troubled Venus (his marital significator) at age 15. He became king at 18, and married shortly thereafter. It was at age 36, in the early part of his Sun dasha, that Henry announced his intention to divorce this wife. A powerful Venus creates a *malavya yoga* in Henry's chart, in the twelfth bhava from the Sun. Venus, occupying the tenth bhava as the tenth lord in the middle of its rashi, creating its own yoga, is good for political power. Venus's presence in the twelfth bhava from the Sun, the significator of political power (and kingship in particular), activates this effect yet further. We can be confident that Ketu exerted its destabilizing influence on Venus, and that this influence was perceptible to Henry during his Venus dasha. Because Venus was so strong in its capacity as marriage significator, however, it was less likely to sour the outcome. It was during Henry's Moon dasha that his vasanas finally caught up with him, for he went through four wives in those ten years. His Moon sits in the eighth bhava, afflicted by Mars, Saturn, and Rahu, creating a scandal-prone situation.

When we examine the potential outcomes that his seventh bhava promises, we find that Henry's seventh lord occupies the sixth bhava. It does tenant its own rashi, but that suggests mainly many separations, with a new partner always waiting in line. His strong marriage significator, Venus, is destabilized by the affliction from Ketu. The fact that his first and seventh lords were Six-Eight to one another suggests that his relationship skills toward his spouses were poor. When we combine all these factors, we are not surprised that Henry found himself in marital hell throughout his Moon decade. During the dasha of the raja yoga karaka, Mars, he married his sixth and final wife, who survived him. We can only speculate as to what might have happened to her had he made it through into his Rahu dasha.

We do not argue here that these nodal influences were the sole cause for marriage breakup in the previous three examples. Many people who are afflicted by the nodes, but whose horoscopes promise good seventh bhava outcomes, end up remaining married, though their married lives may be vexed to some degree. In instances where marriages were likely to break down anyway, these influences act to make the experience of matrimony all the less pleasant. In both Nin's case and that of the anonymous man, out-

Rashi Chart

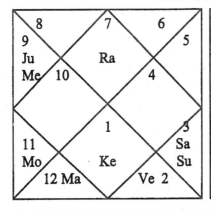

Mo		Ke Ve	Ju Su
	June 28, 1491 8:49 AM Greenwich England		Me
Sa R			
	Ra		Ma

Navamsha Chart

Ma	Ke	Ve	Sa R Su
Mo			
Ju Me		Ra	

Planetary Positions		Vimshottari Dasha		
LG	20°LE 09'	ME	22 Feb. 1482	Yogi Point VI 25-08'
SU	27°GE48'	KE	22 Feb. 1499	
MO	23°PI 60'	VE	22 Feb. 1506	Yogi – MA
MA	09°VI 27'	SU	22 Feb. 1526	
ME	19°CA52'	MO	22 Feb. 1532	Avayogi – KE
JU	07°GE37'	MA	22 Feb. 1542	
VE	13°TA59'	RA	22 Feb. 1549	Duplicate Yogi – ME
SA	19°CP56'R	JU	22 Feb. 1567	
RA	12°SC58'	SA	04 Feb. 1583	Daghda Rasis
KE	12°TA58'			GE & VI

Chart 19. King Henry VIII.

come analysis suggests highly undesirable results for marriage anyway. Moreover, these potential effects were activated powerfully in Nin's life, because she saw the dashas of Mars, Rahu, and Jupiter (three grahas that directly influence her seventh bhava) during some of her prime relationship years (ages 39 to 64).

Paul Newman

A refreshing counterexample of a horoscope that is completely free of the blemish on marriage by either of the nodes is that of Paul Newman (see Chart 3, page 51). His Rahu occupies Cancer, from where it fails to aspect its dispositor Moon. The same Rahu also fails to aspect Newman's seventh bhava and its lord, Mercury. Ketu also declines to aspect its dispositor, Saturn, Newman's seventh bhava, or the lord of his seventh bhava. Both Nodes are, consequently, restrained from creating their typical mayhem in Newman's married life to any substantial extent.

PUNARBHU

Punarbhu indicates an association of the Moon and Saturn, or a full or special full aspect of Saturn on the Moon. Punarbhu indicates a sudden, out of the blue, frequently unanticipated change of heart that occurs between two people planning to marry.

Although Saturn-Moon contacts are common, this combination delivers its promised results amazingly often, particularly in horoscopes that belong to women, when one or the other of these two planets has some connection with the seventh house.

Though it can manifest at any point in a person's life, punarbhu ordinarily does so prior to age 30. When you see a punarbhu birth chart in which Saturn, or the Moon, or both are connected to the seventh bhava, the effect is likely to be very dramatic. For example, one person with Saturn in the seventh in Cancer and, the Moon (the ruler of the seventh) aspected by that Saturn, suddenly changed his mind about marriage, even after the wedding invitations had gone out. The church had been booked, the showers had been given for the bride, and so on, but he changed his mind, and that was that. The very same thing happened to a woman who was due to marry at age 28. Her Saturn occupies her seventh bhava in Aries, conjoined with the Moon. This incident occurred while Saturn was transiting that seventh bhava in debilitation.

Indian tradition says that, after one negative experience, you are certain to marry on the next try, but we have not found this to be always the case. One woman whose Saturn-Moon contact involved her seventh bhava became engaged on three different occasions, and on each occasion each fiancé died suddenly before their impending marriage.

Punarbhu's intensity is greatly reduced when these two grahas have no direct connection with the seventh bhava. When, in such cases, there is a change of heart, it often results in a smoother transition. Many such people will have an important relationship in their late teens or early twenties, in which they start off intending to be married and then gradually change their plans. Some others may live in common-law relationships for a short period without formally marrying before the relationship dissolves.

8

THE AYURVEDA
OF RELATIONSHIP

Although we fragment the human experience by allocating its parts among the horoscope's twelve bhavas, it is impossible to evaluate individual bhavas in complete isolation from one another. The more significant a life event is to us, the more it influences and is influenced by all the other events of our lives, for better or worse. The sacrament of marriage, which is a truly formative experience for most, modifies interactions in every field of human activity.

The simplest sort of synastry gives snapshot images of how generally well a couple will function together. It secures the snapshot by focusing on the details of the alignment between the Sun, the Moon, Venus, and the Ascendant. It determines the image's brightness by gauging the play of light and shadow that the natural benefics and malefics radiate onto these four relationship cornerstones. Another layer of chart comparison, one deeper than those we have addressed thus far, goes further to bring out in considerable detail how the couple will interact in the many key territories of life that the twelve bhavas represent. Such detailed insight comes at a price, for a great deal of experience in astrological analysis is needed, first to assimilate the immense amount of information available, and then to package that information in a compact, focused, meaningful way. Whatever the initial cost in terms of energy and attention, however, in the long run, this sort of analysis works out to be a handsome bargain.

As a jyotishi's mind becomes subtle and graceful, so his or her counseling becomes skillful. A good jyotishi "practicalizes" what he does with a horoscope, often with the help of knowledge that he gains through the study of other branches of the holistic paradigm that makes up Indian classical wisdom. By studying any one of these branches in isolation, you study but one facet of the human jewel. By judiciously combining the facets offered by yoga, dance, music, engineering, the sexual arts, astrology, and medicine, you will eventually get a good picture of the whole human gem. Among the several formulations of India's wisdom, two—Jyotisha and Ayurveda (literally, knowledge of longevity)—are particularly well suited to complement one another. Knowledge of Ayurveda can enhance tremendously a jyotishi's astrological comparisons, and many a skilled Ayurvedic physician successfully employs Jyotisha to enhance his medical evaluations.

We introduce Ayurveda here, in the context of Jyotisha, as an example of how broadening one's horizons beyond the generally accepted canons of Jyotisha can inject insight into what are otherwise formulaic statements. What we say of Ayurveda applies equally well to *niti shastra* (the political arts), *vastu shastra* (the art of construction and configuration), and even *kama shastra* (the arts of love). The more you know of these, the subtler and more sophisticated the culture of your Jyotisha will be—the greater will be its breadth, the profounder its depth. Limit yourself to Jyotisha's technicalities and you restrict your range of potential interpretations and advice. This can jeopardize your efforts to help your clients find paths to enhancing and fortifying their sukha.

In this chapter, we take an Ayurvedic perspective to discuss the impact on a relationship of two of the twelve bhavas: the indispensable first bhava, and the second bhava of food, family, and finances. We try to show how knowledge of Ayurveda can provide an enriching dimension to purely astrological relationship analysis. Most of the simpler relationship portraits, taken by the camera of the horoscope through the filter of Ayurveda, will once again apply the four cornerstones of relationship. The more complex images will focus on the first and second bhavas. You will discover, in the relationship between Ayurveda and Jyotisha, a natural reciprocity much like that found between love and marriage, or between the proverbial horse and carriage.

SUKHA AND THE SECOND BHAVA

Ayurveda deals with each aspect of embodied life from the standpoint of its effect on an organism's physical health, whose rulership Jyotisha principally assigns to the first bhava. Sukha is perpetually compromised when health is poor, in the same way that the many spaces of the horoscope are compromised when the Ascendant is weak. We have seen that sukha is a state in which the many "spaces" of a life are "good." Ultimately, a consistent sukha develops when all the bhavas that make up the facts of your life, as represented by the bhavas of your horoscope, are converted smoothly into satisfying rasas. Having sukha may not guarantee that you will gain shanti (peace), but it certainly makes shanti more likely!

Each bhava of a horoscope does its part to facilitate or impede the development of sukha, but the bhava that most summarizes your overall adjustment to the various spaces of your life is the indispensable Ascendant. The bhava of family, food, and finances, which immediately follows the Ascendant in the visual metaphor of the horoscope, runs a close "second" in providing grist for your sukha-producing mill. What we seek to explore here is your level of "second-bhava sukha." People in relationship are always discussing food, money, and family, for it is quite a chore to make the overall "space" of a couple's life good when its nutritional, financial, or familial "spaces" are misaligned. The very discussion of these topics is, of course, also ruled by the second bhava of speech.

While the first bhava of a horoscope represents your own self, the second bhava indicates the many members of your extended family unit. This sort of "family" includes all relatives (parents, grandparents, uncles and aunts, brothers and sisters, children, cousins, nieces and nephews), even though many of these familial others are ruled more specifically by the horoscope's other bhavas. We use the second bhava to assess the general conditions of this family, which means, for instance, that a well-placed second bhava is likely to indicate that your overall relationship with your family is harmonious, despite your disgust for Uncle Harry and your frequent arguments with your elder sister.

Though family is important to every individual, it is tempting to select money as the most important of the second bhava factors, for, however happy the family, no sukha is possible without the essentials and the comforts that money can buy. Money cannot buy love, however, nor can it satisfy your hunger by filling your belly with gold. Music does sometimes serve as the food of love, but the more reliable path to the heart usually traverses the stomach. While the methodology that we introduce here can be freely brought to bear on any of the matters ruled by the second bhava, we have chosen to develop our Ayurvedic theme primarily in the context of edibles. Food is really more basic to life and to sukha than is family, communication, or money. After all, you can live in near-total isolation for years on end, but you cannot go even a single year without food.

Good common sense joins Ayurveda to point out that our food prefer-ences affect relationships in a number of ways. Food's first effect occurs even before it is consumed, if the dietary habits of one member of the pair are ei-ther repugnant or synergistic to those of the other. Two vegetarians are much more likely to find dining together a satisfying experience than are one vegan and one carnivore. If enough of the four cornerstones are sufficiently well aligned and free of malefic influence to cause the couple to want to work through this quandary, some compromise may be arranged. Jack Sprat and his wife, for instance, adjusted by apportioning fat and lean. Other arrange-ments may be less mutual, but equally effective, as exemplified by the woman who eats her garlic early in the day to avoid being requested by her husband to sleep on the sofa that night.

The effects that food exerts on a relationship after it is consumed are more complex, and more difficult to pin down. One influence arises from the ways in which the pattern of nutrients that the food contains interacts with the organism. All else being equal, for example, a diet that is high in protein tends to foment greater mental activity than does a diet that is high in carbo-hydrate. A high-protein diet may, therefore, act to promote certain relation-ships and inhibit the development of others, depending on how important agile minds are to the relationship in question.

Even more material to sukha are a food's tastes, or rasas. You will re-call that, among the many meanings of the Sanskrit word rasa, are taste and emotion. According to Ayurveda, the flavors of the juices that make up our food interact with our awarenesses to create our personal, subjective emo-tional rasas—what we experience as a result of our bhavas. Each of the tastes contained in each of our foodstuffs contributes to that overall rasa that is the "expression in juice" of that life's unique flavor. As we have seen, pleasing rasas make for a pleasant life, a life of sukha.

We can get some idea of which of the six tastes described by Ayurveda an individual may prefer by examining the grahas that own, occupy, or as-pect his or her second bhava or are somehow involved with the lord of that bhava. In a more general way, much the same can be said of any grahas con-figured with lagna and lagnesha. In this respect:

Sun	governs bitter	Jupiter	governs sweet
Moon	governs salty	Venus	governs sour
Mars	governs pungent	Saturn	governs astringent
Mercury	governs mixed or varied flavors		

This simple listing of correspondences between graha and taste tells only a part of what is a very complex story. Venus, for instance, indicates sour, but also suggests a general elegance and richness of the diet. Jupiter indicates a quality of and a preference for freshness, as does Venus (though rather less so). Saturn indicates the attributes of and a desire for leftover, old, and preserved foods that will produce a secondarily astringent (constricting) effect in the body. The Sun may prefer yellow and golden-colored foods, just as Mars prefers red. The Moon cultivates a raga for dairy products. Mercury encourages vasanas that love variety. Rahu and Ketu can lean in the direction of gluttony, or of other disturbing and distorting food habits. While taste may not be the sole graha descriptor of the qualities of our food and of our food habits, it is the most fundamental.

DOSHAS

To examine the interaction of taste with physiology more deeply, which will assist us in evaluating accurately our potential for bodily sukha through the means of Ayurveda and Jyotisha, we must examine another part of our past karmic inheritance—our genetics. Ayurveda teaches that a certain variety of natural selection will operate, at the time of conception, to determine which traits and tendencies we will inherit from the man and woman who gave us birth. This selection is activated by the state of the bodies and minds of the mother and father, as expressed in terms of Ayurveda's three doshas, the three forces that control all activities of life in all protoplasmic beings. The three doshas are *vata*, *pitta*, and *kapha*, which relate respectively to air, fire and water.

The three doshas are forces, not substances. Kapha is not mucus; it is, rather, the force that, when projected into the body, causes mucus to arise. Pitta is not bile, but the force that causes bile to be produced. Vata is not gas, but increased vata increases gas. Vata, which controls all body movement, concentrates mainly in the nervous system. Body stability and lubrication, and the tissues and wastes of the body, are kapha's province. Pitta's processes all involve digestion or "cooking," including even the cooking of raw sensory data into thoughts. The enzymatic and endocrine systems are pitta's main field of activity.

All three doshas are present in all parts of the body and its mind, at all times. At the cellular level, vata moves nutrients into and wastes out of cells, pitta digests nutrients to provide energy for cellular function, and kapha governs the cell's structure. In the digestive tract, vata chews and swallows the food, pitta digests it, vata assimilates nutrients and expels wastes, and kapha controls the secretions that lubricate and protect the digestive organs. In the mind, vata retrieves previous data from memory for comparison with new data. Pitta processes the new data and draws conclusions, which vata then stores as new memories. Kapha provides the medium in which memories are stored, and the stability needed for the mind to grasp a single thought at a time.

Vata, pitta, and kapha are called doshas because the word *dosha* means "a fault, a mistake, a thing that goes out of balance." As long as vata, pitta, and kapha remain in balance with one another, physical and mental health is likely. Whenever they go out of balance, the system is bound to lose its own balance. Jyotisha also recognizes doshas, including *graha dosha*, which occurs when one or more grahas are sufficiently afflicted to derange those areas of life that they influence. Kuja dosha is one such graha dosha, whose virulence in an individual chart is exponentially enhanced by Mars's natural predilection to unbalance people's relationship lives.

FIRST BHAVA: PRAKRITI

An inborn pattern of relative dominance of the three doshas in our metabolism becomes fixed at the time of conception, inherited from the man and woman who begot us. This constitutional physiological pattern is called *deha prakriti.* We each have a *graha prakriti*, or astrological constitution, as well. The difference between these two constitutions, is mainly one of terminology, for the concepts are fundamentally identical. Where Jyotisha talks of those who display the nature of Mars or Jupiter, Ayurveda identifies them as having the nature of pitta or kapha, respectively. Both describe the same reality in different language. In Jyotisha, this constitutional reality is reflected in the first bhava.

Prakriti literally means "first reaction." Your prakriti, in whatever idiom we choose to define it, tends to determine your first reaction to a perceived stress (even if that stress is a simple change). That reaction is only an effect produced by your prakriti, not the essence your prakriti itself, which is why equivalent Jyotishical and Ayurvedic prakritis produce similar effects. Anger and inflammation are neither Mars nor pitta, but the habitual presence of anger or inflammation in an individual suggests the presence of pitta or Mars in that individual's constitutional makeup. The forces of pitta or Mars act as the causes that create effects like anger and inflammation. Your prakriti, medical or astrological, reflects all the facets of your physical and mental existence that govern the way your body and mind instinctively react when they are confronted by a need to adapt. Many of the traits you prize in your personality and the qualities you hate about yourself arise from and are dependent on these tendencies. Your food preferences and strategies are salient among these traits.

Once your personal physical or astrological constitution is set, you can no more alter it or its accompanying tendencies than you can permanently alter your genes. You can, however, learn to adjust for your constitution, so that you are less affected by its distortions. Using Ayurvedic and Jyotishical principles to manage your own prakriti and understand that of others can help enlighten you as to why the people around you do the things they do. It can suggest ways in which you may be able to foster interpersonal harmony. Knowing your constitution improves your ability to predict how your body and mind are likely to get along with the body and mind of a significant other, which will promote successful relating. Your Ayurvedic constitution and your Jyotishical constitution can both separately assess your nature. When combined, they can produce a satisfyingly multi-dimensional image of your innate tendencies.

Prakriti and the Grahas

We determine deha prakriti through a careful examination of the attributes of our bodies and minds, and graha prakriti through a careful examination of the horoscope in general, and the lagna and lagnesha in particular. The graha that most influences these horoscopic factors becomes the key to a person's astrological prakriti. Some of us are thus "Martian," "Mercurial," "Venusian," or "Saturnian." It is often possible to determine one's personal Ayurvedic prakriti from the horoscope as well, by focusing on the dosha natures of the grahas that influence the lagna, the lagnesha, the Sun, and the Moon. Since the lagna relates to the physical body, the Moon to the astral or subtle body, and the Sun to the causal body, this perspective gives us a reliable snapshot of which among vata, pitta, or kapha is the most essential influence on an individual's fundamental makeup.

We use for this evaluation of the dosha natures of the grahas as follows:

Sun and Mars	are pitta grahas
Ketu	is a pitta graha
Jupiter	is a kapha graha

Saturn	is a vata graha
Rahu	is a vata graha
Moon and Venus	are both kapha and vata grahas
Mercury	can be any of the three doshas, or a mixture of all three

When trying to determine the Ayurvedic prakriti from the horoscope look for the dosha that is most salient, and ask yourself, "Is it a vata, a pitta, or a kapha graha?" Sometimes, the answer is obvious; there is little doubt, for instance, that pitta will predominate in a horoscope that has Sun and Mars together in Scorpio in the lagna, uninfluenced by other grahas. Nor do we hesitate to predict kapha domination when Jupiter occupies the lagna in Cancer and the Moon aspects this lagna from Capricorn, devoid of other influences. Given that extremely mixed influences of the grahas on the lagna, lagnesha, the Sun, and the Moon demand acute insight and considerable practical experience, astrological novices do well to combine impressions obtained from the horoscope with those garnered from a physical examination.

Ayurveda and Jyotisha can often be used collaboratively to establish Ayurvedic or astrological prakriti. Suppose you are certain that, for optimal compatibility, you need a lunar soul mate, but due to its ambiguous placement, you are stumped about whether or not the Moon is strongly expressive or substantially muted in the horoscope of a potential match. You can scrutinize such a Moon by taking advantage of the relationship that exists between a person's innate taste preference and the graha that most influences him or her. An individual who has, since childhood, strongly preferred salty tastes is likely to have a Moon predominance in his or her astrological prakriti. A person who doesn't crave salty tastes at all, or who has only recently begun to crave them, is less likely to have a prakriti that is dominated by vata and kapha. Ayurveda teaches that a recently acquired predilection for salt probably arises out of some temporary imbalance (*vikriti*) that may well be independent of that individual's deeper prakriti.

Knowledge of the deeper principles of Ayurveda enables you to reason back to the horoscope by induction. Our example, though simplistic, illustrates one of many ways in which Ayurveda complements Jyotisha. Jyotisha returns the complement when, confused about a person's Ayurvedic prakriti, despite all attempts at diagnosis through Ayurvedic methods, you turn to horoscope analysis to discover which planets strongly influence lagnesha and the cornerstones.

The dosha natures of the grahas summarize the many effects on the body-mind that each graha displays. The graha-dosha natures are thus the tip of an iceberg whose greater substance is found in the ocean of Ayurveda. For example, Sun, Mars, and Saturn are dry grahas (*sookshma grahas*) that, when configured with the lagna, tend to dry out the body and make it thin. The Sun and Mars are pitta grahas that promote sustained, purposeful activity that dries the organism be heating it (rather like a clothes dryer, or the Sun, will dry wet clothes). Saturn is a vata graha, and vata is wind. Vata's tendency to excessive action, which prompts the native to wander about as if blown by the wind, dries out the organism in the way that a breeze or a fan can dry things out.

Moon, Jupiter, and Venus, the three kapha-causing grahas, are also known as wet grahas (*shleshma grahas*), because of their tendency to cause the body to gain or retain water or fat when they influence the lagna. In Ayurveda, kapha, which indicates cold, wetness, and stability, also promotes weight gain. Of these grahas, Jupiter, who is the most stable, encourages the sort of weight gain that lasts (e.g., deposition of fat). Moon and Venus, who move faster than does Jupiter, often promote more transient weight increases (e.g., retention of water).

Graha constitution is modified or enhanced according to the placement of the grahas in different rashis. When, for example, a watery rashi (Cancer, Scorpio, Pisces) rises in a lagna exclusively occupied and aspected by the wet grahas, the person will typically be stout. Jupiter's wet/kapha nature displays itself more forcefully when it occupies its own, or exaltation, rashi (Pisces or Cancer, respectively) than when it sits in a fiery rashi, even when that fiery rashi happens to be Sagittarius, which it also owns. How strongly or weakly a graha influences an individual's personality fundamentally depends on how influential it is in that individual's horoscope. A graha becomes influential in a horoscope, in our present context, when it:

- Becomes lagnesha;
- Occupies the lagna;
- Occupies the seventh bhava;
- Is associated with or aspects lagnesha;
- Is involved in a mutual exchange of rashis with lagnesha.

The stronger the influencing graha, and the more factors it affects, the greater its influence, according to the usual rules of confluence and strength.

(e.g., a graha that aspects both the lagna and its lord will be more influential than a graha that aspects just one or the other). The stronger a graha is by rashi position—*baladi avasthas, shad bala,* directional strength, *vargottama,* and the like—the more it will "color" a person's constitution.[1]

Whenever, for example, the Sun occupies the lagna, it will radically influence the horoscope in a "solar" way. There will, however, likely be an enormous difference between the constitutions of two people if one of them has the Sun occupying a Leo lagna, which it rules, and the other has the Sun occupying a Libra lagna, in which it is debilitated. Similarly, Sun occupying the ninth bhava of a Leo lagna, in which it is exalted, will make the individual's prakriti very Sun-like, while Sun occupying the sixth bhava of the same lagna, in Capricorn, the constellation of a mutual enemy, will result in a reduced degree of "Sun-like-ness."

Applying this to synastry, ask yourself if your stereotype of Mr. Right is one with a commanding personality who knows how to take charge and show you an exhilaratingly good time. If so, then find yourself someone who has the unmodified influence of a strong Sun and Mars on the lagna, its lord, the Moon, and the Sun. Of course, if you really want to enjoy his company, you will also need to determine how best to deal with his innate ego, anger, hastiness, and despotism! Should your ideal of Ms. Perfect be a woman who is sociable, loves the arts, and is well-padded with flesh, you may do best by finding someone strongly influenced by Venus, the Moon, and Jupiter. If these grahas happen to be weak and afflicted, however, beware of the potential for some not-particularly-attractive characteristics to crop up, including ongoing emotional turmoil, addiction to sensuousness, or allegiance to bizarre cults.

Single and Dual Prakritis

Ayurveda uses simple, easy-to-understand principles to determine individual prakriti. These principles examine individuals through the lenses of the three doshas. The prakriti that is derived from their use is expressed in terms of vata, pitta, and kapha. Knowledge of these tendencies enables navigators on the seas of relationship to take useful compass readings on both their own tendencies and the proclivities of others in relationship.

Vata-type people literally are more airy and ethereal than others. Their bodies tend to produce more intestinal gas, and their minds tend to be

---

[1] For a detailed explanation of these forms of strength, the reader should consult a classical work on Jyotisha.

more scattered and "spacey." Pitta-type people literally have more fire in them than other types. They have better appetites and better digestion, can withstand cold better, and are more hotheaded. Kapha people tend to have heavier, earthier bodies than other types, and tend to store watery substances like fluids and fat more readily than others.

Most people are not, however, ruled by a single dosha, in the same way that the most people are not ruled by a single graha. Understanding an individual's deha prakriti is often a matter of understanding the complex interplay of several dosha influences, just as graha prakriti is frequently determined through the interactions of two or more grahas.

There are, effectively, two main groups of Ayurvedic constitutional types:

• Single, in which one dosha predominates in strength over both the others. This group includes the vata, pitta, and kapha constitutions.
• Dual, in which one dosha is primary and another secondary. This group includes the vata-pitta and pitta-vata, pitta-kapha and kapha-pitta, and vata-kapha and kapha-vata constitutions.

Your personal dosha constitution operates most strongly when you are put into a situation in which you must react. Relationships being cauldrons inside which two people are "cooking" together, the relationship that exists between the personal Ayurvedic constitutions of two individuals often has a critical effect on how their interpersonal relationship will develop. Even when strongly positive connections exist among the four cornerstones in two horoscopes, and even when benefic influences are strong and confluent and malefic influences few and weak atop those cornerstones, imbalances can still occur in relationships where the predominant doshas of the couple do not jibe. Ultimately, it is the insights provided by several disciplines of the classical Indian holistic paradigm that enable us to align the spaces of our lives into an elegant confection of sukha.

Single Constitutions

Vata people reflect the energies of the Moon, Venus, and Rahu in their quickness to act and their determination to spend their energies impulsively. Vatas are prone to unstable stamina, for their energy comes in spurts or bursts. They love intensity, and tend to seek out opportunities to overstimulate themselves (especially if Rahu is overshadowing their lives). Their short-term memory is usually good, but they tend to forget things quickly.

Exploring theory is often more important to them than putting that theory into practice. Vata people often have trouble falling asleep or staying asleep (for neither Rahu nor Saturn encourages sound slumber), but sometimes become so exhausted that they sleep as if dead. They tend to feel both cold and pain more intensely than other types. Loud noise is also less tolerable to them, for their nervous systems seem to have less "insulation" than the norm (Saturn rules the nerves). Saturn and Rahu also promote fear or anxiety, often the first emotion that a vata will feel when stressed. Vata people tend to live lives that are as erratic as the phases of the Moon, for they find great difficulty in creating routine. The word that best characterizes them is "changeability."

Pitta people are as intense as the Sun and as hot-blooded as Mars (who rules blood). They tend to be irritable and anger easily, but do not always lose their tempers outwardly. They carefully calculate each energy expenditure, except when their natural boldness decays into recklessness (which strong influences of Mars or Ketu may encourage). Fire's intensity gives them a love of food and confrontation. They can be as helpful and kind to their friends as the Sun is generous to the Earth, and as unforgiving as Mars to their opponents. Their memories are sharp, particularly for insults and slights. Their minds are acutely logical and intelligent, and they tend to become impatient quickly around people who are slower or less focused than they. They are not particularly sentimental. Pitta people can usually sleep well, but when they become obsessed with something, they may banish sleep for nights on end. They apply the same intensity, strong willpower, and competitiveness to everything they do, in work or play.

Kapha people do not crave excitement and stimulation in the same way that vata and pitta people do. Once they are well stimulated, however, their appetites awaken like those of an aroused Tauran bull or Jovian centaur. They make up for being intellectually slower than the other types by generally displaying the stable, consistent, efficient, kind, considerate, and loyal traits that characterize Jupiter. Attachment to the status quo can, however, make kaphas averse to change. They may become complacent, greedy, stubborn, or reactionary (especially if the Moon is ill-placed). They usually prefer to remain close to their families and communities. The Lunar and Venusian qualities of love and affection, and Jupiter's propensity for empathy, come naturally to them, but these can deteriorate into sentimentality when kapha is unbalanced, or when the grahas that create these emotions are afflicted. The typical kapha type is a heavy-boned individual who is a natural athlete when exercising properly and a natural sloth when neglecting exercise. Though kaphas do not feel the intense physical hunger that other types do, they sometimes use food as a means of emotional fulfillment. This can cause them to balloon out, since Jupiter rules the body's fat. Kaphas sleep soundly, and enjoy oversleeping. They need time to consider things before deciding on a course of action, but once decided, they stick tenaciously to their path. Kaphas need motivation and stimulation as much as vatas require balance and pittas require challenge.

Dual Constitutions

Individuals whose constitutions reflect the influence of only one dosha (or one graha) are lucky, in the sense that, once they know themselves, they know precisely how they will react to specific stimuli. People with dual constitutions have personalities that are always, in a sense, "split." Under one set of circumstances, one dosha will predominate, and under other circumstances, the other. The inherent cohesion of personality that characterizes single-dosha people is more difficult to come by for those of us who have to struggle to balance the demands of two dissimilar principles. Most humans are dual in constitution.

Vata-pitta and pitta-vata people show physical and mental characteristics of both vata and pitta, sometimes simultaneously. At other times, these influences alternate—as, for example, when fear alternates with anger as a response to stress. This alternation can lead to bullying and domination, particularly when Saturn and Mars are involved, for, while the pitta aspect feels the need to command, the vata presence creates self-doubt about the individual's capacity or fitness for command. Vata and pitta have lightness and intensity as their common qualities. Proper direction of this intensity calls for harnessing the lightness for intensive self-development. Otherwise, the vata tendency toward addiction to pain control (a Rahuvian trait) and the pitta predilection for addiction to amplified intensity (which both Mars and Ketu love) can drag such people into deep states of addiction. Vata-pitta and pitta-vata types most need stability. They need to be weighted down with Jupiter, whose heaviness reflects the power of kapha, the least influential factor in their personality equation. The sweet taste is most important for them, but it should be the healthy sweet of whole grains, root vegetables, and fruits that they rely on, rather than the empty sweet of white sugar, alcohol, or saturated fat.

Pitta-kapha and kapha-pitta people tend to adjust better to the constant change that characterizes today's world than other types. The combination of kapha (Jovan) stability with Pitta (Martian or Ketuvian) adaptability promotes good physical health, and the pitta anger is well tempered by kapha's quest for harmony to encourage good mental balance. The dark side here derives from the shared oiliness of pitta and kapha. Ease at worldly success can magnify the solar arrogance and overconfidence of pitta and the smug self-satisfaction of Jupiter-kapha. Pitta-kapha people may let criticism run off them like "water off a duck's back," an attitude that can make a successful pitta-kapha or kapha-pitta very difficult to live with. These types lack vata's dryness, which they can and should imbibe through introspection or spiritual discipline (a Saturnian quality), or by exposing themselves to unpredictable situations (Rahu) to prevent the aridity of overconfidence. Bitter and astringent are their best tastes.

Vata-kapha and kapha-vata types are usually zealous about what they do, and often overdo things by neglecting to use discretion. They can be, by turns, light, open, and airy (Venus and Moon) and deep and secretive (Saturn and Rahu). Their diametrically opposite vata and kapha natures, which are united in their coldness, lack the strong pitta fire that makes personality integration easy. They must, therefore, be especially wary of jumping to conclusions without proper preliminary investigation, and must continually strive within themselves to create a stable center. Vata-kaphas and kapha-vatas need the warmth of the Sun more than anything else, and should, overall, employ more "hot" tastes (sour, salty, and pungent) than "cold" (sweet, bitter, and astringent) in their diets.

If your Ms. Ideal was born swaddled with a "Vata-Queen-of-the-Universe" ribbon, then you will most certainly not wish to overstimulate her with endlessly fascinating nocturnal activities and discussions that run until dawn. If you happen to foolishly provoke her prakriti in such ways, do not feel insulted if she falls into a Sleeping Beauty slumber from which no sane amount of shouting, poking, or prodding can rouse her. Even you, as Prince Charming, may have difficulty getting her organism to cooperate with you once her vata is aggravated. Similarly if your ideal man was decorated at birth with a "Mr. Kapha-of-the-World" medal, do not ceaselessly regale him with your subtle pet theories without occasionally permitting him a sandwich.

SECOND BHAVA: FOOD AND TASTE

The qualities that characterize your personal constitution help to determine what effect specific rasas are likely to have on you. Remember that rasa means, among other things, both "taste" and "emotion." This suggests that taste is to the body what emotion is to the mind; that the same fluid reality appears as taste in the body and as emotion in the mind. Emotions tend to produce their corresponding taste, and tastes promote the development of their corresponding emotions. Your life is much more likely to be filled with satisfying juice when your food, career, and other life activities are appropriate to your body type. When they are not, life can become dry and tasteless, deteriorate into bitterness, or drown you in cloying sweetness.

The horoscope's first bhava reflects personal constitution; its second tells us what effect foods and tastes are likely to exert on that constitution. Each taste influences all three of the doshas:

Sweet	cold, oily, and heavy; increases kapha while reducing vata and pitta
Sour	hot, oily, and light; increases kapha and pitta, and relieves vata.
Salty	hot, oily and heavy; increases kapha and pitta and relieves vata
Pungent (or Spicy)	hot, dry, and light; increases vata and kapha, and relieves kapha
Bitter	cold, dry, and light; increases vata, and relieves pitta and kapha
Astringent	cold, dry, and heavy; increases vata, and reduces both pitta and kapha

In this context, let us consider a prediction that our Jyotisha guru made one day when examining the second bhava of a prashna chart in which he found Venus prominently placed. He said to the pregnant woman who was consulting him, "You are craving sour things now, aren't you? Your child will be very smart." This prediction was an inspired union of Ayurveda and Jyotisha. His rationale was that, because her fetus was inducing a craving for a Venusian taste, Venus (who rules the arts, and is said, in particular, to be a *kaviraja*, a king of poets) would be prominent among the graha influences in the child's life. Ayurveda asserts that the sour taste increases pitta and, as our brief description of pitta as a single constitution specifies, its qualities of logic, focus, and sharp memory are all directly linked to acute intelligence. That woman's child is, at this writing, twenty-four years after the prashna, enrolled in Princeton, busily obtaining her Ph.D. at a precocious age.

The tastes you prefer and consume will influence your lover's tastes, as surely as your emotions will influence his or hers. If your prakriti disagrees with that of your mate, the two of you will probably adopt variant food habits, which (particularly if the food is more junk than nourishment) will probably further misalign you. Taste maladjustment will likely encourage subsequent poor food choices, entrenching you deeper in a maladapted downward spiral. Collaborate, instead, on a mutually beneficial diet and you will slowly extricate yourselves from the alienating effects of your former food choices.

When your prakriti aligns with that of your mate—when you consume mutually agreeable food of high quality, and digest that food well—the likelihood that the rasas thus produced will agree improves dramatically. Even well-digested mutually agreeable food, however, may not guarantee good rasa alignment if your diet aggravates your predominant doshas. Two dyed-in-the-wool carnivore pittas are much more likey to roar at one another like aggressive lions than are two equally pitta vegetarians. Pittas (like Martians) are always tempted to compete, and when two pittas contend for the upper hand in a relationship, open war can break out. Two pitta people who want to relate successfully should always ensure that they are equally strong (a first-bhava matter), to prevent either from being able to gain the upper hand permanently. They should always select for themselves a pitta-pacifying diet (second bhava), to discourage fruitless harsh rivalry.

Similarly, two vata types who live together will end up more vata-provoked if they fall into the trap of feeding off one another's chaotic, Rahu-style energies. Should such a couple elect to subsist on raw foods, their vata levels may climb so high as to exhaust them. A diet of dairy products and chocolate will encourage two kapha types to become more lunar, which can make them so weepy that they may begin to tilt at one another like jousting elephants, or so lethargic that they retire sulking into their corners, never to interact substantively again. When you promote dosha harmony in these and similar toxic circumstances through dietary and life-style change, however, seemingly intractable situations may become salvageable.

SIMILAR OR DIFFERENT?

Two people of the same prakriti type who live together under one roof often find persisting in innate habits too tempting to resist, for each will constantly be reinforcing the other's built-in tendencies. There are benefits, however, to having a partner of similar prakriti type. In a sort of Ayurvedic version of yoni poruttham, Indian sexology suggests that individuals of like constitution be paired together—vatas with vatas, pittas with pittas, and kaphas with kaphas—because of their inherent sexual proclivities. Kaphas, for example, are often not as instantly arousable as vata or pitta types can be, but they become seriously lusty once they get going. Because of their well-matched innate physical strength, two aroused kaphas will not easily wear each other out with persistent readiness for intercourse. Two vata partners usually excite each other easily and become easily exhausted, which is fine, if there is mutuality. Two pittas who are equally matched in their general levels of strength and activity can usually find a mutually satisfactory level of passion.

Most people do not have pure prakritis, however, which makes the issue murkier. A vata-pitta and pitta-kapha couple is well equipped to form a stable relationship, for both have sufficient fire energy to solder themselves together, and to balance the vata of the one with the kapha of the other. A vata-kapha and a pitta-kapha can also form a good match, though their shared kapha stubbornness will tend to amplify the differences between them. A vata-kapha and a vata-pitta may make a good spiritual pair, but the stability of their mundane life will always be at risk because of the shared vata influence. In such pairings, appropriate foods must be carefully selected to redress doshic tendencies and promote sexual compatibility.

In general, pitta will always try to dominate a relationship, in the same way that Sun or Mars tries to dominate its surroundings. Vata tends to follow pitta's lead (often out of fear of potential repercussions), but will often feel suppressed or repressed (which are Saturnian qualities) while doing so. Kapha will often give in to pitta or vata, hoping to promote harmony (Venus). They may also proceed, hoping that imbalances will ebb with the passage of time (Moon), or they may be willing to sacrifice in exchange for peace (Jupiter). Adolf Hitler, in whom Mars and the Sun predominated, was a perfect example of pitta taken to the "nth" degree. His relationship with the world was so totally out of control that, having driven one of his lovers to suicide, he tried to consume the world itself.

Pitta people who learn to manage their pitta will find that their relationships magically improve as they stop aggravating their partners. Vata people who bring their vata under control will find their partners loving them for no longer being spaced out. Kaphas who reduce their kapha will find themselves better able to keep pace with their more strongly vata or pitta partners.

In general, if you want a stable relationship with a compatible spouse, select someone of your own constitutional type (first bhava) and make sure that you share a diet (second bhava) that will keep your doshas under control. Each member of a couple that shares constitutional similarities (who may well also have their Ascendants aligned) intuitively understands the forces that motivate the other, because the same forces motivate both. If you do not want to have to put undue energy into a relationship, look for a spouse who is of your dosha type.

If you wish, instead, to use a relationship as a vehicle for self-evolution, then, by all means, select a partner who will stimulate you and shake you up, who will offer you what you lack and to whom you can provide complementary energy. Be warned, however, that the constitutional variance may drive you and your spouse to live two lives as different as those lived by two people whose cornerstones misalign. The mutual excess in same-prakriti pairings is usually easier to endure than is the strained dynamic inherent in a pairing of two people whose constitutions differ radically.

How relationships develop for you depends fundamentally on the attraction or repulsion of the auras of you and your partner. A balanced relationship is far easier to accomplish when your physical prakritis are similar. Each misalignment in a relationship translates into a potential conflict, and when a couple's sheaths of food are seriously maladjusted, the one may tend to feel a physical revulsion for the diet (and eventually the body, since we are what we eat) of the other. Such a situation requires serious compromise on both parts if it is not to deteriorate into emotional revulsion.

SECOND BHAVA: FINANCES

Prakriti's influence on second-bhava matters extends to finances as well. Knowledge of constitution will at least promote an understanding of why one partner saves every penny when the other is busy spending money as if it were going out of style. Vata people often do not manage money well, because vata represents motion, which is the antithesis of the kind of stability that is necessary for wealth accumulation. Those vatas who are influenced strongly by Saturn compensate for this tendency by becoming miserly. Other vata people fritter their money away on enjoyments (Moon, Venus), in get-rich-quick schemes (Rahu), or with no apparent design (also Rahu). Pitta people, on the other hand, calculate and plan well (Sun), and save and spend their money with conscious design. A pure pitta and a pure vata, married to one another, may thus end up tearing out their mutual hair over their partner's fiscal habits. Kapha people tend to accumulate money, and may take a dim view of a partner who feels any urgency to disburse it freely.

Grahas that influence the second bhava exert their own graha-prakriti effects, often in addition to the patterns of the Ayurvedic prakriti. For example, both Jupiter and Venus are kapha grahas, and both accumulate. Indeed, when either Jupiter or Venus appears in the second bhava, the person is generally good at accumulating money. Because Venus is not a purely kapha planet, however, but also displays a vata nature, Venus in the second bhava is more likely to spend accumulated money on opulent indulgences (which are signified by Venus) than is Jupiter. Saturn, as a vata-producing planet, discourages a healthy attitude toward money. A Saturn in the second bhava may be very miserly, or have erratic spending or saving habits. Such a person may even bury (Saturn) money in the ground (Saturn) in a tin can (Saturn = base metal). Sun or Mars in the second bhava may tend to extend their pitta control natures into the finances of their partners. Mercury, the commercial graha, represents all three doshas, and may find fascination in the many ways in which money can be manipulated.

When we combine constitutional tendencies with specific graha influences on the second bhava, our interpretation becomes more complex, which forces our predictions to depend heavily on confluence. We will be confident, for instance, that a purely kapha person whose Jupiter and Moon occupy the second bhava is likely to become very successful at earning and preserving money. Moreover, there are likely to be times when a vata person who has a weak Moon in his second bhava will have not a penny to his name.

One word of warning: You may discover, as you study your own situation, that you and your spouse are totally incompatible from the point of view of prakriti. While this may be a concern, it is no cause for despair. Prakriti is but one of many important relating factors. When other influences (in the horoscope, perhaps, or in the spiritual path) are strong, the influence of misaligned prakritis can be held at bay. Under no circumstances should you use prakriti misalignment as an excuse for divorce!

When we turn to assessments of vasana compatibility for the second bhavas of two horoscopes, we re-invoke the simple principles already introduced by looking to the relative planetary placements of the two rulers of the two second bhavas. If Jack's second bhava is ruled by Jupiter, and Jill's second bhava by Saturn, we compare the placement by rashi of Jack's Jupiter to

Jill's Saturn. Favorable mutual placements of these two grahas will be those that render them associates, opposites, or open and secret supporters. Unfavorable placements are those that link this Jupiter and Saturn in relationship as open or secret adversaries, or (to some degree) contrasts.

Next, we assess the reciprocal friendship, animosity, or neutrality of the two grahas. By gauging the relative placement of the two grahas to each other by rashi and by assessing their relationship as friends, enemies, or neutrals, we arrive at a wealth of detail about how the vasanas will align for a couple regarding the several themes of their second bhavas.

What Ayurveda permits us to do here is amplify our analysis and make it more sophisticated, by adding the influence of prakriti into the situation. Two people of similar or complementary prakriti, all else being equal, will likely have relatively better negotiating skills (because of their innate similarities of preference and outlook) than another couple whose prakritis do not agree. Prakriti alignments will, in general, enhance vasana alignments, and constitutional clashes will tend to promote vasana collisions.

Suppose that Jack's Jupiter and Jill's Saturn (which are mutual neutrals, an important consideration from the vasana compatibility point of view) are both in the seventh bhavas of their respective horoscopes, Jupiter tenanting Leo, and Saturn, Gemini. In this situation, both are strong by both bhava and rashi position, and they create a desirable Three-Eleven alignment, one of secret supporters. Based on these data, our prediction is one of good vasana compatibility. Now, however, let us add in constitution.

If Jack and Jill have prakritis that accord with one another, the influence of these prakritis is likely to reinforce our prediction. Suppose, however, that Jack's prakriti is predominantly kapha and Jill's predominantly vata. This will make Jack all the more Jovian, and Jill all the more Saturnine. In this case, it is quite possible that, since Jupiter and Saturn are strong, well aligned, and mutually neutral, the couple's positive astrological constitution will surpass their potentially problematical Ayurvedic prakritis, particularly in the second bhava arenas of food, finance, and family.

Now, suppose that Jack's Jupiter sits debilitated (in Capricorn) in his horoscope's third bhava as its second lord, and Jill's second lord Saturn occupies Leo in her eighth bhava. In this situation, both grahas are weak by both bhava and rashi position, and they create an undesirable Six-Eight alignment, one of active adversaries. Our prediction here would ordinarily be one of poor relating skills.

If we now factor in constitution, and discover that Jack and Jill have prakritis that are in unusual accord with one another, the influence of their prakritis may be able to attenuate, to some extent, the undesirable interaction abilities that the couple is likely to display. The imbalance between the two lords of their second bhavas may, however, be virulent enough to thwart the couple's ordinary well-intentioned attempts to align themselves agreeably. Should, for instance, the couple both be pitta types, their innate pitta competitiveness may be so aggravated by their vasana misalignment that it may actually accentuate the adversarial nature of the Six-Eight placement. The pair may then spend their free time brawling, instead of interacting in some substantive way that might advance their mutual harmony.

Adolf Hitler

Hitler's exceptional example (see Chart 14, page 115) demonstrates how very useful it is to know a person's prakriti. When we examine the influences on his lagna, lagnesha, Sun, and Moon, we discover that Sun and Mars, Jyotisha's pitta archetypes, both aspect the Ascendant. These aspects are superlatively strong (since the Sun is exalted and Mars occupies its own rashi), which gives great power to their expression, particularly in the body (which the Ascendant represents). Hitler's lagna lord Venus is associated with those two exceedingly pitta grahas, in a rashi ruled by the fiery Mars. The intensity of these pitta grahas completely overwhelms Venus's mild, vata-kapha nature (particularly since Venus is weak, as a result of being defeated in a planetary war). Both Sun and Moon are themselves pitta-permeated, by virtue of occupying fiery constellations, with Mars conjoining the Sun and the blazing Ketu conjoining the Moon. Pitta's influence becomes yet more exaggerated when we look to Hitler's navamsha, where we again find Mars in his own rashi, which happens to be identical with the navamsha lagna. All our constitutional factors thus show stunning confluence of a preposterously extreme pitta predominance in Hitler's nature.

Knowing how pitta expresses itself, we can, no matter what the cornerstone alignment or the karmic outcome, understand how this person will function in his relationships. The massive force of his pitta instinct makes astrological analysis superfluous, for pitta becomes the keynote to his method of relating. Pitta seeks to dominate in any relationship, and history reminds us how totally he wanted to dominate.

In his personal life, Hitler totally dominated his mistress Eva Braun. Things might have been different with him had he chosen to involve himself with a strong pitta partner, even one whose pitta nature was not as well developed as his. Such a pairing would have been a prescription for arguments, strife, challenges to his authority, and serious contests of will, of course, regardless of how their cornerstones aligned. With a worthy adversary, however, Hitler might have found the sort of challenge to occupy his relationship energies in a healthier way.

Had Hitler been able to admit a strong spouse into his life, such a mate might have helped redirect his energies from war into less destructive contests. In such a situation, positive relationship vasanas could have been buoyed by strong and beneficial cornerstone alignments. Although such alignments would not directly have assuaged his pitta, they might have encouraged that pitta to be rather more manageable in the context of the relationship.

This is, of course, all after-the-fact speculation. What is not speculative is that Hitler's is a very unusual case of being able to identify prakriti so clearly from the horoscope. We do run across well-defined horoscopes of stereotypical Kapha people who are sweet and rock-solid but slug-like. And we do find purely vata types who are as effervescent and changeable as the breeze, but also anxiety-ridden. In that large majority of people whose dosha indications are much more mixed, however, we must employ other techniques, in addition to purely astrological ones, if we are to gain a clear image of who the couple is and can be, alone and together.

VENUS & MARS IN LOVE

For this exercise, refer to the charts given in figures 22 and 23 (see page 234). It would be very difficult to diagnose prakriti from these two fictional charts using astrological principles alone. A trained Ayurvedic practitioner, however, might use Ayurvedic means (e.g., pulse and body-type assessment) to discover that she (figure 22) is overwhelmingly vata and he (figure 23) possesses a clear predominance of kapha, with vata a close second.

We can thus be confident that she will bring typical vata characteristics to the relationship: she will be somewhat indecisive, perhaps overly inclined to adapt and accommodate, or prone to anxiety (especially about rejection). His predominance of kapha will tend to make him slow-moving, slow to speak, hard to motivate, or reluctant to confront. Put these two together and we can predict, before we even begin vasana analysis, that Ms. Vata will try to motivate Mr. Kapha to get up and do something just at the moment that he is looking forward to resting at home in front of the TV or the computer. She may exert herself to get him to improve himself, and may become frustrated if she finds him hard to motivate once he has settled into the comfort of his routines.

Since, when we examine the lords of the second bhavas of these two charts, we discover that Mars rules her second bhava and Venus his, we accordingly compare her Mars and his Venus. We pay no attention here to his Mars and her Venus (as we might if we were teasing out secondary links among the cornerstones). Mars and Venus are mutually neutral to each other, which is good, but her Mars occupies Aquarius and his Venus Capricorn, which puts them in a Two-Twelve relationship, one of secret adversaries.

That the lords of the second bhavas of these two charts sit in a Two-Twelve relationship suggests that these two people will regularly find themselves at odds in terms of their own habits and their expectations of each other (their vasanas) regarding second-bhava matters. A Two-Twelve relationship is difficult to resolve under the best of conditions, but it is exacerbated here, because it involves one predominantly kapha person and one predominantly vata person.

Two people of the same dosha typically share an affinity that is more likely to encourage understanding between them than would the general lack of affinity that two people of different doshas tend to feel for each other. In this instance, the lack of affinity is multiplied by the fact that the Ayurvedic relationship tends to recapitulate the graha relationship of secret enemies, for, though vata and kapha frequently disapprove of one another's habits, neither is particularly adversarial. They are more likely to brood or stew in secret than regularly to erupt in the kind of open conflict that pitta enjoys (and, when unbalanced, craves). That Mars and Venus are mutually neutral is another reason why this couple is likely to indulge in mostly passive second-house skirmishes.

Readers will recall that the person whose bhava lord occupies the second position in a Two-Twelve misalignment frequently feels disappointed by the person whose bhava lord occupies the twelfth position. Prakriti here further exacerbates the situation, since vata is usually far more proactive when it comes to doing anything than is kapha. A vata Two who lives with a kapha Twelve will find his or herself repeatedly frustrated with an inability to conform to a conception of who he or she should be, and will repeatedly let the partner know of this frustration, to the detriment of the relationship as a whole. Where the frustration is focused is usually determined by the rulership of the bhava in question.

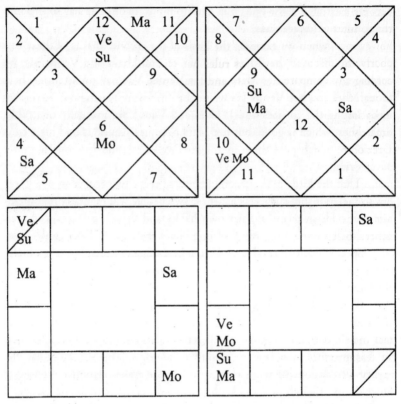

Figure 22.Vata partner.　　　　Figure 23. Kapha/Vata partner.

In the case of food, let us assume that Ms. Mars is as carnivorous as Mr. Kapha is vegetarian. Vata people often find it beneficial to consume some animal protein, but the Mars who rules her second bhava may inspire in her a substantial taste for flesh. This predilection may make it exceedingly difficult for the two to establish an in-house cuisine that can satisfy them both. Moreover, when they want to eat out, their communication may easily break down over the question of spending money for a meal that neither is likely to appreciate fully, no matter which restaurant they visit. Food is so important a bonding item for most people (consciously or otherwise) that eating can truly become a disruptive dynamic in this relationship.

We may suppose that he (kapha and Venus love harmony) will eventually agree (more or less) to become an omnivore. This potential for agreement in second-bhava matters is shown by the Seven-Seven alignment between her Aries second bhava and his Libra second bhava, which, you will recall, automatically occurs whenever the lagnas align Seven-Seven. This is, however, a general indication, a statement of potential alone. How well or poorly this potential is activated differs from horoscope to horoscope, according to the relative placement of the bhava lords. Consequently, even though the second bhava alignment here provides some potential for accommodation, the misalignment of the lords of those second bhavas is likely ultimately to prevail. This couple is thus likely to find it impossible, finally, to agree on reasonably common ground in their food habits.

With regard to money and finances (another primary second-bhava matter), the misalignment of their second bhava lords will probably cause her to feel that he is letting her down financially as well. She may believe him to be wasteful and extravagant, and generally unstable around his finances, particularly if he borrows money from her and then fails to repay it.

Speech is also a second-bhava matter. Kaphas commonly speak slowly, and are generally disinclined to speak. The malefic influences in this chart will probably encourage Mr. Venus to prevaricate, especially if he thinks that fibbing may encourage his partner to let him alone. This is not to suggest that a Two-Twelve (or any other) misalignment will guarantee lies, just that their communication will always tend to be misaligned. The potential for dissonance is intensified, in this case, by the prakriti misalignment, for regular verbal communication is more important to vata than to kapha. Moreover, vata's high-strung nature is likely make her quicker and more erratic in her speech than he.

The second bhava also rules family, and the Two-Twelve misalignment of the bhava lords here suggests that the couple's family backgrounds also show misalignment. In fact, each and every matter ruled by the second bhava is likely to become a matter of contention in this relationship, simply because the lords of the second bhavas are misaligned.

Note that there are compelling cornerstone alignments between these two charts, indicating a strong potential for relationship should they actually get involved. The lagnas here are Seven-Seven to each other, the Moons Five-Nine, and the Venuses Three-Eleven. Only the Suns sit in a less benefic Four-Ten relationship, an alignment that can, however, be made to work, with time and energy. Is such a relationship likely to persist if they actually were to get involved? Or would the couple eventually separate?

The strong cornerstone alignment here is so indicative of general vasana compatibility (no matter what their specific differences around the second bhava) that this young couple could well go head-over-heels for each other. Unfortunately for them, their cornerstone alignments are tainted by the malefic influence of Saturn. When we take his Gemini Saturn and place it in her chart (where Gemini is the fourth bhava), we find that Saturn aspecting her lagna, the Sun, and Venus (three of the four cornerstones). Reversing the process, we place her Cancer Saturn into his chart, where Saturn aspects his lagna, the, Moon and Venus.

We have already seen how malefic influences can ruin otherwise positive cornerstone alignments. In this case, Saturn, who is neither lagnesha nor the raja yoga karaka for either horoscope, will act as a thoroughgoing malign influence on the relationship. The exceptionally close and bilateral influence of both Saturns on three of the four cornerstones in the other's chart will act as the harbinger of the agonies of emotional isolation, regular disappointments, unfair distribution of responsibilities, and of other similar Saturnian motifs in their relationship. Saturn is likely to make the skills that the pair bring to their association significantly less capable of mitigating these influences than they seem at first blush. Their prakriti misalignment will serve to intensify this. Still, skills are not outcomes, and Saturn, on his own, may not be sufficiently malevolent to separate the two. To be certain that they would, in fact, discontinue their relationship, we would need confirmation from karmic outcome analysis of their navamshas and dashas.

Hitler and Churchill

One pair of actual horoscopes in which similarly complete second-bhava maladjustment occurs is that of Adolf Hitler (see Chart 14, page 115) and Winston Churchill (see Chart 15, page 116). Their malign relationship was rendered even rougher by misalignment among their cornerstones and by the exceptionally intense pitta nature that they shared. Hitler, as we have seen, was pitta through and through; Churchill, with Mars in his lagna, lagnesha conjoined with Ketu, Sun in the Martian rashi Scorpio, and Moon in the fiery rashi Leo, surely also had a substantial pitta component to his prakriti.

We have already noted that Hitler and Churchill had Ascendants that were Two-Twelve to one another, which means that their second bhavas were similarly misaligned. Their second lords (Mars and Venus, respectively) create a Six-Eight relationship, one of open adversaries. Curiously enough, Hitler was a vegetarian. Although history may never have brought these two gentlemen together to sup at the same banquet table, we may presume that Sir Winston's very English dietary propensities would have been way out of line with the pitta-driven, but meat-free, menu of Herr Hitler. With regard to other second-bhava matters, we can conclude (metaphorically) that the results of their adversarial relationship extended even to their "families" (i.e., their countrymen), whom each man led to war against the other. Their speaking styles differed dramatically as well, as did (most likely) their attitudes toward fiscal policy. Their second bhavas were, in short, thoroughly out of sync.

9

THE NAVAMSHA

In its analyses, Jyotisha uses a number of micro-zodiacs created within the horoscope's natural (macro) zodiac. The production of these *varga* or *amsha* charts, which are similar to what Western astrologers call harmonic charts, is analogous to the duplication of the fixed sequence of notes in a musical scale in different octaves. A single note elicits two different bhavas in its listener, depending on the octave in which it is sounded. Similarly, though each amsha contains the familiar twelve constellations of the zodiac, each describes a different aspect of an individual's life, with one micro-zodiac highlighting career, another health, and so on.

Jyotisha's classical literature describes methods for constructing at least twenty of these micro-zodiacs. The micro-zodiac known as the *dvadashamsha* (the twelfth division), for example, duplicates the order of the natural zodiac within each of the 30° constellations of a horoscope's macro-zodiac. The constellation of Aries thus contains an evenly distributed dozen dvadashamshas that starts from Aries and ends with Pisces, each portion being 2½° (since a division of 2½° when repeated twelve times equals a standard rashi's 30°). In Taurus, the 30° rashi that follows Aries, the twelve dvadashamshas are duplicated in a sequence that begins with Taurus and ends with Aries. The situation is similar for each of the macro-zodiac's other 30° rashis.

Though no other varga duplicates the whole of the zodiac within one rashi as neatly as does the dvadashamsha, the general idea remains the same for each. Because this process involves dividing into smaller portions the 30° span of one rashi, the rashis of these micro-zodiacs are duplicated in segments that are always less than 30°.

Table 9. Sequences of Navamshas.

DEGREES	AR	TA	GE	CA	LE	VI	LI	SC	SA	CP	AQ	PI
00°00' to 03°20'	1	10	7	4	1	10	7	4	1	10	7	4
03°20' to 06°40'	2	11	8	5	2	11	8	5	2	11	8	5
06°40' to 10°00'	3	12	9	6	3	12	9	6	3	12	9	6
10°00' to 13°20'	4	1	10	7	4	1	10	7	4	1	10	7
13°20' to 16°40'	5	2	11	8	5	2	11	8	5	2	11	8
16°40' to 20°00'	6	3	12	9	6	3	12	9	6	3	12	9
20°00' to 23°20'	7	4	1	10	7	4	1	10	7	4	1	10
23°20' to 26°40'	8	5	2	11	8	5	2	11	8	5	2	11
26°40' to 30°00'	9	6	3	12	9	6	3	12	9	6	3	12

In the context of primary relationships, the dvadashamsha micro-zodiac relates to everything about parents. Other micro-zodiacs relate to siblings and to children. The most widely used of these micro-zodiacal divisions is the navamsha (the ninth division), whose every portion is 3°20' (30° divided by 9). Continuous sequences of this micro-zodiac run in order, from the first degree of the 30° rashi of Aries, as illustrated in Table 9. The navamsha is such an essential ingredient of Jyotisha that it is almost always written or printed next to a horoscope's main chart.[1] The navamsha's influence is so commanding that it has even found a place in some forms of Western astrology.

The great sage Parashara itemizes the uses of Jyotisha's various amshas.[2] He specifies that the navamsha be used for marriage. In the modern context of relationships, we may take marriage to include the whole potpourri of quasi-marital arrangements: heterosexual and homosexual, common-law and platonic, and even circumstantially convenient liaisons (such as contractual matrimony for immigration or monetary purposes). It is in the spirit of this simple dictum on the specific use of the navamsha that we will explore examples of how the navamsha can be and has been used to shed light on various mysteries of relationship.[3]

As we illustrate the use of the navamsha in synastry, bear in mind that accuracy of interpretation for any amsha is heavily dependent on possessing an accurate time of birth. Even a few minutes of distortion in the birth time can cause each of the micro-zodiacs (including the navamsha) to become so distorted that the indications in them for success can be interpreted to promise failure, or vice versa. This difficulty, which becomes a pitfall for many, proves a boon when one seeks to rectify distorted times of birth, a process that involves working backward from the known facts of a person's life to create an estimate of their astrologically correct birth time.

---

[1] To understand the method of calculating a navamsha, consult any Jyotisha primer, such as our *Light on Life* (London: Penguin, 1996).

[2] Maharishi Parashara, *Brihat Parashara Hora*, vol. I (New Delhi: Ranjan Publications, 1984), ch. 10.

[3] There are many contexts other than marriage in which the navamsha also plays an important role. Here we confine the use of the navamsha to the subject of synastry.

USING THE NAVAMSHA IN CHART COMPARISON

One way to utilize the navamsha when comparing two horoscopes for marriage compatibility is this:

- Locate the graha that rules the seventh bhava in the navamsha chart of Individual A, and find this same graha's position by bhava in the rashi chart of Individual B;
- If the graha under consideration falls in the sixth, eighth, or twelfth bhava of Individual B's rashi chart, tensions are likely to result should those individuals marry (and, rightly or wrongly, B is likely to blame A for the problems);
- Now reverse the process and look at the ruler of the seventh bhava of the navamsha of B's horoscope. If that graha falls in the sixth, eighth, or twelfth bhava of A's rashi chart, tensions that A blames on B may result.

When the placement is unfavorable in both directions, an incompatibility develops that actively augments tensions bilaterally. A single-sided placement suggests that some unidirectional obstruction may arise to the detriment of the couple's mutual compatibility. Isolated one-way placements imply, perhaps, a tractable dissatisfaction on the part of one of the individuals in the relationship. When such unilateral tensions are unsupported by other incompatibility confluence, they need not generate undue concern, as they will tend to resolve themselves amicably over time. When the placement is unfavorable in both directions, however, and there is no compatibility confluence to redress it (or such confluence is weak), the tensions that develop have little scope for release. Reciprocal unfavorable placements that are actively supported by other incompatibility confluences are likely to become untenable.

If, in both horoscopes, the lord of the navamsha's seventh bhava is placed in the rashi chart of the other in a good bhava (one other than six, eight, or twelve), we can predict that the couple's compatibility will be very good indeed. Remember, however, that, as useful as this navamsha-based principle, is it should be used, neither in isolation, nor in lieu of a comparison of the four cornerstones and other factors. Also, since amshas become accurate only when you have an accurate birth time, remember not to predict boldly on this principle unless you are confident that the chart is correct.

Kennedy and Onassis

JFK's lagna was 27°18' Virgo (see Chart 7, page 79), making Pisces the seventh bhava of his navamsha. Jupiter, who rules Pisces, occupies the eighth bhava of Jackie's horoscope (see Chart 8, page 80). In return, Jacqueline Kennedy Onassis had a lagna of 25°06' Libra, making Scorpio the seventh bhava of her navamsha. Scorpio's lord, Mars, occupies the eighth bhava of JFK's birth chart. These placements are unfavorable in both directions, permitting us to predict an incompatibility that would actively interfere with the relationship. We can even learn something about the nature of the interference by the bhava placement of the two grahas involved, particularly since they occupy the same bhava in both charts. The eighth bhava rules major intrigue, manipulations, sexual affairs and adventures, death, and legacies (both of substance, and of image or notoriety). All these themes cropped up acutely at one time or another during their relationship.

We dare not predict on this principle alone, however, without confirmation in the form of confluence elsewhere in their horoscopes. Let us first search for such confluence among their cornerstones. He had a Virgo lagna, and she a Libra Ascendant. This creates a Two-Twelve alignment, one that is disappointingly potent, because the degree positions of his Mercury and her Venus are within 7½° of one another. The couple's Suns are Three-Eleven, within 7½° (which is strong, though Three-Eleven is the weakest of the positive cornerstone alignments, because it operates in secret). Their Moons are Five-Nine, far distant from one another, and their Venuses are One-One, within 7½°.

Our tally: one powerful secret enemy, one strong secret supporter, one weak active supporter, and one powerful associate. The sum of the confluences among the cornerstones suggests a strong bond of vasanas between the couple. The Two-Twelve placement of their lagnas, however, implies strong disappointment on Jackie's part (since her Libra lagna sits in the second to his Virgo lagna, his in the twelfth to hers). The navamsha placements of their seventh lords in the respective eighth bhavas of their respective horoscopes reinforce the implications of the Two-Twelve placement of their lagnas. It may well be that the turbulence of those placements were, nevertheless, somewhat contained by the majority evidence of well-aligned cornerstones (they didn't divorce, after all). Who knows, on the other hand, what might have happened to their marriage had death not separated them?

Newman and Woodward

Contrast the previous situation with that of Paul Newman (see Chart 3, page 51) and Joanne Woodward (see Chart 9, page 106). Newman's lagna is 20°23' Sagittarius, which makes the seventh bhava of his navamsha Aries. Mars, lord of Aries, sits exalted in the second bhava of Woodward's chart. Woodward's lagna of 18°57' Sagittarius gives her a navamsha as the seventh bhava of Pisces, whose lord, Jupiter, occupies Newman's lagna in its own rashi. Our conclusion? All will generally be well with this couple, which we have already seen to be the case.

We can flesh out our interpretation of this finding by noting that Mars sits exalted in Woodward's second bhava. We can already assume that Woodward will do well financially, by virtue of having an exalted graha in her second bhava. Navamsha analysis adds a layer of texture to this conclusion by implying that one of Newman's chief functions in her life will likely be to help her achieve a level of financial prosperity that will be greater than whatever she might be capable to achieve on her own. Furthermore, the conjunction of her Mars and Mercury creates a raja yoga (a dharma karma adhipati yoga, with Mars as fifth lord and Mercury as seventh and tenth lord) in her second bhava. Here again, Newman, who is represented by Mars, will play a catalytic role in helping her activate the full promise of that yoga.

Reversing our viewpoint, we find that the seventh lord of Woodward's navamsha is Jupiter, who appears in its own rashi in Newman's lagna. Jupiter there creates one of the highly extolled mahapurusha yogas (viz. hamsa yoga), and is a full participant in a chamara ("regal fly whisk") yoga. Chamara yoga is formed because the lagna is tenanted by benefics and lagna lord Jupiter occupies the lagna associated with benefics. (Jupiter's strength and Saturn's exaltation here permit us to regard as minimal the potentially noisome influence of natural malefic Saturn on both lagna and lagnesha). Jupiter also participates in a dharma karma adhipati yoga (with Jupiter as first lord and Mercury as seventh and tenth lord). Woodward will help (in the person of Jupiter) to promote the full realization of all these yogas. Whether or not she does this wittingly, willingly, or deliberately, the fact is that her very presence in his life will facilitate the development of the morality, charisma, philanthropy, fame, health, and prosperity that his hamsa, chamara, and raja yogas foretell.

This navamsha-lord principle thus provides yet further evidence that Newman and Woodward have come together to facilitate each other's karmas. Whenever the graha in question activates something exceptionally good or bad in the horoscope of the other, that other will help the native to activate his or her karmas, for good or ill. Facilitation will occur, for better or worse. Fortunately for Newman and Woodward, it appears that, much of the time, they facilitate one another for the better.

Queen Elizabeth II and Prince Philip

The Queen's lagna is 28°33' Sagittarius (see Chart 10, page 108) and Mercury, the lord of her navamsha's seventh bhava, occupies the seventh bhava of the Prince's chart. In return, Philip's lagna is 20°48' Sagittarius (see Chart 11, page 109) and Mars, lord of his navamsha's seventh bhava, occupies her second. Here, we may again conclude that good results are likely, since the second and seventh are fundamentally good bhavas.

Once again, we find that the relevant grahas, Mercury and Mars, are very well placed in the horoscope of the other. The Prince's Mars occupies the second bhava of the Queen's chart, involved in a raja yoga that is potent (since, even though Jupiter is debilitated, Mars is exalted). Also, a Moon that occupies its own rashi sits opposite this pair of grahas, creating both a kesari yoga and a chandra-mangala yoga in the Queen's chart. These strengths permit us to conclude that the Prince has not served as a mere poster boy in her life, but has been a catalyst who facilitates her powerful karmas.

In turn, the Prince's Mercury sits in his seventh bhava in its own rashi, creating another famous mahapurusha yoga (bhadra yoga), as well as a dharma karma adhipati yoga (with Mars as fifth lord and Mercury as seventh and tenth lord). There is not the least doubt that the Queen has activated this raja yoga in the seventh bhava (which promises benefit through marriage, and a highly-placed partner). In this case, in fact, his raja yoga became literally a "kingship combination" for him, for it was his marriage that elevated him to princely status. These powerful interactive placements of the lord of the navamsha/seventh bhava across their horoscopes parallels the potent placements of the relevant grahas in the charts of Newman and Woodward, and what was said of them largely applies to this couple as well.

HETU

Our Jyotisha guru taught us that miracles and calamities do not arise from nothing. When your luck is about to change (to your benefit or your detriment), the change will arrive in your life via a *hetu*, a proximal or concomitant cause that delivers you new energy *(shakti)*. A diseased person who is about to find a cure will, for example, happen upon a hetu in the form of a talented doctor, a new remedy, a change in life-style, or some other factor that will activate the relief. Similarly, raja, dhana, and other powerful yogas do not operate in a vacuum; some hetu arises (a lottery ticket that flutters down from an overhead window into an outstretched hand, or an expert who pops up in a life and starts to teach) to deliver the goods. In beneficial relationships, like the one that Newman and Woodward share, the partners act as hetus for one another, perpetually reactivating the potentials promised in the horoscopes of their partners.

Let us now refine our principle further. We have seen that marital concord is likely when the lord of the seventh bhava of the navamsha chart in one horoscope occupies any bhava other than six, eight, or twelve in a potential partner's chart, particularly when such placements are mutual. Since we must not forget any of Jyotisha's conventional principles, we must add here: provided that the grahas involved are strong and unafflicted. Two heavily afflicted lords of the seventh bhava of the navamsha are likely to interfere with a couple's achievement of marital happiness, however good their potential may seem when measured by bhava position alone.

For example, good results are particularly likely in the Elizabeth-Philip match-up because both grahas have dignity (Mars is exalted and Mercury occupies its own rashi). In the Queen's chart, Mars sits within about a degree of the natural benefic Jupiter (who is, no doubt, debilitated). In the Prince's chart, Mercury combines with natural malefic Mars, but remains 19° distant from him. Even here, the rule of 7½° applies, strengthening the impact of the natural benefic Jupiter on the Queen's Mars and weakening the impact of the natural malefic Mars on the Prince's Mercury. These factors permit us to confidently confirm that the navamsha seventh bhava lords in these two charts are both strong and reasonably well placed to one another.

Prince Charles and Princess Diana

To illustrate the converse of this situation of strength and non-affliction, we will consider the case of the Queen's famous son and daughter-in-law, whose well-publicized marital problems ultimately led to their separation prior to Diana's death. The seventh lord of Diana's navamsha is the Sun (see Chart 13, page 113). Although the Sun occupies the beneficial fourth bhava in Charles's chart, it is debilitated there and attains its weakest *dig bala* (directional strength) position. The nodal axis, moreover, afflicts the Sun, which is also aspected by Saturn. Venus, the Sun's dispositor, is debilitated as well. The seventh lord of Charles's navamsha is Mars (see

Chart 12, page 111), who, though in Leo in the tenth bhava in Diana's horoscope sits within 2° of the nodal axis. Its dispositor, the Sun, resides in the obstructive eighth bhava.

In this instance, even though both Sun and Mars appear in good bhavas in the requisite horoscopes, the negative influences on them prevent these bhava positions from delivering on their promise, particularly since, in both directions, the relevant grahas are not favored by the glance of any benefics. (Moon does aspect Mars in Diana's chart, but this is more a problem than a blessing; see below.) Contrast this situation with that of the Newmans, where Woodward's strong Mars is aspected by benefic Jupiter, and Newman's Jupiter tenants its own rashi, conjoined with two benefics (benefic influence that is sufficient to overcome the effects of Saturn's gaze).

Since the grahas involved are weak, they transmit their weaknesses to the matters indicated by the bhavas they inhabit. That the Sun is very weak in the fourth bhava of mother in Charles's chart suggests (rightly, as it turns out) that Diana would never be able to establish a very good relationship with Charles's mother. That Charles's Mars occupies Diana's tenth bhava of public persona, with Rahu (a significator for the masses) unmodified by any benefic suggests that he will sometimes be perceived by Diana's adoring multitudes as one of the chief causes of her misery.

The navamsha seventh lord will activate whatever combinations, good or bad, involve that graha in the horoscope of the partner. If it can activate yogas, it can equally well activate astrological taints. Since Charles's seventh lord is Mars, we must examine the implications in Diana's life for that Mars to activate combinations in her chart. On inspection, we find that Diana's Mars creates both a chandra-mangala yoga and kuja dosha. Because indications in Jyotisha are cumulative, we can predict that this activated Mars will deliver the results of both these combinations. Indeed, the chandra-mangala did give her wealth (as an angular chandra-mangala yoga usually does), and the kuja dosha (afflicted by the close conjunction with Rahu) also delivered its influence.

Diana's Mars creates a double kuja dosha, since it sits in the fourth bhava, as counted from Venus, and the seventh bhava, as counted from the Moon. When we search for modification to these doshas, we discover that amelioration does exist, since Mars tenants Leo (which works for both positions) and Mars sits in the seventh bhava from the Moon in a woman's chart (which works for the Moon-based kuja dosha). However, as we made clear in our discussion of kuja dosha, all bets are off if Mars is afflicted, which it certainly is here. The close affliction by Rahu permitts Mars to play its promised role, and acts as another reason for the breakdown of their marriage that was not as apparent when we analyzed this horoscope from the point of view of the cornerstones alone.

Prince Charles also has a kuja dosha (his Mars sits in the eighth from his Moon), but it is modified (for it occupies Scorpio) and is unafflicted. Their union thus violates the first rule for matching kuja doshas for marriage, that the horoscopes of the two people should belong to the same category of dosha. Moreover, Diana got married before age 28, which further empowered her kuja doshas ultimately to end her marriage.

It is instructive to contrast the kuja dosha activated in Diana's chart by Charles's Mars, the ruler of his navamsha's seventh bhava, with that of Prince Philip's Mars, lord of his navamsha's seventh bhava, which, in the Queen's, chart activates her own triple kuja dosha (from lagna, Moon, and Venus). The Queen's Mars also has a cancellation (it sits in Capricorn, exalted), but here it is a cancellation that is reinforced by benefic influence and by participation in good yogas. Mars's conjunction with the debilitated-but-rehabilitated benefic Jupiter (for its neecha bhanga, see page 139) creates a dharma karma adhipati yoga. Moreover, the aspect of its own-rashi benefic Moon creates a chandra-mangala yoga as it cancels the kuja dosha that occurs from that same Moon.

OTHER WAYS TO EMPLOY THE NAVAMSHA

Many jyotishis estimate the attributes of a partner-to-be from an individual's navamsha. Some jyotishis use the graha ruling the navamsha Ascendant as key for these purposes, and others take the navamsha seventh lord. Which should the fledgling astrologer use? Aside from certain esoteric interpretations (e.g., if the navamsha lagna lord occupies a rashi of Mercury and is aspected by Saturn, the partner will be impotent), this choice seems to be a personal matter, one that cannot necessarily be predicted. Due experience and diligence usually leads a good astrologer eventually to the one he or she should use for this sort of horoscope analysis.

Let us turn again to the examples that we have consistently used, both to display that special internal consistency that confluence provides, and to show the reader the depth to which chart analysis can proceed. Remember that, for these analyses, we are now plugging this navamsha lord into the chart from which it was derived and *not* into the horoscope of the partner.

Princess Diana

We will begin by examining the seventh lord of Lady Diana's navamsha (see Chart 13, page 113), which is the Sun. The Sun will, therefore, be key to the attributes and sensations of the spouse-to-be, which we can analyze from its condition in her birth chart. For example, given that the Sun and Mercury form a budhaditya yoga, we may infer that her spouse has a good chance of being intellectually inclined and well educated, an interpretation that is exceptionally well supported, since Mercury occupies the intellectual rashi Gemini, which happens to be its own domicile. Given that the Sun is in the eighth bhava, the spouse may be rather idiosyncratic, especially since both Sun and Mercury are in Ardra, a nakshatra that is ruled by the eccentric Rahu. He may also provide her a legacy, since legacies are also eighth-bhava matters. Yet another meaning of the eighth bhava may come forward: the partner may be involved in, or may involve her in, intrigues, manipulations, and scandal, as was the case with the Kennedys.

If we now rotate Diana's horoscope to make her seventh bhava into his lagna, we see that the Sun now occupies the second bhava, conjoined with second and fifth lord, Mercury. This is the aforementioned budhaditya yoga, which is now rendered particularly potent by virtue of the fact that one of its participants is the lord of the fifth bhava. Because the combination of the Sun and Mercury occurs so frequently, a budhaditya yoga will only display its true qualities of intellectual culture if it distinguishes itself in some essential way. Here, it is distinguished because Mercury, the intellectual graha, sits in its own rashi as lord of the fifth bhava of intellect (as counted from her seventh bhava, of course).

The combination of the Sun with Mercury now also creates a raja yoga (here, the combination of the fourth and fifth lords, as counted from Diana's seventh bhava). This raja yoga is also a strong combination for wealth, since one of its components is the second lord sitting in the second bhava. The partner is also likely to possess much wealth in the form of property (since the fourth lord also occupies the second bhava, as a participant in the raja yoga). Actually, we know that Diana came into immense money from her husband, a pattern that may have repeated itself with another spouse had she lived to remarry.

This disposition of eighth lord in eighth bhava similarly appears in the charts of Jackie Onassis and Prince Philip, who came by their wealth in similar ways. The pattern recurs in Jackie's case with her second spouse, Aristotle Onassis, for, in this marriage as well, she greatly benefited from her partner's money. Queen Elizabeth's eighth lord also appears in her eighth bhava, but, in her case, it represents not her partner's money, but inherited money. Of course, Jackie and Diana also benefited significantly from inherited money. In the Queen's case, however, the magnitude of her personal inheritance merely overshadowed other potential connotations of this combination for legacies.

The strength of these combinations is multiplied in Diana's chart by the presence of Venus nearby, for, when a powerful Venus occupies the twelfth bhava to a positive combination of powerful grahas, it vastly enhances the person's ability to enjoy the effects of that combination. The twelfth bhava is classically known as the *bhoga sthana*, and the planetary significator for bhoga (enjoyment, indulgence) is Venus. This tradition suggests that a Venus placed in the twelfth bhava of a horoscope immensely enhances the capability for bhoga for that person (represented by the first bhava), provided that the first bhava of that horoscope is strong. In selected circumstances, this principle can be extended to a Venus that occupies the twelfth bhava to any graha or bhava. Here, a Venus in its own rashi appears in the twelfth bhava to the combination of second and fifth lord Mercury, who occupies the second bhava involved in a raja yoga (having rotated the chart), promising, therefore, that immense wealth and influence will flow from the partner.

Suppose that we now do this the other way round, as some jyotishis would be inclined to do, and take, instead, the lord of the first bhava of the navamsha as the indicator graha for spouse. In this way, we obtain a powerful profile of the husband from Diana's chart, for there, Saturn (the lord of her navamsha's first bhava) tenants his own rashi, conjoined with Jupiter. This combination falls in the ninth bhava, as counted from Diana's seventh bhava, with Saturn as the raja yoga karaka and Jupiter as lord of the eleventh, as counted from her seventh bhava, thereby concurrently forming a dhana yoga.

In Diana's case, both the Sun and Saturn paint a compelling portrait of a spouse of some means and power, a portrait much supported by the Venus that occupies its own rashi in Diana's seventh bhava. This clear confluence is, however rare, for similar results when taking either lord are not so easy to find, as the horoscope of Jackie Onassis informs us.

In Jackie's case (see Chart 8, page 80) the lord of her navamsha's first bhava, Venus, works well for this purpose. It occupies Jackie's eighth bhava (as Diana's Sun, the lord of the seventh bhava of her navamsha, occupies

Diana's eighth bhava), thereby reinforcing the sense of manipulation, intrigue, and scandal that touched her married life. When we rotate Jackie's chart to make her seventh bhava into the first bhava of her partner's chart, we find Venus in its own rashi in the second bhava, conjoined with Jupiter, lord of the ninth bhava. This powerful dhana yoga reinforces the notion of a wealthy partner (as it did with Diana). When we use Mars, the lord of the seventh bhava of Jackie's navamsha, for the same sort of analysis, we do not find the same sort of powerful indications, for Mars, though well placed and unafflicted, does not participate in any yogas that would reflect JFK's status.

An astrologer needs an intuitive sense to determine what to do, without falling into the trap of viewing every factor all of the time. A good jyotishi (or Ayurvedic physician) looks at the one thing he needs to see, touch, or feel, and makes a leap—and that leap is often correct, if his intuition has properly blended with his experience. Some exceptionally gifted, intuitive jyotishis are bold enough as to read from the navamsha the direction from which the spouse will come, what the spouse will look like, when and how the two will first meet, and many other things. In fact, in our limited experience of these principles, it seems to be very much a hit-or-miss process (perhaps because so many horoscopes remain unrectified).

We mention these and similar principles only because they are still so much used by native jyotishis. Perhaps these processes worked better in older, traditional societies in which people tended to remain near their birthplaces than it does in the exceptionally convoluted modern world, where many people move (and divorce and remarry) with great regularity.

KARAKO BHAVO NASHTO

Karako bhavo nashto ("the karaka destroys the bhava") is a situation that occurs when the significator of a relative or spouse sits in its own bhava. Such a graha "destroys" the indications of that bhava. While destruction *(nashto)* suggests that the beings indicated are somehow rendered null and void, in practice, such placements suggest that the significations are in some way blemished. Jupiter occupying the fifth bhava, for example "blemishes" one's children (the individual may not have any, or may be troubled through or by them). The Sun in the ninth "blemishes" father, Mars in the third, younger siblings, Jupiter in the eleventh, elder siblings.

Venus in a horoscope's seventh bhava, even if in its own rashi, is a blemish, as in Princess Diana's chart. This damages marriage, regardless of what it may imply about the partner's position, wealth, or attributes. Even when the spouse remains "unblemished" (remains strong, healthy, athletic, rich), the marriage may not work (it may "die"). Diana's Venus is further detrimented by attaining just slightly more than one degree of the rashi, a position that is a "dead degree" for the even-numbered rashis.

Karako bhavo nashto can be applied to the navamsha lagna as well. Venus in the navamsha lagna often creates a kind of equivalent to Venus in the birth chart's seventh bhava, with the important exception that a Venus that happens to occupy its own rashi in the navamsha lagna is in a good position for marriage. This is true even though a graha that occupies the lagna of the navamsha is regarded as being equivalent to appearing in the seventh bhava of the birth chart (in which instance, Venus becomes less than ideal for marriage, even when in its own rashi).

Paul Newman (see Chart 3, page 51) has Venus in his navamsha lagna, but in its own rashi, which is the exception to this rule. Adolf Hitler (see Chart 14, page 115) had Venus in the lagna of his navamsha, but in Scorpio (not in its own rashi); he married only once, immediately before the end of his life. This detriment to marriage is reinforced in his birth chart by karako bhavo nashto in the seventh bhava, and that, too, with a heavily afflicted Venus. Fascinatingly, Hitler's nemesis, Churchill (see Chart 15, page 116), also had Venus in the lagna of his navamsha; exalted, to be sure, but not in its own rashi (exaltation is not an exception to this rule). He was, however, married, and since his horoscope has not been rectified to the minute, this is not a good point to predict on in his case. It is always best to rectify a horoscope before beginning to rely on its varga charts predictively.

Some Indian jyotishis go as far as to treat the navamsha as if it were itself a birth chart, and to read it in the same way that they would read a natal horoscope. When used in this way, for analyzing compatibility, it is probably better to confine the analysis in the main to outcome analysis, with the aim of getting some additional insight for the relationship of interest. For example, to examine relationship with a spouse, look to the seventh bhava, lord, and karaka in the navamsha, and investigate the same factors in the birth chart, applying the general 80/20 rules to evaluate which grahas are benign and which malign. Should these factors be benefic and strong in both the birth chart and the navamsha chart, it indicates the best of all worlds for a successful marital outcome. If bhava, lord, and karaka are malefic and weak in both charts, however, beware.

TIMING

Few people, when assessing compatibility, consider the question of choosing a propitious moment to formally inaugurate the coupling. Most of us would probably agree that we humans remain part of the natural scheme of things, and there is evidence aplenty to prove that "to everything there is a season, and a time to every purpose under heaven." Millions of Canadians know from personal experience that seeds planted in the frigidity of a Canadian winter will not fructify. Millions have also learned from experience that the majority of those seeds that are planted in that same soil during the spring season will sprout, grow, mature, and multiply.

It is a well-known and time-tested principle that the life and death of living beings depend substantially on the ways in which those beings interact with their environments. The external cosmos forms a significant portion of our environment. Few astrologers would disagree with the proposition that the constellations that were rising and the planets that were setting at the time of a birth reflect something about the reality of the child being born. Many declare, however, that such knowledge is merely symbolic, that it does nothing more than resonate with a reality that is wholly internal to the human in question.

In Jyotisha, we suggest that a deeper, less comprehensible sort of causation is at work here, and that the rashis and grahas of the sky do influence, in inscrutable but substantial ways, our lives here below. Though the correlation of the cosmic environment and the human senses is not as obvious as the correlation of plant with soil, Jyotisha suggests that the nature of that interaction, is nonetheless, very real. Jyotisha teaches that some of the less physical aspects of existence still reflect, albeit with greater subtlety, the same principles that we find to be abundantly real in material nature. Cultures of antiquity worldwide, for whom the culture of the sky was more immediate than it is with us, have maintained that astral realities can influence mundane existences, even though most of us are unlikely ever to be able to enjoy direct sensory perception of the celestial realms.

ADRISHTA AND MUHURTA

In classical India, these unobserved, but puissant, influences are often grouped together under the term *adrishta*, which literally means "unseen." Adrishta is something that may affect you, even without your seeing it, as a dog whistle can affect a dog at a distance. A third party may both see the dog react to the whistle and notice the whistle being blown, and may correctly draw the conclusion that these two events are related. A jyotishi performs the same job for his clients when he shows them the nature of the adrishta that is present in their charts, and what effects those influences are likely to deliver.

Adrishta is, fundamentally, the soil in which we plant our actions. Specifically, what we plant in adrishta is our kriyamana karmas (current actions) and agama karmas (actions planned for the future). If bumper crops are desired, good seeds should be planted during appropriate seasons. One aim of Jyotisha is to develop methods that can select that season, the most cosmically propitious environment, under which to inaugurate any project or endeavor, including partnership. Commitment to a partnership gives birth to a new entity, one that will grow, mature, and die according to its own innate timeline. To a certain degree, we can orchestrate the life of a partnership by orchestrating its birth, according to the principles of *muhurta*.

Muhurta, or electional astrology, is the art of optimizing our free will by selecting astrologically auspicious moments for beginning any endeavor. Relationship outcome being a three-legged stool (with outcome analysis and synastrical comparison being the stool's first and second legs), we are left with a wobbly stool if we ignore muhurta, the stool's third leg. Muhurta helps us select a beneficial astrological time to serve as a moment of intent (a wedding vow, the signing of a partnership or loan document, one's official entry into a new home or office). The moment of intent focuses your purpose; it becomes the seed impulse from which the outcome will grow. Plant your seed with focused intent at a propitious moment and your desired re-sult will ripen with a maximum of efficiency and a minimum of obstruction.

General Muhurta Rules for Marriage

We do not pretend here to address anything more than the absolute basics you should consider when selecting a muhurta for something as important as a marriage. There is a vast body of detailed, comprehensive principles that make up the muhurta procedure, for muhurta forms an independent limb of Jyotisha. What we have extracted from muhurta's long and respected tradi-tion are some basic, useable principles that will hold generally true. As these principles are very general, some specific exceptions to them will to be sure arise—for example, simply because Saturday is generally the least desirable day for a wedding does not mean that all marriages conducted on that day are doomed. All of us, in fact, know people who married on a Saturday and did just fine in their relationships. Sugar may be generally unhealthy, but rock candy may be good in a specific context—e.g., for soothing a sore throat or calming an upset stomach. Just as regular consumption of sugar deranges most organisms, however, violations of the rules of muhurta will, for most people, disturb the production of beneficial results on the imper-ceptible plane of adrishta.

Select an appropriate day of the week. The worst weekday for a wedding is Saturday, with Tuesday following a close second. The best days are, in or-der, Thursday, Friday, Monday, and Wednesday, with Sunday bringing up the rear. Thursday, which is ruled by Jupiter, the largest of the planets, is generally auspicious for commencing things that you wish to grow, espe-cially if those things are primarily spiritual in their nature. Jupiter also pro-motes progeny (being the significator for children), and children are often viewed in India as the *siddhi* (extraordinary achievement) obtained by fol-lowing the *sadhana* (spiritual discipline) of marriage. Venus, who often dominates the early morning or early evening sky as one of its brightest jew-els, is great for celebration of the senses at the festivities of a wedding. Friday nuptials carry an implication that the union will organize itself along Venu-sian lines (i.e., a relationship that celebrates the senses through such pur-suits as art, food, amusements, and dalliances).

Many cultures revere the Moon as mother-archetype of our sky. Mar-rying on a Monday will thus bring domesticity, the household, and nurtur-ing into focus. Wednesday matrimony activates Mercury, which suggests contractual affairs and communication in general (of which marriage is a specific form, communication being essential to marriage). Sunday is on the borderline for wedlock; it is neither optimal, nor to be completely avoided. One reason for this ambivalence is its very importance. The Sun, given its position in the solar system, is not prone to taking true partners. Consequently, the Sun, in matters of business, prefers independence, or prefers to be the enterprise's director rather than a co-equal team player. Similar tendencies may arise in a romantic relationship begun on a Sunday.

In the red planet, Mars, we have an entity whose sense of independence is typically associated with truculence, calculation, unbridled passion, and challenge. These ideas have probably become associated with this graha because of the erratic nature of its retrogression cycle (compared to those of the other four, true planets in Jyotisha) and its perceptible redness (red is associated with dominance and heat). Ayurvedically, this has led Mars into association with pitta, one of whose primary negative emotion is anger (and the potential for violence, via abusiveness or in accidents). None of this has ever been, or will ever be, conducive to a happy, harmonious union. Marriage on Tuesday tends to activate Mars.

Saturn, as the outermost planet visible to the naked eye, is visually dim (due to its distance from the Sun). These two qualities (distance and dimness) have caused this planet to be associated with coldness, isolation, lack of luster, and a nondescriptness that borders on invisibility. Most people rarely think of such qualities when they think of espousal. More commonly, they think of life's "positive" qualities—brilliance, passion, juiciness, and warmth. Particularly in India, a wedding is a feast for the senses: a bride opulently attired and bedecked with jewels, her hands and feet hennaed; a groom atop a striding stallion, followed by a long column of singing and dancing relatives, friends, and well-wishers; sumptuous food, clouds of incense, the flames of the sacred fire. None of these traditional spectacles have much to do with the nature of Saturn. Probably the overriding reason why most Indians prefer to avoid beginning anything that they would like to see endure on a Saturday is that, among all the grahas, Saturn is the significator of death.

None of this weekday symbology should be interpreted narrowly, for, taken together, the weekdays cover everything that may occur in a marriage, or a life. In a broad sense, however, the days of the week do carry these implications, which they transfer to whatever enterprise is commenced on that day.

Venus should be visible. Because Venus is the natural significator of marriage (at least in the Parashari system of Jyotisha), as well as the primary indicator of socialization (as in the celebration of marriage), for muhurta purposes, we must pay considerable attention to its cosmic state. In particular, we want Venus to be visible in the sky, either as the Morning or Evening Star, on the day that a marriage is solemnized. When Venus (or any other planet) is very close to the Sun, it is lost to the naked eye in the Sun's glare, even when it should be visible (e.g., during its rising or setting). Such planets are combust—in Sanskrit, *asta*. *Asta* literally means "set," this "setting" refers to a planet's loss of its own luminosity in that of the Sun—a loss that occurs because it has moved too close to the Sun, not because it has disappeared below the western horizon.

Combust planets are weak, unable to deliver what they promise. A natural intuitive correlation for ancient sky watchers was that Venus, which is typically the third most-brilliant object in our sky, should not be invisible (as if fallen from the sky) at the time of the celebration of a marriage. Different planets become combust within different orbs. Venus becomes combust at different positions, depending on whether or not it is retrograde. For our purposes, Venus can definitely be assumed to be combust if its longitude is within 6° of that of the Sun (on either side of the Sun).

Avoid Pitri Paksha. The year's seasons reflect themselves in the cycle of waxing and waning light and dark that is the day. Conversely, day and night reflect themselves in the seasons of the year. Ancestors, those who have "fallen away" from us, are worshipped in India (and elsewhere) at the "dusk" of the year, the fall, when the Sun is "falling" away from Earth. This time of "falling away," of discontinuance, is not preferred for marriage celebrations. The two weeks of the year during which ancestor veneration alone is an appropriate form of ritual worship is called, in Sanskrit, the *pitri paksha* ("the forefather fortnight"). This occurs during the dark half of the lunar month of Bhadrapada. Any Indian *panchanga* (ephemeris) will include the dates for the pitri paksha, which changes annually due to fluctuations in the lunar year. If you are unable to consult a panchanga, but are interested in exploring this principle, be advised that this period can happen at any time during September or the first half of October.

Wed during daylight hours. Based on similar reasoning (of a peculiarly astrological type), the night represents all that is invisible in life. Night is a time associated with loss of awareness, with the temporary death that is sleep, with the diminishment of all that is associated with active, productive human life. One should, therefore, wed during the day, and well before dusk, before the Sun losses its vigor and heads toward its diurnal disappearance from our world.

Select a bright Moon. The Moon, the other of our two luminaries, also possesses dignity. Marriages should, in general, be avoided within five days before and after the New Moon (specifically, during that period that stretches between the tenth tithi of the dark fortnight and the fifth tithi of the bright fortnight). The other twenty-odd days of the lunar month are generally acceptable, provided that the Moon is unafflicted (by being debilitated, or associated with natural malefics, unless they are attenuated by benefics).

Because the Moon changes its position and shape so swiftly, however, and thus its character, classical Jyotisha has filled volumes with criteria to be considered for selecting a strong Moon. Each of the thirty tithis, twenty-seven nakshatras, twenty-seven soli-lunar yogas, and eleven lunar karanas possesses its own attributes and degree of beneficence or malevolence to be evaluated and accounted for in muhurta.

Protect the seventh bhava. At the time a wedding takes place, you should try to optimize the natal horoscope by boosting the strength of any grahas that are associated with the seventh bhava therein. These include the seventh lord, the significator (Venus or Jupiter), and (in some cases) any occupant of that seventh bhava as well.

DASHAS AND GOCHARAS

All who live are busy, either growing or deteriorating, for life allows no permanent repose other than the grave. For any relationship, we need to know whether it is developing or dying, and also how swiftly and consistently that change is occurring. To perform this and many other types of horoscope appraisals, it is always useful to maintain a clear awareness of the distinction between static and dynamic astrological interpretation. Static interpretations generate general descriptions that set parameters of possibility over the total course of any experience, such as marriage. Dynamic interpretations focus more on specific segments of time during that overall experience.

To say that someone has difficult marriage karma is a static interpretation that glosses over personal bests in marriage, sacrificing them to the bottom line of the marital dynamic. A person may have been madly in love for a couple of years in each of five marriages, but if each of those marriages led to years of chaos and ended in divorce, then these marriages were clearly difficult. Periods of love and alignment are thus discounted in the overall assessment of the marriage patterns.

Dynamically, the individual described above is said to have had great marital encounters during years of love and bitter marriage experiences at other times, the highs and lows being valued equally as parts of the astrological interpretation. Everything that has been introduced in this book so far has revolved around static analysis. Now it is time to address the question of dynamic analysis. From now on, our examinations, both of individual charts and of comparisons, will make use of both static and dynamic analyses.

To reiterate, a static evaluation assesses a horoscope's permanent potential, and a dynamic assessment predicts when these potentials are likely to develop. Static interpretation tells us whether or not a horoscope promises a successful marriage, while dynamic interpretation predicts at what age such a marriage is likely to begin and when we may expect its highs and lows. In Jyotisha, static evaluations derive from analysis of houses, their lords, and their significators, while dynamic assessments involve the use of progressed time periods known as dashas and bhuktis, and of the ongoing movements of the planets known as gocharas (transits).

Sometimes, a horoscope with good innate potential for success in relationships will temporarily promise relationship hassles because of the dasha and/or bhukti in progress. The reverse also happens, when a chart with difficult placements promises temporary relief during a favorite dasha/bhukti. Such phenomena may cause a long-term chart comparison to ring untrue over the short term. On rare occasions, the temporary indications may even overwhelm the general indications for compatibility, causing the relationship to break.

We do not wish, by drawing a distinction between static and dynamic analysis, to suggest that they are insulated from one another. There is, rather a spectrum or continuum of methods that range from the exceedingly static at one end to the exceptionally dynamic at the other. Outcome analysis, for example, hovers close to the far static end of the static-dynamic spectrum, with cornerstone analysis closer to its center. One evaluation that combines both static and dynamic analysis involves comparing what the natal chart promises with what the dasha promises when these two factors disagree. If natal chart and dasha both promise positive results, or both promise negative results, the conclusion is clear. If, however, the dasha is fundamentally positive when the natal chart is negative, or vice versa, greater judgment will be necessary.

One example of an evaluation that may be found further toward the dynamic end of the continuum is the process of comparing the positions of the dasha lords in the two natal charts. If, for example, both dasha lords are influencing both Ascendants in the two charts under consideration, even if there is otherwise no foundation in synastry between them, there may be the possibility for some affiliation to occur, at least for as long as that dasha continues. Perhaps the most dynamic method of dynamic analysis are those that involve transits, both of grahas in general, and of dasha lords specifically. Before we examine transits, however, let us first consider a few of the implications of dasha periods in synastry.

Dasha Sandhi

The most widely used of the many different dasha systems that grace Jyotisha is the *vimshottari dasha,* in which a prototypical 120-year human life is divided into nine unequal periods, each ruled by one of Jyotisha's nine grahas. The Sun, for example, is assigned 6 years, the Moon, 10, Mars, 7, Rahu, 18, Jupiter, 16, Saturn, 19, Mercury, 17, Ketu, 7, and Venus, 20. Each of these dasha periods is further subdivided into smaller periods known as bhuktis, each bhukti possessing a length that is proportionate to its length as a dasha. For example, based on this proportion, the Venus bhukti in the Jupiter dasha lasts for two years and eight months, and the Mars bhukti during the Venus dasha endures for fourteen months.[1]

The sequence of dashas is identical for everyone; where a particular individual's dasha sequence begins depends on the precise position of the Moon, the fastest moving of the grahas, at the time of birth. Obviously, any two people are unlikely to be running precisely the same dasha at precisely the same time, because of the many different positions that the Moon attains within a single month. It is not uncommon, however, for two people to begin the same dasha within a few years of one another. In such cases, the overlapping of some portion of one set of dashas will be followed, generally, by the overlapping of some portion of the rest.

The period during which one dasha ends and the next begins is technically known as a *dasha sandhi.* As with gandanta (see page 171), dasha

[1] de Fouw and Svoboda, *Light on Life* (London: Penguin, 1996).

sandhi is one of the joints (sandhi = "joint") of time. Just as the joints of your body are threatened when they lack support, a dramatic difference in the placement of two dasha lords who are consecutive can readily dislocate the "joint" that they form. When time gets disjointed, people change. If their partners cannot cope with these changes, cracks can appear in the relationship's backbone. Just as overdeveloped thighs and underdeveloped calves can combine to place the knees at risk during exercise, the dynamic of a relationship can be put at risk when the dasha of a strong well-placed graha is followed by that of a weak, afflicted graha (or vice versa).

Jyotisha's tradition has it that people's lives tend to destabilize during these dasha sandhis, when the two dasha lords are not similarly placed. The period of greatest destabilization usually begins toward the end of the previous dasha and continues through the beginning of the next. We usually consider roughly 10 percent of a dasha's length to be expended in sandhi. To calculate this period, take the total of the durations of the two dashas, divide by ten, and apply one half of this amount, both to the end of the previous dasha, and the beginning of the next.

For example, we can calculate the length of the dasha sandhi that ends the Jupiter dasha and begins that of Saturn by taking the number of years present in the Jupiter dasha (16) plus the number assigned to Saturn (19), which gives us 35. Divide 35 by ten to give 3.5 years, then divide that in half to give 1.75 years, which is the amount of time isolated as sandhi at the end of Jupiter's dasha and the start of Saturn's. The sandhi that joins these two dashas thus constitutes the last year and nine months of the Jupiter dasha, and the first 21 months of Saturn. This period commonly begins with a gradual buildup of the new energy of the dasha to come, which climbs to its apex at the actual moment of transition. Thereafter, the influence of the dasha that has passed gradually winds down, until the full flow of the new dasha prevails.

A broader approach to dasha sandhi and the "spillover" effect is to think of the last bhukti of the dasha just ending and the first bhukti of the dasha just beginning as being flavored with crossover energies. This may be one reason why there is a general rule that grahas do not deliver their promised results during *svabhuktis*. A graha's *svabhukti* is its own bhukti, the bhukti that occurs at the very beginning of a graha's dasha. Jupiter-Jupiter is a svabhukti; so is Saturn-Saturn.

However one reckons it, dasha sandhi tends to cause things that may have been of central importance to you for many years to begin to lose their significance. Because the momentum that the new dasha will deliver is still feeble, however, the person, though beginning to feel his or her way forward, often cannot yet see clearly what is approaching. Like dusk and dawn, when neither day nor night is truly present, dasha sandhis are joints in time at which the world is run neither by one dasha lord nor the other. In such ill-defined epochs of life, change becomes possible. Such change may propel a person further in the direction he or she is already moving, or may create such a wrenching bend in a previously familiar road that it may precipitate a personality crisis. Such crises can spur people to question their self-definition, thereby giving them an opportunity for new growth. How these opportunities play out, and how that activity is perceived, rests squarely on the conditions of the grahas involved.

Dasha sandhis can be difficult in all areas of life, but they are often particularly problematical for relationships, for humans generally resist change. When, under the influence of an authoritative graha, one member of a couple begins to change, neither of the two may know any longer who the other "is." We can imagine four possible scenarios for this change, beginning with the best case, in which one good dasha glides smoothly into another similarly good one. In such cases, the re-evaluation that occurs will often lead to constructive changes in the relationship. A bad dasha that shifts into a good one may provide some initial uncertainty, but also delivers a generally optimistic feeling that improvement is on the way. When a good dasha veers into one that is less than wholesome, the essence of the sandhi is to make things look less rosy. And when a bad dasha skids into another dasha that promises nothing better, new problems tend to pile up atop the old. These obstacles can, when combined with the uncertainty that prevails during a sandhi, lead to a breaking point.

A unique case of dasha sandhi occurs when two people happen to come to the end of their dashas at almost the same time, a development that complicates their interactions markedly. If both new dashas in both charts are similarly well placed, the destabilization phenomenon of transitioning energy will be minimized. This is rare, however. More typically, the partner who goes from a worse dasha to a better one will struggle to understand the change of attitude on the part of the one who is going from better to worse. If both are headed from good to bad, their mutual distaste for their new circumstances will itself be stressful, and they may find that the variations in their new stresses enhance pre-existing divisive tendencies. Two people who go from bad dashas to dashas that are worse are likely to find themselves headed to divorce court.

For an example of dasha sandhi let us turn to the horoscopes of Prince Charles (see Chart 12, page 111) and Princess Diana (see Chart 13, page 113). Charles entered his Rahu dasha in January 1995, and Diana was due to enter her Saturn dasha in February 1998. Dasha sandhi would have operated for Charles between the beginning of the last bhukti of his Mars dasha (Mars-Moon, which began June 1994) and the end of the first bhukti of his Rahu dasha (Rahu-Rahu, which ended September 1997). Dasha sandhi would have operated for Diana between the beginning of the last bhukti of her Jupiter dasha (Jupiter-Rahu, which began September 1995) and the end of the first bhukti of her Saturn dasha (Saturn-Saturn, which would have ended February 2001). The dasha sandhi overlap between them thus transpired between September 1995 and September 1997.

Considering their respective charts, these do not appear to be dramatic dasha changes (though this appearance is somewhat misleading, as we shall see). Considering the lengths of their dasha sandhis, the overlap was not dramatic either. The fact is, however, that there was overlap, and the stresses of trying to save their marriage while living in a regal fishbowl were certainly extreme, extreme enough to inflate dramatically any lurking instabilities. The couple had announced their separation on December 9, 1992, well before dasha sandhi actually began for either. The actual divorce decree was issued only on August 28, 1996, however, a year and three days before Diana's untimely death and almost precisely in the middle of the overlap of their dasha sandhis.

When we examined the relationships of the four cornerstones in these two horoscopes, however, we found the two natives to be deceptively well aligned. Then on examining their navamshas, however, we discovered a significant challenge to that alignment, and now we find a further vulnerability, one that attacked at a critical juncture. Both were headed into the dasha of a major malefic, which made matters worse.

For Diana, it was a move from the dasha of natural benefic Jupiter into that of natural malefic Saturn. For Charles, it was a move from the dasha of one malefic into another, though, in his case, Mars acts less like a malefic than it might for most people because it is his raja yoga karaka, and occupies its own rashi. Rahu, in his chart, sits close to Moon (within our $7\frac{1}{2}°$ rule), and aspects the Sun and Mercury. Since Mercury and the Moon are two of the indicators of mind, Rahu's influence on them is very destabilizing, producing cloudy judgment, particularly during the Rahu-Rahu bhukti.

Diana was also moving from the dasha of a debilitated graha (Jupiter) to that of a graha who occupied his own rashi (Saturn). This, in and of itself, creates a potential for huge change, sufficient to have permitted her to stabilize herself, to "find" herself as it were. All aspects of her life would have stabilized generally, but particularly with regard to this relationship. In chapter 47 of his treatise, Parashara states that a graha that occupies its own rashi is *svastha* (a word that means both "healthy" and "self-established"). An exalted graha is *garvita* ("proud" or "haughty"), a graha that occupies an enemy's rashi is *dukhita* ("miserable"). A graha that occupies an enemy's rashi while conjoined with an enemy (which well describes Charles's Rahu) is *kruddha* (angry).

Diana's Jupiter was debilitated, and conjoined with malefic Saturn. Her Saturn was in its own rashi, and conjoined with benefic Jupiter (who is also the fifth lord). Her Saturn's condition is preferable to the condition of her Jupiter, for the Sanskrit term that another text uses to describe a debilitated graha is *dina* (wretched). One could argue that, since there is neecha bhanga for this Jupiter, who also participates in a dhana yoga and a raja yoga, such a graha could not be particularly wretched. This, however, would be to ignore the fact that indications in Jyotisha are cumulative; they do not always cancel. Jupiter's potent yogas displayed their effects in the high status Diana achieved during her Jupiter dasha, and the misery she underwent during that period reflected Jupiter's debilitation.

Sama Dasha

Sometimes, two people whose dashas run parallel to each other become involved in a relationship. This potent situation is known in Sanskrit as *sama dasha* or *dasha samya*. Two people who are attracted to each other, when both are in the same dasha, will discover much common ground between them, because the tone of that dasha will provide a similar vantage point that is conducive to rapport. A traveler who, while in a foreign country, meets a compatriot often finds an instant recognition and understanding pass between them, a common ground of experience that they can share, even if they are otherwise wholly different from one another. Daily encountering the influences of their dasha lord, the couple will share a quality of awareness that can often suffice to create a supportive common ground for their relationship, even when none of their four cornerstones agree. Each change of dasha then serves as a change of the lens through which they perceive their experiences of life. Re-evaluations will still roll around, but the glue of the commonality that is implied by the common dashas will allow the couple to continue to relate without significant interruption.

For example, suppose a couple begins their relationship when both are running their Mars dashas. Martian things are likely to bring them together: adventure, travel, bungee jumping, teasing, verbal fencing, or similar excitements. After their Martian encounter, they will find themselves together in a Rahu escapade, and then in a Jupiter tutorial, during which the couple will relate to each other in Jovan ways (providing sage advice and counsel to each other, perhaps). Later, when they move into Saturn, they will understand the value of solitude, detachment, and forbearance in relationship.

While there is no one rule to determine how close the inception dates of two dashas should be, roughly speaking, they should occur within a year and a half of each other for the benefits of dasha samya to be activated. Suppose a couple both have ongoing Saturn dashas that overlap by only five or six years. For those five or six years, they will experience a fragmentary sort of sama dasha. As soon as the one enters the Mercury dasha and leaves the other behind in Saturn, however, that shared Saturnian perception will be lost, and a transition must be braved. Should Mercury be well placed for marriage, the marriage will continue with strength and dynamism, but if that Mercury is poorly placed for marriage, inescapable stress will develop in the relationship. In either case, the new dasha samya-free situation will demand some adjustment.

What we have described thus far is only a general principle—one that becomes more specific when more factors are evaluated. We can, for instance, factor in the position of the two dasha lords relative to each other, to provide us information on the nature of the interaction between the partners. A couple who are moving from Saturn dashas whose Saturns were Six-Eight to one another into Mercury dashas are likely to find that they are suddenly doing better together if those Mercuries are Five-Nine to one another. Similarly, a couple that is moving from Moon dashas in which their Moons were Three-Eleven to each other into Mars dashas where their Marses are Two-Twelve to each other are probably going to find themselves walking into relationship difficulties as they cross the threshold into their new dashas.

This principle applies even when dasha samya is absent between two people. Take a couple who are running the Mars and Venus dashas whose respective Mars and Venus are Five-Nine to each other. They are more likely, all other factors being equal, to have an agreeable time of it than are another couple with the same ongoing dashas whose Mars and Venus are Two-Twelve or Six-Eight to one another. Similarly, a couple running the dashas of a Mars and Jupiter who are Five-Nine to each other are more likely to enjoy the experience than would another couple who are running the dashas of a the Sun and Saturn who are Five-Nine to each other. Mars and Jupiter are mutual friends, after all, and Sun and Saturn are mutual enemies. In these and similar instances, the Rule of $7\frac{1}{2}°$ applies when estimating intensity of effect.

It is the potential for such unpleasant surprises that makes it not necessarily beneficial for dasha transitions to occur too close to one another. If, for example, a couple is running dasha samya within a few months, and if the grahas involved are positioned in radically different places in their birth charts, the jarringly different surge in perception that may transpire could easily give rise to problems instead of resolving them. This is the primary negative exception to this otherwise positive rule, for such moments could certainly pull the couple apart.

TIMING OF MARRIAGES AND OTHER RELATIONSHIPS

We cannot hope to do justice, in this chapter, to the exceptionally complex question of timing. What we have included here are some relatively straightforward and simple methods that may provide hints toward the timing of marriages and other romantic involvements.

Dasha-based Principles

1. Dashas of grahas that own, occupy, or aspect the seventh bhava are key indicators of marriage during those periods;
2. The dasha of Venus, who is the natural significator for marriage, may prove productive, particularly if Venus has some connection with the seventh bhava and/or is involved somehow with grahas that are connected to the seventh bhava;
3. The lagna lord, the fifth lord, and the occupants of the first and fifth bhavas will also tend to give marriage during their dashas;
4. The dasha of an exalted graha (except the nodes), whether or not connected to seventh bhava or seventh lord, may activate marriage;
5. Sometimes the twelfth lord as the natural indicator of bhoga (here, pleasures of the bed) can indicate marriage and/or a sexually intimate relationship during its periods;

6. The *vivaha saham* ("point of marriage"): Subtract the longitude of Saturn from that of Venus and add the longitude of the lagna (if the position of Venus is less than that of Saturn, add 360°). Chances for wedlock will occur during the dashas and/or bhuktis of the lord of the rashi and the nakshatra in which that point falls.

Transit-based Principles

1. Add together the longitudes of the lagna lord and the seventh lord, and cast out 360° if need be. When Jupiter transits that rashi then marriage, the inception of a relationship, or even the meeting of someone that one marries later may ensue. This is especially true in the Western context, where there are more opportunities for multiple overt relationships. This also holds true for cases in which Jupiter transits the rashis that hold the trines of this point, or its opposite rashi. Although this principle is widely known in Jyotisha, none of the standard texts will tell you that the principle can be refined by considering, from those three points, whether Jupiter will aspect the seventh bhava, and/or the seventh lord, and/or Venus. The more of these factors it influences the better, from the confluence point of view.

2. When Jupiter transits the seventh bhava or the seventh lord or their trines *(Phaladipika)*. Indian jyotishis use many more such Jupiter trine-transit principles, searching always for confluence. When Jupiter is strongly placed in one of these places of transit, and/or it aspects multiple marriage factors (seventh bhava, seventh lord, Venus), and/or the dasha-bhukti happen to agree, such a transit becomes more likely to produce results with every added confluent factor.

Remember as you seek to combine the influences of dasha-bhukti with gochara, the salient rule that a transiting graha cannot provide other than what it promises by static analysis. What can change is the degree to which it will cooperate. An exalted or own-rashi graha is likely to transmit the most of what can be expected, while a graha that is debilitated in transit is unlikely to deliver on its pledge.

Examples of Timing

The glittering royal wedding between Charles and Diana transpired on July 29, 1981, during Charles's Moon-Jupiter period. Moon is empowered to give marriage to Charles according to principle 3 above (see page 266).

Principle 3 also operates for Diana, who married in her Rahu-Mars period. On the day of the wedding, Jupiter occupied Virgo, which, in both charts is a rashi that trines the seventh bhava.

These nuptials took place when an already-wan Moon (closely conjoined with Mars) was continuing to wane. More significant as a timing criterion, however, was the planetary war that Jupiter was fighting with Saturn. Planetary war is hardly ever good in a muhurta chart, no matter which graha wins. It is never appropriate for two grahas to vie for the same space, for such conflicts are bound to distort their energies. This conjunction takes on paramount importance in this muhurta, because Saturn·is the lord of Charles's seventh bhava. Would a better muhurta have prevented their divorce? We will never know, but there is a good possibility that it might have.

Newman and Woodward married when Jupiter was transiting Libra, one of the trines to Gemini, the seventh bhava in each of their charts. Since Newman's Saturn-Saturn was ongoing at the time of his marriage, Jupiter in Libra happened to be transiting his dasha lord. Saturn is, here, empowered to give marriage, because he is exalted (see page 266), particularly because he also aspects both the seventh lord and Venus, the significator of marriage. Saturn is yet further empowered to deliver wedlock to Newman, for he is lord of the rashi in which falls this horoscope's vivaha saham (22°05' of Aquarius). This effect is compounded because Saturn was lord of Newman's bhukti at the time, as well as lord of his dasha.

Woodward's dasha and bhukti at the time of marriage was Jupiter-Ketu. Jupiter is empowered, by principle 3 above (see page 266), to give matrimony, by virtue of being lord of Woodward's Ascendant, especially since Jupiter aspects her seventh lord, as well as her twelfth lord and twelfth bhava. Moreover, Jupiter is lord of the nakshatra (purva bhadrapada) in which Woodward's vivaha saham falls (22°22' of Aquarius). How impressive that the vivaha sahams of the couple are but 17' of arc apart!

Newman and Woodward married January 29, 1958, an appropriate weekday (Wednesday) when the Moon was bright and strong (being exalted). One downside to this muhurta is that Venus is exceptionally combust (being a mere 1°40' distant from the Sun), a weakness that is partially modified by the fact of its also being retrograde. Had Woodward and Newman requested the assistance of a competent jyotishi before the fact, they would likely have been given a better muhurta; this rather second-rate one sufficed because of the multiplicity of the strengths in their synastry.

CONCLUSION

One final, perhaps most important, reminder to our readers: Even when we find two people with good individual relationship skills and outcomes, whose chart comparison shows good shared relationship skills and outcomes, there is no guarantee that those two people will get involved with one another! Nor is there any guarantee that people whose shared relationship skills are impaired will not get involved. Involvement is the interplay of adrishta and free will, of pre-existing karmas and those that are currently being planned and performed. An alchemical approach to relationship acknowledges the karma and vasana realities that exist, and takes them as raw materials that can be transmuted into relationship gold. Sufficient patience, diligence, and enterprise can often make even grim situations more tolerable. Some interactions that, at first, seemed doomed can bear rare blossoms. The Philosopher's Stone in relationship is the talisman that provides us the eyes to see where we are karmically, how our vasanas are impelling us to cope with our situation, and what we can do to transform ourselves.

APPENDIX

Table of Nakshatras (showing the position of each of the 27 lunar nakshatras in the sidereal zodiac and their planetary rulers).

To determine the nakshatra that a graha occupies in a horoscope, transfer the position of the graha to this Table of Nakshatras. A graha that occupies 14°26' of Aries falls in Bharani, and the nakshatra ruler of such a graha is Venus. The same method is used to determine rulership of a bhava cusp. If the cusp of the seventh bhava (or any other bhava, for that matter) falls at 25°47' of Libra, then it falls in the nakshatra of Vishakha, and the nakshatra ruler of such a bhava cusp is Jupiter.

Name & Number	Zodiacal Position	Ruler of (Lord)
1. Ashvini	00°00' ♈ to 13°20' ♈	Ketu
2. Bharani	13°20' ♈ to 26°40' ♈	Venus
3. Krittika	26°40' ♈ to 10°00' ♉	Sun
4. Rohini	10°00' ♉ to 23°20' ♉	Moon
5. Mrigashirsha	23°20' ♉ to 06°40' ♊	Mars
6. Ardra	06°40' ♊ to 20°00' ♊	Rahu
7. Punarvasu	20°00' ♊ to 03°20' ♋	Jupiter
8. Pushya	03°20' ♋ to 16°40' ♋	Saturn
9. Ashlesha	16°40' ♋ to 30°00' ♋	Mercury
10. Magha	00°00' ♌ to 13°20' ♌	Ketu
11. Purva Phalguni	13°20' ♌ to 26°40' ♌	Venus
12. Uttara Phalguni	26°40' ♌ to 10°00' ♍	Sun
13. Hasta	10°00' ♍ to 23°20' ♍	Moon
14. Chitra	10°00' ♍ to 23°20' ♎	Mars
15. Swati	06°40' ♎ to 20°00' ♎	Rahu
16. Vishakha	20°00' ♎ to 03°20' ♏	Jupiter
17. Anuradha	03°20' ♏ to 16°40' ♏	Saturn
18. Jyeshtha	16°40' ♏ to 30°00' ♏	Mercury
19. Mula	00°00' ♐ to 13°20' ♐	Ketu
20. Purva Ashadha	13°20' ♐ to 26°40' ♐	Venus
21. Uttara Ashadha	26°40' ♐ to 10°00' ♑	Sun
22. Shravana	00°00' ♑ to 23°20' ♑	Moon
23. Dhanishtha	23°20' ♑ to 06°40' ♒	Mars
24. Shatabhisha	06°40' ♒ to 20°00' ♒	Rahu
25. Purva Bhadrapada	20°00' ♒ to 03°20' ♓	Jupiter
26. Uttara Bhadrapada	03°20' ♓ to 16°40' ♓	Saturn
27. Revati	16°40' ♓ to 30°00' ♓	Mercury

GLOSSARY

adhipati: Lord, especially of a rashi.

adridha karma: Adridha (unfixed) karmas produce results that can be easily altered by the concentrated application of creative will.

adrishta: Literally, "unseen"; unobserved but puissant influences that may affect you even without your seeing it. Adrishta is the soil in which we plant our actions.

ahamkara: The I-forming power of consciousness.

amsha: A micro-zodiac or calculated chart, also known as a varga, similar to what Western astrologers call harmonic charts. Jyotisha's classical literature describes methods for constructing twenty or more of these amshas, each of which describes a different aspect of an individual's life.

ascendant: The lagna or rising sign of a horoscope. The Ascendant is an important general indicator for overall sukha in one's life. Both the Ascendant and its lord should be strong for all of the areas of one's life to be aligned. Jyotisha reads the physical body from the Ascendant.

ashtaka varga: The "eightfold interrelationship" of the grahas, a method for determining the effects of transits that is also used as an system of interpretation.

asta: Literally, "set"; an "asta" graha is combust, so close to the sun that it is lost to the view of the naked eye. Combust planets are weak, unable to deliver what they promise.

auras: Human interchange involves the attraction or repulsion of auras (chaya), the fields of energy that surround living organisms. The human aura is the shadow that matter creates when illumined by consciousness, and the luster that radiates when consciousness reflects itself in the mirror of matter. The auras and rasas of those people with whom you associate will influence your own auras and rasas. The degree of aura alignment or misalignment determines to a substantial degree how aligned or misaligned a couple will be. Jyotisha endeavors to determine how well or poorly the auras of two humans will interact by comparing the mutual influences of each of the nine grahas in the individual auras of the couple.

avayoga nakshatra: The nakshatra that contains the avayoga point.

avayoga point: The avayoga point is found by adding 186°40' to the yoga point, and expunging multiples of 360° if possible. The avayoga point always occupies the fifteenth nakshatra from the yoga nakshatra, counted inclusively.

avayogi: The avayogi is the lord of the avayoga nakshatra. The avayogi obstructs a person's prosperity.

Ayurveda: India's classical healing art; literally, "the knowledge of life."

baladi avasthas: One set of avasthas (planetary states or conditions) which evaluates a graha's strength or weakness via its degree position in a bhava.

bhava: A state or condition of existence. The twelve bhavas (astrological houses) of Jyotisha each defines the state of karma of one portion of life. Taken together these twelve bhavas house the totality of your external existence as they are experienced by the internal states of your being.

bhoga: Enjoyment, indulgence.

bhukti: A sub-period, a smaller division of time within a dasha.

budhaditya yoga: A combination that occurs when the Sun and Mercury occupy the same rashi.

chandra lagna: The lagna obtained by taking as the Ascendant the rashi that the Moon occupies. We examine the chandra lagna to evaluate the astral or subtle body.

chandra managala yoga: A combination that occurs when the Moon and Mars occupy the same rashi.

chaya: Shadow, reflection, luster; in the context of human beings, the aura.

chaya grahas: Rahu and Ketu, the Moon's Nodes, are chaya grahas ("shadow planets") who project life's "shadows," the fears, phobias, hang-ups, and secret lives that many of us lead or dream of leading.

chi: The Chinese word for prana, the life force.

dasha samya: Occurs when two people whose dashas run parallel to each other develop a relationship. Such people will discover much common ground between them.

dasha sandhi: The period during which one dasha ends and the next begins is technically known a dasha sandhi. A dramatic difference in the placement of two dasha lords who are consecutive can readily dislocate the "joint" that they form, and many relationships cannot cope with such disjunctions.

dasha: A dasha is a "planetary period," an interval during which a particular graha's influence on a person will be paramount.

dasya: The humble devotedness of a servant for his master.

debilitation: A graha's weakest degree position in the zodiac.

deha prakriti: Constitutional physiological pattern. An individual's prakriti is his or her innate proportion of doshas. This prakriti can often be determined from a horoscope, by focusing on the dosha natures of the grahas that influence the lagna, lagnesha, Sun, and Moon.

deva: A divinity, deity; divine.

dhana yoga: An astrological combination for wealth.

dharma karma adhipati yoga: This yoga is formed when the lord of a trinal bhava (a *dharma* bhava-bhavas 5 & 9) combines in a horoscope, either by aspect or by association, with the lord of an angular (karma) bhava (bhavas 4, 7, & 10).

dina poruttham: Another name for nakshatra poruttham, which evaluates the health and longevity of the partners with reference to one another.

dosha: A fault or mistake. When a graha is very afflicted it causes a graha dosha, of which kuja dosha is an example. The three doshas of Ayurveda are the three forces that control all activities of life in all protoplasmic beings; they are vata, pitta and kapha. Sun and Mars are pitta grahas; so is Ketu. Jupiter is a kapha graha. Saturn is a vata graha, as is Rahu. Moon and Venus indicate both kapha and vata. Mercury can indicate any of the three doshas.

dosha parihara: Mitigating or modifying circumstances for an astrological dosha, especially for kuja dosha.

dridha karma: Dridha ("fixed") karmas give fixed pleasurable or painful results; they are so difficult to change that they are practically non-changeable.

dridha-adridha karma: Dridha-adridha ("fixed/unfixed") karmas are karmas whose potential to give good or bad results can be changed with considerable effort through the concentrated application of creative will. Dridha-adridha karmas give fixed or unfixed results according to the quantum of effort employed toward the goal of change.

duplicate yogi: The lord of the rashi in which sits the yoga point.

dushkriti yoga: A "miscreant combination" that exists when a horoscope's seventh bhava is occupied or aspected by malefics and the lord of that bhava is afflicted and is not influenced by any benefics.

dussambandha: A dussambandha ("poor relationship") yoga, which portends substantial relationship difficulties in life, is formed when a large number of inimical dispositions occur between the lord of the first bhava and other grahas in its horoscope.

dvadashamsha: The dvadashamsha ("twelfth division") reduplicates the order of the natural zodiac within each of the 30° constellations of a horoscope's macro-zodiac, each of the dozen portions of that 30° being 2½°. In the context of primary relationships the dvadashamsha micro-zodiac relates to everything about one's parents.

dvesha: Repugnance; two people whose relationship "chemistry" is completely off will progressively develop an ever-deepening mutual revulsion (dvesha) that will drive them apart.

gandanta: Gandanta occurs when a child is born with the Moon (or sometimes the Ascendant) occupying the last 3°20' of Ashlesha, Jyeshtha, or Revati nakshatras or the first 3°20' of Ashvini, Magha, or Mula nakshatras. Grahas located at gandanta points are very weak, and indicate major problems in the native's life (or that of a poshaka) unless appropriate remedies are used to mitigate the karmic implications of such placements. The principles of gandanta should not be used in isolation; they must be supplemented by a fuller analysis of the horoscope.

gaja kesari yoga: Jupiter occupying the bhavas 1, 4, 7, or 10 as counted from the Moon, with both grahas occupying good bhavas as counted from the Ascendant.

gana: Gana ("class or category") poruttham evaluates a couple's general sukha by classifying them according to three categories as shown by the nakshatra positions of their Moons. A sort of natural rapport exists between people from the same gana, who can often adapt to one another more readily than can people of different ganas.

gocharas: Transits.

graha: The nine "planets" of Jyotisha: Sun, Moon, Mars, Mercury, Jupiter, Venus, Saturn, Rahu, and Ketu.

graha dosha: Graha dosha occurs when one or more grahas are so afflicted that they derange those areas of life that they influence. Kuja dosha is one such graha dosha.

graha prakriti: Astrological constitution.

guru kripa: Divine grace.

hamsa yoga: Is formed when Jupiter occupies its own or exaltation rashi while in an angular bhava.

hetu: a proximal or concomitant cause that delivers new energy (shakti) to a person.

janma: Natal astrology, which examines the karmic balances or imbalances that the couple brought forward into this lifetime. Janma assesses the way in which a couple will relate.

Jyotisha: The "study of light"; Indian astrology.

jyotishi: A practitioner of Jyotisha.

kala sarpa yoga: The "Serpent of Time" yoga, formed when all the grahas from Sun through Saturn are situated between Rahu and Ketu.

Kali: The goddess of death and transformation.

Kali Yuga: The "Iron Age," the age during which civilization deteriorates greatly.

kama shastra: The study of the arts of love.

kama yoga: A "desire/passion combination," which is formed when a horoscope's seventh bhava is aspected by benefics, the lord of the seventh bhava occupies a good bhava while associated with benefics, and the seventh bhava is not afflicted by malefics.

kapha: Kapha, which arises from the water element, controls body stability and lubrication. The tissues and wastes of the body are kapha's province.

karaka: The karaka (literally, "agent, doer") of a bhava is its natural significator.

karako bhavo nashto: Karako bhavo nashto, which occurs when the significator of a relative or spouse occupies its own bhava in the birth chart, "destroys" the indications of that bhava. In the context of marriage, a Venus that occupies the seventh bhava "destroys" the seventh bhava. Karako bhavo nashto can also be applied to the navamsha.

karma: The sum of all our actions is our karma. Relationships are coordinated by both the singular individual karmas that partners bring to the interaction and by the shared karmas that the couple generate together. Jyotisha is a karma-measuring apparatus, which evaluates the karmas for any one bhava from the conditions of the bhava, the lord of that bhava, and its significator.

karyesha: ("Lord of the effect/purpose") The lagnesha is the lord of the Ascendant, and the karyesha is the lord of the bhava whose effect you wish to analyze. For marriage the karyesha will be the lord of the seventh bhava.

kendras: The angular bhavas (bhavas 1, 4, 7, 10) of a horoscope.

kona: The trinal bhavas (bhavas 1, 5, 9) of a horoscope.

koshas: The bodies or "sheaths" of an organism that represent consciousness expressing itself at different levels of matter. Five koshas are commonly described in classical Indian traditions.

kriyamana karma: Our current actions, which will give results in the future.

Kubera: The Indian god of wealth.

kuja dosha: Kuja dosha ("the blemish of Mars") is defined as a birth that occurs whenever Mars occupies bhavas 1, 2, 4, 7, 8, or 12 in a horoscope as counted from the Ascendant, the Moon, or Venus. Kuja dosha becomes stronger when it appears in two of these three positions, and is particularly malignant when it recurs from all three positions. Kuja dosha has the potential to severely disrupt a marriage, though one should predict abject marital misery only where there is no mitigation. There is disagreement as to what constitutes a legitimate modification to kuja dosha.

kusanga: Kusanga ("bad blending") takes place when you overexpose yourself to people who are predominantly selfish.

kutams: Kutams (roughly, "a group with a purpose"), also known as porutthams (q.v.), are methods of synastry that determine the degree of a couple's compatibility by using a system of points derived solely from the interaction of the Moons in each birth chart.

lagna: The Ascendant (q.v.) or rising sign of a horoscope.

lagnesha: Lord of the Ascendant.

Lakshmi: The Indian goddess of wealth.

madhurya: The intensely fervent craving that a passionate woman feels for her lover.

maha bhava: Literally, "super bhava," a samadhi (spiritual trance) in which one goes mad with uncontrollable love and joy.

mahendra poruttham: Mahendra ("great lord") poruttham evaluates both a couple's ability to have children (the "fruit" of coupling) and the happiness they will derive from their progeny.

malavya yoga: Formed when Venus occupies its own or exaltation rashi while in an angular bhava.

manas: The astral or subtle body; loosely, the mind.

mangala: "Auspicious"; a name for the graha Mars.

mangala sutras: The wedding necklaces that most Indian women wear instead of wedding rings.

manomayakosha: The "sheath of mind"; the astral or subtle body.

manushya: Human.

mrita avastha: A "dead state," which occurs to a graha that occupies the last 6° of an odd-numbered rashi or the first 6° of an even-numbered rashi.

muhurta: Electional astrology, the art of optimizing free will by selecting astrologically auspicious moments for beginning any endeavor.

nadi poruttham: In nadi poruttham the nakshatras are classified into three groups, known as the kapha, pitta, and vata nadis, respectively, referring to the three principle constitutions of Ayurveda, India's classical system of medicine.

nakshatra: One of Jyotisha's 27 or 28 sidereal lunar asterisms (see Appendix for details).

nakshatra poruttham: This poruttham, which is also known as dina poruttham in southern India, evaluates the health and longevity of the partners with reference to one another.

napumsaka: Sexually ambiguous.

navamsha: The navamsha (ninth division) is a harmonic chart that reduplicates a micro-zodiac whose every portion is 3°20'. It is primarily used in Jyotisha for marriage analysis. Accurate analysis based on navamsha is totally contingent on an accurate birth time.

neecha bhanga: "Cancellation of debility"; any of a group of combinations that mitigates a debilitated graha's condition.

ojas: An exceptionally subtle form of rasa that creates an organism's aura.

padas: One of the four equal segments into which each nakshatra is divided.

panchanga: Indian ephemeris.

parama rasa: "Supreme rasa," the transcendental flavor of God-consciousness.

Parvati: The goddess who is the consort of Lord Shiva.

pitri paksha: The two weeks during the year during which ancestor veneration alone is an appropriate form of ritual worship. The pitri paksha ("forefather fortnight") occupies the dark half of the lunar month of Bhadrapada. The dates for the pitri paksha change annually due to fluctuations in the lunar year, but fall sometime during September or the first half of October.

pitta: Pitta arises from the fire element. Its processes all involve digestion or "cooking." The enzymatic and endocrine systems are pitta's main field of activity.

porutthams: The porutthams (loosely, "a compatible union"), or kutams, are methods of synastry that determine the degree of a couple's compatibility by using a system of points derived solely from the interaction of the Moons in each birth chart. Traditionally ten in number, these principles can also be extended to the Ascendants as well. The porutthams are secondary methods of chart compatibility analysis whose principal utility is their ability to highlight specific areas of relationship strength and weakness.

poshaka: "Nourisher," the person who nourishes a baby or small child, its provider.

prakriti: Prakriti literally means "first reaction." Your prakriti is an inborn proclivity that tends to determine your first reaction to a perceived stress.

prana: The life force, the power that strings together body, mind, and spirit.

prashna: Horary astrology; literally, "question." In the context of synastry, prashna can evaluate a couple's present karmic prospects, and can suggest whether two people will pursue a relationship or not.

primary links: Primary links arise through the contacts of the four cornerstones of relationship life as mutually exclusive pairs: Ascendant to Ascendant, Moon to Moon, Sun to Sun, and Venus to Venus. The primary links forged by these mutually exclusive pairs are exceptionally potent, and the nature of the interactions of these four pairs of cornerstones are potent indicators of whether a healthy relationship will develop between two people. Two people will rarely enter into a lasting harmonious relationship unless some strongly positive primary link exists between their birth charts.

punarbhu: Punarbhu, which is an association of the Moon and Saturn, or an aspect of Saturn on the Moon, indicates a sudden, out of the blue, frequently unanticipated change of heart that occurs between two people planning to marry. Punarbhu delivers its promised results particularly in horoscopes that belong to women. Though punarbhu can manifest at any point in a person's life, it ordinarily does so prior to age 30.

raga: The word *raga* means "rage, passion, redness, inflammation." The many modes of Indian music are called ragas. Two people who share relationship "chemistry" will tend to promote intensifying passion (raga) in their relationship, which will tend to transform their bhavas into delightful rasas.

raja yoga karaka: A raja yoga karaka is a graha who in and of itself fulfills the requirements for creating a dharma karma adhipati yoga in a horoscope by virtue of owning both an angular bhava and a trinal bhava.

rajju poruttham: Rajju ("rope") poruttham evaluates longevity, both of the spouse and the relationship.

rakshasa: Demon, demonic.

rasa: *Rasa* in Sanskrit represents "juice," in all senses of that word. Rasas are "fluid realities." The flavors of the juices that make up our bodies and minds combine together to create our personal emotional rasas, the subjective perceptions that are the juices that water our soul. Your rasas (juice, essence) are what you experience as a result of your bhavas. Individual bhavas produce individual rasas, and the overall bhava of your life produces an overall rasa that is the "expression in juice" of your life's unique flavor. Delicious rasas make for a life of sukha. Relationship "chemistry" is a function of rasa.

rasa vidya: Indian alchemy.

rasahina: "Dry and tasteless"; an existence that is bereft of emotions.

rasatmaka: Filled with rasa.

rasayana: Rejuvenation; literally, "the path of rasa."

rashi: Any one of the 12 astrological constellations.

rashi poruttham: Rashi ("heap or mass") poruttham evaluates the impact of a potential union on the overall prosperity of the social systems within which the couple exists.

rashi sandhi: The boundary between two rashis; grahas are weak when posited in these regions.

rashyadhipati poruttham: Rashyadhipati ("rashi lord") poruttham evaluates the prospects for a couple to have strong children, and the prospects for prosperity in the lives of those offspring.

retrogression: The seemingly backward motion of the planets.

rnanubandhana: Bonds of karmic debt.

sadhana: Spiritual discipline.

sakhya: The friendly camaraderie of two near-equals.

sama dasha: Occurs when two people whose dashas run parallel to each other develop a relationship. Such people will discover much common ground between them.

samasaptami: Literally, "same/seventh"; this happens when a couple's Moons occupy the same or the opposite rashis.

sambandha: Affiliation, connection, relation.

sandhi: A joint, boundary.

Sankhya: The Indian philosophical system that is the basis for Jyotisha, Ayurveda, and Tantra.

Saraswati: The Indian goddess of knowledge.

satsanga: Satsanga ("true blending") occurs by interacting primarily with people who pursue generally altruistic goals.

secondary links: Secondary links arise through the cross-contacts across two horoscopes of any two of the four cornerstones of relationship. Six pairs of secondary links can arise between two horoscopes: Ascendant-Sun, Ascendant-Moon, Ascendant-Venus, Sun-Moon, Sun-Venus, and Moon-Venus. These are calculated twice, from the first horoscope to the second and then from the second back to the first. Secondary links means that they can be "mutual" or "unilateral." Unilateral secondary links are less meaningful than primary and mutual secondary links, but they add to the overall pattern of attraction, in a one-sided sort of way.

shad bala: The "six strengths," a group of mathematical formulas often used in Jyotisha to generate precise numerical values for each graha's overall strength.

shanti: Peace.

shuddha patrika: "Pure chart," a horoscope that contains no kuja dosha.

siddhi: "Extraordinary or supernatural achievement," especially one obtained as a result of sadhana.

sidereal: "Pertaining to the stars"; the sidereal zodiac is the zodiac whose starting point is fixed in relationship to certain fixed stars.

significator: The significator (karaka) of a bhava is that graha which has a natural affinity with the life themes of that bhava. Evaluation of a natural significator can provide support and color when evaluating a bhava. The natural significator for a bhava assumes great importance when the Ascendant lord owns that bhava.

stri dirgha poruttham: Stri dirgha ("long woman") poruttham evaluates the partners' prosperity, of which wealth is the main but not the sole criterion.

sudarshana: Sudarshana ("good sight") is a principle whereby horoscopes are tied down from three angles: the Ascendant, the Moon as Ascendant, and the Sun as Ascendant. Sudarshana is "good sight" because it makes embodied life visible to us from its three most fundamental perspectives: the physical (Ascendant), the mental/emotional (Moon), and the spiritual (Sun).

sukha: Literally, "good space," a state in which all the many "spaces" of a life are "good." It appears in a life only when internal satisfaction blends with material sufficiency.

sukhahina: "Bereft of sukha"; unhappy.

surya lagna: The lagna obtained by taking as the Ascendant the rashi that the Sun occupies. We examine the surya lagna to evaluate the causal body.

susambandha: Literally, "good relationship"; a susambandha yoga occurs when multiple grahas in a horoscope create harmonious "skill" placements with the Ascendant lord.

svabhukti: A graha's own bhukti, which occurs at the very beginning of a its dasha.

synastry: The art of assessing the relationship dynamic between two or more people by comparing their horoscopes.

Tajika: The system of Jyotisha that uses many Arabic astrological methods.

Tantra: A body of Indian religion and spiritual practices that requires both intellectual knowledge/understanding and ritual participation. Tantra teaches that the highest of human aspirations is to re-create the divine act of creation by harnessing and cultivating will, action, and knowledge through sadhana.

tithi: The thirty different phases of an Indian lunar month.

trikona: Trinal bhava.

tropical: "Pertaining to the turning"; the tropical zodiac is the zodiac whose starting point changes each year according to the position of the sun in relation to the zodiac's fixed stars at the moment of the vernal equinox.

udaya lagna: The Ascendant lagna.

upachaya: "Improvement"; the upachaya bhavas of a horoscope (bhavas 3, 6, 10, 11) are bhavas of improvement.

upaya: Astrological remedy.

varga kundalis: The horoscope's harmonic sub-charts; amshas.

vasanas: Our relating abilities (our skills) arise from our vasanas (psychic residues created by karmas). Vasanas can be examined by comparing the positions of the lords of the first bhava (which represents the individual) and of the bhava that represents the person with whom the native relates. To compare the vasana alignment between any two specific bhavas of the horoscopes of a couple, check the relative rashi placements of the lords of the two bhavas.

vashya poruttham: Vashya ("obedient") poruttham evaluates the couple's mutual attraction and respect. It comments on the couple's mutual harmony.

vastu shastra: The art of construction and configuration.

vasumati yoga: Occurs when the benefics occupy all the upachaya bhavas (3, 6, 10, 11) as counted from the Moon or from the Ascendant.

vata: The dosha that arises from the air element. Vata controls all body movement, and concentrates mainly in the nervous system.

vedha poruttham: Vedha ("pious, virtuous, wise") poruttham evaluates the couple's resilience, their ability to ensure long-term happiness by driving away all misfortunes.

vimshottari dasha: The most widely used of the many different dasha systems of Jyotisha. The vimshottari dasha system divides a prototypical 120-year human life into nine unequal periods each ruled by one of Jyotisha's nine grahas.

visha kanya: Visha kanya is the general name of a set of astrological combinations that are traditionally said to portend widowhood but more often indicate proneness to hypersensitivity. Each combination involves births that occur when a specific nakshatra and specific tithi fall on a specific weekday. Part of the effect that a visha kanya produces in India is likely to be due to cultural and psychological factors, with fear of the influence of such women tending to produce a self-fulfilling prophecy. When a visha kanya combination appears in conjunction with the "poison line" (visha rekha) of palmistry the tendency toward hypersensitivity amplifies dramatically, especially in a very long and narrow hand.

visha rekha: The "poison line" is a horizontal line on the ulnar side of the palm about one inch above the main crease mark at the wrist. The line, which is typically about one inch long, runs from the outside of the hand toward its center, parallel to the wrist. When present it is usually quite visible, though it is typically much fainter than the main flexion lines of the hand.

vivaha saham: "Point of marriage," calculated by subtracting the longitude of Saturn from that of Venus and adding the longitude of the lagna (if the position of Venus is less than that of Saturn, add 360°). Chances for wedlock will occur during the dashas and/or bhuktis of the lord of the rashi and the nakshatra in which that point falls.

yoga: An astrological combination.

yoga nakshatra: The nakshatra that the yoga point occupies.

yoga point: The point obtained by adding the longitude (from 0° Aries) of the Sun to that of the Moon, then adding 93°20', expunging multiples of 360° if necessary, and restating the result in rashi terms.

yogi: The yogi is the graha that is the nakshatra ruler of the yoga point. The yogi provides prosperity to a person.

yoni poruttham: Yoni ("womb") poruttham evaluates the couple's generative organs, with a view to ensuring successful mating. This poruttham evaluates the nature and degree of satisfaction and bonding that sexual contact will bring a couple.

BIBLIOGRAPHY

The Bhagavadgita. 22d ed. Gorakhpur, India: Gita Press, 1975.

Campbell, Joseph. *The Inner Reaches of Outer Space.* New York: Harper-Collins, 1986.

de Fouw, Hart, and Robert Svoboda. *Light on Life: An Introduction to Indian Astrology.* London: Penguin, 1996.

Dhundhiraja. *Jatakabharanam.* (Hindi) SitaRama Jha, trans. Varanasi, India: Thakurprasad and Sons Bookseller, 1977.

Dikshita, Vaidyanatha. *Jataka Parijat,* 3 vols. V. Subrahmanya Shastri, trans. New Delhi, India: Ranjan Publications, n.d.

Iyer, H. R. Seshadri. *New Techniques of Prediction:* vol. I and II. 2d ed. Bangalore, India: Rohini Printers, 1970.

Kakar, Sudhir. *The Analyst and the Mystic: Psychoanalytic Reflections on Religion and Mysticism.* New Delhi, India: Viking, 1991.

Kalidas. *Uttarakalamrita.* V. Subrahmanya Shastri, trans. 4th ed. Bangalore, India: Shri Mallikarjuna Press, 1981.

Kalyana. *Manasagari.* (Hindi) SitaRama Jha, trans. Varanasi, India: Thakurprasad and Sons Bookseller, 1983.

Kalyan Varma. *Saravali,* vol. I and II. R. Santhanam, trans. New Delhi, India: Ranjan Publications, 1983.

Mahadeva. *Jataka Tattva.* V. Subrahmanya Shastri, trans. 2d ed. Bangalore, India: Sadhana Press, 1967.

Maharshi Jaimini. *Jaimini Sutram.* P. S. Shastri, trans. New Delhi, India: Ranjan Publications, 1992.

Maharshi Parashara. *Brihat Parashara Hora Shastra,* vol. I. R. Santhanam, trans. New Delhi, India: Ranjan Publications, 1984.

_____. *Brihat Parashara Hora Shastra,* vol. II. G. S. Kapoor, trans. New Delhi, India: Ranjan Publications, 1988.

Mantreshwara. *Phaladipika.* V. Subrahmanya Shastri, trans. Bangalore, India: Yugantara Press, 1961.

Moore, Thomas. *Soul Mates.* New York: Harper Perennial, 1994.

Narasimha. *Kalaprakashika.* N. P. Subramania Iyer, trans. New Delhi, India: Asian Educational Services, 1982.

Neelakantha. *Tajika Neelakanthi.* (Hindi) Kedaradatta Joshi, trans. Delhi, India: Motilal Banarsidass, 1992.

Podumanai Chomadiri. *Jatakadesha Marga.* S. S. Sareen, trans. New Delhi, India: Sagar Publications, 1992.

Prashna Marga, 3 vols. J. N. Bhasin, trans. Delhi, India: Ranjan Publications, 1987.

Prithuyashas. *Horasara.* R. Santhanam, trans. New Delhi, India: Ranjan Publications, 1982.

Rosen, David. *The Tao of Jung: The Way of Integrity.* New York: Viking/ Arkana, 1996.

Sharma, Vyankatesh. *Sarvarth Chintamani.* J. N. Bhasin, trans. New Delhi, India: Sagar Publications, 1986.

Varahamihira. *Brihad Jataka.* V. Subrahmanya Shastri, trans. Bangalore, India: Sadhana Press, 1981.

_____. *Brihat Samhita: Part I & II.* M. Ramakrishna Bhat, trans. Delhi, India: Motilal Banarsidass, 1981.

INDEX